Virtual Economies

Information Policy Series

Edited by Sandra Braman and Paul Jaeger

The Information Policy Series publishes research on and analysis of significant problems in the field of information policy, including decisions and practices that enable or constrain information, communication, and culture irrespective of the legal siloes in which they have traditionally been located as well as state-law-society interactions. Defining information policy as all laws, regulations, and decision-making principles that affect any form of information creation, processing, flows, and use, the series includes attention to the formal decisions, decision-making processes, and entities of government; the formal and informal decisions, decision-making processes, and entities of private and public sector agents capable of constitutive effects on the nature of society; and the cultural habits and predispositions of governmentality that support and sustain government and governance. The parametric functions of information policy at the boundaries of social, informational, and technological systems are of global importance because they provide the context for all communications, interactions, and social processes.

Virtual Economies

Design and Analysis

Vili Lehdonvirta and Edward Castronova

The MIT Press
Cambridge, Massachusetts
London, England

MIT Press books may be purchased at special quantity discounts for business or sales promotional use. For information, please email special_sales@mitpress.mit.edu.

This book was set in Stone Serif Std by Toppan Best-set Premedia Limited, Hong Kong. Printed and bound in the United States of America.

Library of Congress Cataloging-in-Publication Data

Lehdonvirta, Vili.
Virtual economies : design and analysis / Vili Lehdonvirta and Edward Castronova.
pages cm.—(Information policy)
Includes bibliographical references and index.
ISBN 978-0-262-02725-0 (hardcover : alk. paper) — 978-0-262-53506-9 (paperback)
1. Electronic games. 2. Shared virtual environments—Economic aspects. 3. Virtual reality
—Economic aspects. 4. Computer-aided design. I. Castronova, Edward. II. Title.
GV1469.15.L44 2014
794.8—dc23
2013037348

For Mika and Doris

Contents

Acknowledgments

The idea for writing this book came to us at the Game Developers Conference 2010 in San Francisco. At a panel chaired by William Grosso, a developer whose name we never got asked us to recommend a book for designing and analyzing virtual economies. Of course, none existed.

This book represents a culmination of many years of research and engagement with developers. Many people have helped us and contributed ideas over the years. We especially mention the following people: Annie Lang, Juho Hamari, Kai Huotari, Mikael Johnson, Tuukka Lehtiniemi, Olli Pitkänen, Marko Turpeinen, Antti Ukkonen, Sulka Haro, Marjoriikka Ylisiurua, Thor Olof, Eino Joas, Patrick Geuder, John Buckman, Tatsuo Nakajima, Yoshiaki Hashimoto, Mirko Ernkvist, Tim Kelly, Hiroshi Yamaguchi, Koji Fukada, Pekka Räsänen, Harry Barkema, Jun-Sok Huhh, Sang-Min Whang, and Taiyoung Ryu.

The following people read the manuscript at various stages and offered feedback that significantly improved the end result: Robert Bloomfield, Ian Bogost, Yanis Varoufakis, Juha Tolvanen, and Ning Wang. We are also grateful to our series editor, Sandra Braman, and our editor, Marguerite Avery, at MIT Press. Our thanks go, as well, to Dominic Zou, who served as a diligent proofreader.

Eyjólfur Guðmundsson of CCP Games has contributed to our research in many ways over the years. He made it possible to use data from *EVE Online* to illustrate concepts in this book, for which we are grateful.

We also thank the institutions that have employed us and so enabled us to strike out in this direction: University of Rochester, California State University at Fullerton, Indiana University, Aalto University, London School of Economics, and University of Oxford. Our work has obtained crucial financial support from Finland's Foundation for Economic Education, Kone Foundation, and Tekes.

Finally, we thank our wives—not merely for supporting us and tolerating our whims, as you often find written in book acknowledgments, but for their important contributions to the content of this book as our intellectual equals and life partners.

1   Introduction

Lionel Robbins, a former head of the economics department at the London School of Economics, defined *economics* as follows: "Economics is the science which studies human behaviour as a relationship between ends and scarce means which have alternative uses."

Scarcity is a central concept in economics. It means that something exists in a lesser quantity than would be required to satisfy all desire for it. Not everyone can have everything; people need to make choices. Economics studies those choices, and the patterns or laws of give-and-take that emerge when many people make such choices in interaction with each other. A set of scarce resources together with processes like production, trade, and consumption that arise from people's economic interactions is called an *economy.*

In the digital world, things seem different. Bits are not scarce: information can be duplicated indefinitely. Instead of choosing which of two music albums to buy, you can simply download both and share them with your friends. Because there is no need to choose, there is no need for economics. The dynamics of online interactions are sufficiently explained with concepts such as status and identity, which are the domain of sociology and psychology. In the digital world, a set of resources coupled with interactions is not called an economy but a community.

But sometimes an anomaly arises: a digital good that is also scarce. Consider the following example, an early case. An instant messaging system called ICQ (pronounced "I seek you") was launched in 1996. Instead of identifying users by a nickname, it gave every user a number—like a phone number that users could give to their friends. Those who joined first were given five-digit numbers. When the five-digit numbers ran out, ICQ started handing out six-digit numbers, then seven digits, and eventually eight. By 2001, the number of accounts surpassed 100 million, and ICQ was distributing nine-digit numbers. Now the original five- and six-digit numbers had become extremely rare: fewer than one account in a hundred had such a short number. Having a six-digit on your contact list was something you could brag to your friends about. Claiming to have talked to a five-digit was like claiming to have dined with a celebrity.

Then something even stranger happened: people started buying and selling ICQ numbers. It probably started casually, as someone who sold a used computer throwing in their number as a sweetener or someone giving an extra number to a friend in exchange for a favor. But it soon developed into a fully fledged market, where ICQ numbers were listed on eBay and traded for U.S. dollars. Semiprofessional traders sold six-digit numbers at list prices ranging from a few dollars to dozens of dollars. Five-digit numbers, on those rare occasions that one became available for sale, were sold for hundreds of dollars. Triple digits and other notable numbers could cost even more: we once saw the number *11111111* listed at $3,000. A custom ICQ number was like a vanity car license plate: it made its owner stand out. It was something that people could genuinely consider their own in the digital world, where everything else was quickly copied.

Seeing that there was a big demand for catchy ICQ numbers, semiprofessional traders began to "farm" them by creating lots and lots of new accounts. Notable numbers were listed on eBay, while ordinary numbers could be placed in storage in case they would later turn into valuable vintage. In other words, people were now producing, warehousing, trading, and consuming a scarce digital resource in the ICQ network. This was no longer just a community; it was now an economy. The digital dynamics of status and identity had become intertwined with the ancient dynamics of give-and-take.

We use the term *virtual economy* to refer to an economy that is based on scarce digital resources. We use the term *virtual goods* to refer to the scarce digital resources themselves. Most studies of digital business and economics have focused not on scarcity but on the implications of abundance and sharing. The current trend is to predict the end of scarcity and look for business models fit for a postscarcity world. But the ICQ example, one of countless, shows that there is still a place for scarcity even in the twenty-first-century digital world. In fact, if anything, virtual economies are growing. When ICQ was launched, the idea of selling virtual goods for real money was almost unheard of. Today some of the largest digital media companies in the world use it as a revenue model. It turns out that there is yet a need for the science of scarcity.

Understanding virtual economies is important not only to designers and businesspeople, but also to social scientists, scholars of culture and communication, and policymakers. Virtual economies, whether emergent or planned, overt or subtle, influence the landscape of digital media—who has power, who has voice, what is valued, and what kind of participation is rewarded. The study of virtual economies thus adds a crucial dimension to social scientific and cultural studies of digital media. While the first and foremost audience of this book are the practitioners who create and manage virtual economies, we have also tried to make it useful to scholars and policymakers, to teachers who want to introduce elementary economics in a novel way, and even to gamers seeking a deeper understanding of the games they play.

Real business from virtual goods

ICQ numbers became valuable by accident. The designers never intended for people to become so attracted to them as to start trading them for real money. Today, over fifteen years after ICQ was launched, the number trade continues on eBay. But ICQ itself, now greatly diminished by competition, still earns most of its meager revenues from advertising.

One of ICQs successors, a Chinese instant messaging system named OICQ, took a different path. OICQ's developers understood the lesson from the number trade: that people were willing to pay for goods with personal and social meaning in digital environments, just as they were willing to pay for vanity plates and fashion items in physical environments. Armed with this realization, they set out to design a commercial virtual economy.

OICQ's developers knew that instant messaging was popular among young people. They let each user be represented by a virtual character, an avatar. They then created a selection of virtual clothes, accessories, and gifts for the avatars, which they started selling for real money. OICQ and its avatars were a phenomenal success—a landmark in the history of the Chinese Internet. By 2010, under the new name Tencent QQ, the system claimed over 600 million active users. Its publisher, Tencent, earned more than $2 billion a year from avatar accessories and value-added services and was the third-largest Internet company in the world by market capitalization.

A few years later, Facebook and Apple lead similar virtual goods breakthroughs for Western consumers. They went further than just selling virtual goods to their users: they set up relatively open virtual economies where any third-party developer could come and sell virtual offerings—while paying a share of their revenues to the hosts. This helped create a number of billion-dollar companies whose revenues are based almost exclusively on the sales of virtual items, add-ons, map packs, and even virtual camera lenses. Anywhere you look, digital publishers are increasingly making their money from artificially scarce virtual goods.

Yet virtual goods offered for sale are only the tip of the iceberg. Behind every such offering, there has to be a social dynamic or a cultural context that makes the offering desirable in the first place. There also has to be some mechanism for ensuring its scarcity in order to preserve its market value. And there has to be a virtual currency or other micropayment system for carrying out the transaction in practice. In other words, every virtual good is always part of some kind of a virtual economy. Simple ones do little more than invest virtual goods with some value, ensure that they cannot be duplicated, and provide a storefront. Complex ones do much more, maintaining large portfolios of goods, allowing users to produce them according to predefined rules, and letting users exchange them between each other.

In many cases, the primary purpose of a virtual economy is not even to earn revenues directly, but something more subtle yet equally powerful: to attract, hold, and manage attention; to reward referrals and incentivize contributions; to allocate resources; to lock users into a platform or to guide them around it. These mechanisms are found not only in games and interactive entertainment services, but also in online communities, knowledge banks, retail sites, payments, and marketing, and they are coming to business software. If virtual goods offered for sale are the visible tip of the iceberg, then the subtle virtual economies embedded deep into the infrastructure of our digital environment are the mountain underneath. As software turns into services and our lives are increasingly mediated by technology, virtual economies will come to shape our options and influence our choices in much the same way as conventional economies do today.

A new tool for digital design

Even when virtual economies are intentionally created rather than emerge spontaneously, they can take highly unexpected trajectories. This is part of their fascination, but it is also a challenge for anyone hoping to use them for a specific purpose. To illustrate this unpredictability, let us continue the story of the Chinese instant messaging system.

When Tencent started its virtual goods business, it faced a common problem for online businesses in China at the time: lack of credit cards or other online payment methods among potential customers. Tencent's solution to this problem was to create a *virtual currency*—the Q coin, launched in 2002.[1] Q coins are virtual coins that sit on the user's instant messaging account. Users could buy the coins, typically from a brick-and-mortar corner shop, and then use the coins to buy virtual goods from Tencent. Q coins could also be earned as rewards from things like advertising supported games. For those who frequented Tencent QQ, the virtual currency was as good as money, and Tencent was in the happy position of being the mint.

As the reach of the instant messaging network grew, something unexpected happened once again: online entrepreneurs not affiliated with Tencent started accepting Q coins as payment for their services. A company would open a QQ account, ask its QQ-using customers to "friend" them, and then accept payments as Q coin gifts, which the system facilitated. Such an arrangement was much easier and cheaper to set up than

1. This account of China's Q coin economy is based on research by Lehdonvirta and Jiaping Xu in 2007–2008, some of which has previously been published online at the Virtual Economy Research Network, http://virtual-economy.org. Many of the major developments in virtual economies occur in Asia, especially Korea and China, but news of them travels slowly due to language barriers and weak links between researchers. Opportunities exist for multilingual scholars and analysts to communicate innovations back and forth between Asia and the West.

any official payment system, and it was accessible to a far bigger audience. Accepting payment in a virtual currency was also an effective way to avoid scrutiny by authorities. Gambling and adult entertainment sites, both illegal in China, quickly adopted Q coins in their business.

What could online entrepreneurs do with a pile of virtual coins earned in this way? To some extent, they could use the coins to pay for goods and services purchased from other vendors that accepted the virtual money. But as long as their landlord and grocer refused to accept the coins, the entrepreneurs would also need some national currency. Entrepreneurs therefore sold the Q coins they accumulated to private traders, who then sold the coins back to users on local markets and e-commerce sites. Q coins thus circulated back and forth between firms and consumers. By 2006, the Q coin, which was originally intended as a medium through which users could buy value-added services from Tencent, had became a general online currency in China. You could buy anything from compact discs and makeup to *World of Warcraft* game items using Q coins.

With a private virtual currency increasingly used in place of China's official currency, the yuan, the People's Bank of China began to get worried. Every new Q coin that Tencent released into circulation increased the country's money supply—the total amount of cash, bank account balances, and other money equivalents in circulation. Left unchecked, this monetary expansion in theory could lead to general inflation. The central bank had tools for managing the amount of yuan in circulation, but virtual currencies were totally outside its control. Other government agencies started to develop similar anxieties. How does one tax virtual currency earnings, for example?

In 2007, the People's Bank of China and fourteen other agencies issued a joint announcement according to which the central bank would start enforcing governance over virtual currencies in the country. According to the statement, strict limits would be imposed on the volumes of virtual currencies issued by publishers and the amounts purchased by consumers. Virtual item trading would have to be clearly distinguished from e-business transactions, and virtual currencies could not be used to buy physical goods, only virtual goods and services provided by the companies that issued the currencies. The redemption of virtual currencies for value exceeding their original purchase price would be forbidden. According to the announcement, violators would be subject to prosecution for financial crimes detailed in China's banking law.

Yet despite these strictures, the Q coin economy continued to boom. Participants quickly invented a way to circumvent a limit imposed on the amount of coins that could be remitted from one QQ account to another. Instead of remitting coins using the gifting feature, the payer would send the payee a password that allowed the latter to take over the entire account, which would contain the agreed sum of Q coins. Sometimes several accounts were sent. In effect, accounts became a new currency—something that could be used as money even if no remittances between accounts were allowed at all. In June 2011, e-commerce site Taobao carried over 800,000 listings for Q coins—up from 20,000 listings in April 2007. In total, Taobao featured over 3 million listings for QQ-related virtual goods, ranging from avatar accessories and pets to game trophies and currencies.

The central bank's intervention was not without some effect, however. Because of the threat of prosecution, the Q coin was never adopted by mainstream online stores and e-commerce sites. It remains mostly a currency of the informal (and sometimes outright illegal) digital shadow economy. Yet without the central bank's crackdown, China's netizens might by now have entirely eschewed the yuan in favor of a virtual currency.

This story illustrates a key challenge with virtual economies. Forces arising from the participants' economic interests and expediencies can lead systems on trajectories that differ significantly from what their designers originally intended. Sometimes the new trajectory is so radical that it even puts the system on a collision course with authorities; the Q coin example is not the only one in this book. This is a problem for design. How can you design if you don't know what the consequences of your decisions are? Creating something without any outcome in mind is not design but experimentation.

In order to be able to anticipate how a virtual economy will play out in practice, you need to understand the economic forces that govern its behavior. In addition, any effective intervention to an economy that has already gotten out of hand depends on an analysis of the economic forces at play. Therefore, with this book, we seek to introduce the discipline of economics into the toolbox of digital design and game design, which so far has been dominated by other disciplines. For those already familiar with economics, we seek to show how it can be applied to analyzing how scarcity-based digital interaction and business functions. In our economic models, we also include a healthy dose of other social sciences and practical knowledge from game design.[2]

The economics of virtual spaces

We are not the first to propose using economics for designing games. In fact, respected economists have been designing games for years—not just theoretical model games like

2. Some insightful pieces of virtual economy design have already been written by game designers who have picked up the skill through practical experience. Richard Bartle is a coinventor of the first MUD (text-based virtual world), and his 2003 textbook is a classic source on virtual worlds design that also includes economic insights. Raph Koster was the guiding spirit on *Ultima Online* in the 1990s, and his online essays are eye-opening. We also urge readers to make use of general game design literature. Some of our favorites include Crawford (1984), Salen and Zimmerman (2003), Rollings and Morris (2003), and Schell (2008). Koster (2004) offers an accessible theory of fun. Fullerton (2008) and Braithwaite and Schreiber (2008) offer wonderful learn-by-doing approaches.

prisoner's dilemma, but actual games intended to be played for real. When a government needs to allocate radio frequencies to telecommunications companies or a consortium of nations decides to reduce greenhouse gas emissions, it turns to economists to design a game for the purpose. Frequently the task involves dreaming up a synthetic commodity, such as spectrum bands or carbon credits. Companies are then invited to play this game and to take its results seriously, whatever the outcome. For example, the spectrum auction game, also known as the "simultaneous ascending auction", was created by economists Preston McAfee, Paul Milgrom, and Robert Wilson. It has been run successfully by governments around the world since its debut in the United States in 1994.

If economists already know how to design complex games that run flawlessly, what is this book needed for? Couldn't digital designers simply pick up an ordinary economics textbook instead? Or is there something different about conventional economic design of the sort we have described and the virtual economy design practiced by digital designers? The fundamentals of human behavior do not change: they are the same in both contexts, as we argue later. Both online games and spectrum games involve agents seeking favorable outcomes in light of their preferences. Basic economic tenets should therefore be equally valid in both. But something tells us that the matter is not quite as simple. Consider the following example of what happens if we analyze an online game economy as if it were a conventional economy.

In the massively multiplayer online (MMO) game *EVE Online*, hundreds of thousands of players trade minerals, spaceship components, and other commodities with each other on a number of regional marketplaces. The marketplaces are highly sophisticated, resembling real commodity spot markets. Participants can submit buy offers and sell offers, and execute trades immediately by accepting someone else's offer.

If a textbook economist was asked to assess *EVE Online*'s economy, they would doubtless point out several places where its efficiency could be greatly improved. For example, players can see only prices quoted in their current region. A better deal might be available in the neighboring region, but a player will miss this opportunity unless they exchange information with distant friends or regularly travel to other regions themself. Every time a player misses such an opportunity and pays an unnecessarily high price for a commodity, the market is said to be operating inefficiently.

The textbook economist knows that, other things being the same, providing more information to market participants increases the efficiency of a market. They might thus suggest that the game be modified in such a way that all players gain instant access to price information in all the regions across the galaxy. This way, everyone could easily locate and make use of any better deals nearby. This would have the effect of evening out price differences between regions and therefore improving the overall efficiency of the galactic market. In physical commodity markets, prices are instantly broadcast across the world so that no one will pay much more for gold in Tokyo than they would have to pay in New York.

Of course, this change would be a blow to players who have specialized in gathering and trading price information. It would also reduce the opportunity for arbitrageurs: players who rummage the galaxy for underpriced goods and transport them to regions where they can be sold for a profit. These professions would no longer be needed. But these players could always turn themselves into haulers, the space equivalent of truck drivers. Increased efficiency should increase cross-regional trade, which means plenty of new opportunities for haulers.

But wait—realizing the infinite malleability of virtual economies, the textbook economist might actually decide to eliminate regions altogether. Distance is what economists refer to as a transaction cost: the economy would run much more efficiently without the need to transport things around. In the physical world, distance is a necessary impediment, one that logisticians strive to minimize. In a virtual environment, there is no need to encumber the economy with it at all. The textbook economist would therefore give the order to either modify the game in such a way that all goods and characters can be instantly teleported to their desired locations or simply collapse the whole galaxy into a single, dimensionless point. With these changes, the efficiency of the virtual economy would certainly be greatly improved: everyone could get anything they wanted instantaneously. But whether anyone would still like to participate in this economy, let alone pay a subscription fee for the privilege, is a different matter!

Although virtual economy design and conventional economic design are based on the same fundamentals, there is a major difference in their objectives. Governments try to develop economies that are efficient. Digital publishers try to put out products that attract users, satisfy them, and make money. For this reason, solutions that work in conventional economic design can be destructive if transported wholesale into virtual economy design, despite both being based on the same understanding of human behavior.

What virtual economy design can achieve

Virtual economies can be created for many kinds of reasons: to act as a living lab for research, complement a local economy, or simply serve as someone's personal hobby, for example. But most virtual economies today are created and operated by companies that publish digital content and services, especially game companies. What the creator hopes to achieve with the economy obviously has a great impact on its design. In this section, we outline what kinds of things virtual economies can be used to achieve, especially in the games and digital publishing industries. This is not an exhaustive list of what virtual economies can be useful for, but it does give a good idea of how they are used in these particular industries.

Digital publishers are usually for-profit companies that aim to make money. Their specific approach to making money is providing digital content to consumers. On a very abstract level, their business consists of three processes: creating content, attracting users, and monetizing. Virtual economy design, like every other function in the company, must somehow contribute to these processes. In the following sections, we examine each process in more detail and outline how it is pursued through virtual economy design. This yields us a set of objectives for virtual economy design: reasons that virtual economies are created in the first place. In later chapters, we refer back to these objectives to explain why one design decision might be better than another.

Creating content

When digital designers talk about content, they usually mean things like text, images, music, and video. When game developers talk about content, they similarly refer to things like 3D models, textures, animations, sounds, maps, and storylines. Content is distinguished from platforms and game engines, which provide the mechanics and physics of a service, that is, the rules that govern how objects interact with each other and the user. This distinction reflects the division of labor in a typical development studio: programmers create engines, and artists populate them with content.

The topics we deal with in this book cut right across conventional disciplinary divisions. They have implications not only for artists and programmers, but also for publishers, marketers, and even lawyers and policy analysts trying to get to grips with virtual economies. For this reason, we need to use the term *content* in a much wider sense: content is anything that can be delivered digitally that users find desirable.

In a game, content certainly includes attractive graphics, groovy soundtracks, and gripping storylines. But it also includes the pleasures derived from fun game mechanics: the adrenaline-laced excitement of a rapid feedback loop, the contemplative joy of discovery through experimentation, and the sense of accomplishment from beating a difficult puzzle. Most content, in games and other digital services, is a combination of art and programming. In multiplayer games and online communities, huge amounts of content are also created by the users. The simplest and most pervasive user-created content are the social interactions that users have with each other: discussions, conversations, and relationships. The measure of content is not data; it is experience (but see box 1.1).

An important thing to realize about content is that it is a consumable good. Once someone has seen a film or read a book, typically they are much less interested to experience it a second time. The same is true in games. As players advance to new levels and areas, they expect to see new kinds of terrains, units, storylines, items, and game mechanics. As they experience this new content, they are said to consume it because it loses its novelty value. Once all content is consumed, it is gone, and players are likely to start leaving. Reintroducing old content with scaled-up numerical attributes or even

Box 1.1
What is "good" content?

> From a business perspective, good content is something that is effective at attracting users. But being effective is not always the same as being fun or satisfying. Sometimes we are drawn to respond to a forum post out of anger rather than out of interest. Sometimes what prompts us to check in and water our virtual plants is a feeling of obligation rather than accomplishment. In other words, the moral value of content can sometimes diverge from its economic value. For developers, it can be worthwhile to occasionally stop and think about whether their content appeals more to the positive or the negative in humans.

algorithmically generated variations will not restore more than a small part of its novelty value. Content is one of the few naturally scarce resources in a virtual economy.

Digital content publishers must constantly provide new content to their users. When *World of Warcraft* was first launched in 2004, it had content for sixty levels of game play, developed at a cost of approximately $63 million. When players reached level 60 and completed all the dungeons, there were no more areas left to explore, and many stopped playing. In 2007, Blizzard released The Burning Crusade, an expansion pack that added ten new levels' worth of content to the game. It sold over 3.5 million copies in the first month and convinced many of those who had stopped playing to return to the game. Since then, three more expansions have been released. Each expansion costs millions of dollars to create, but the game could not hold on to its subscribers without them.

Clearly, creating content must be one of the objectives of virtual economy design. The simplest way in which virtual economy design can contribute to this objective is that virtual economy features can themselves be a form of content. Economic processes such as production, logistics, and trade are not simply means toward ends but can also be fun in themselves. In *World of Warcraft*, harvesting natural resources, refining them into raw materials, producing goods, managing inventories, and trading goods on the market are all a core part of the game experience. In the expansions, the developers added more economic processes for players to enjoy. Game content does not always have to be inspired by adventure and combat. It can also be about trade and industry.

User-created content Since developing content is costly, many games and digital services also look to user-created content to keep their users happy. In MMO gaming, a particularly notable example of such a strategy is *EVE Online*. Instead of advancing along storylines and levels defined by designers, *EVE*'s players focus on pursuing careers in player-run corporations and alliances, some of which have thousands of members. Player organizations compete for control over territories and resources, wage wars, trade, and build infrastructure. Player-to-player politics gives rise to heated nego-tiations, fantastic double-crosses, and epic space battles. This is perfect space opera, yet no designer was paid to script it; it was created by the players themselves.

This is not to say that professional developers had no part in the creation of *EVE*'s player-to-player space opera. On the contrary, developers intentionally designed the game in such a way that player-to-player interactions and dependencies would be max-imized. The biggest part of this design is *EVE Online*'s virtual economy. It places a big emphasis on player-to-player transactions. Most objects are not dropped by computer-controlled enemies or purchased from nonplayer characters (NPCs). Instead, they are manufactured by player industrialists from raw materials mined by player mining cor-porations. Players specializing in trade and logistics distribute the goods across the galaxy, using player-run transport ships protected by player-run security corporations. Pirate players seek to steal the cargo and sell it to the highest bidder. In other words, virtual economy design can contribute immensely to user content creation by provid-ing an interaction framework in which it can emerge.

Incentivizing contributions   The world of social media runs almost entirely on user contributions. Facebook, Twitter, Quora, and Pinterest are completely reliant on con-tent created and posted by users and third-party content developers. Some games and virtual environments, too, make use of 3D objects and landscapes created by users. A well-known pioneer was the virtual world *Second Life,* where almost every object, from buildings to pieces of clothing, is designed by a user or a third-party developer. A recent success story is *Team Fortress 2*, a first-person shooter game, where weapons and acces-sories designed by players can become items that circulate in the game's economy.

Sometimes positive attention, goodwill, and the joy of self-expression are sufficient to motivate users and third-party developers to contribute content. In other cases, it is necessary to provide more concrete incentives. The simplest incentive systems reward every contribution in the same way, but this often leads to a deluge of low-quality contributions. More sophisticated incentive systems involve a market where user con-tributions are rewarded in accordance with their value. Creating incentive systems is something that virtual economy design is perfectly suited for.

Allocating resources efficiently   Even in a virtual economy, some resources are natu-rally scarce. Content is one such resource, but there are also two others: computing resources and user attention. When we facilitate the creation of content by users, we must ensure that these naturally scarce resources are used efficiently, delivering the best experience possible within the resources available. This is another area where vir-tual economy design can contribute.

In *Second Life*, land is divided into regions of 256 meters by 256 meters. Each region is hosted on a server computer, and the technical specifications of that computer place a limit on the magnitude of activities that are possible in that region. A standard region can simultaneously hold a maximum of 100 avatars and 15,000 primitives. Primitives are basic components from which all objects in *Second Life* are constructed. This limit is not artificial: *Second Life*'s publisher has determined that this is the maximum load that the current servers can reliably handle. Increasing the limit would require costly hardware upgrades. Primitives in *Second Life* are therefore a naturally scarce resource. For similar reasons, the polygons that objects in *Team Fortress 2* are constructed from are a naturally scarce resource. The demand for polygons exceeds their supply because everyone would like to use a large number of polygons in the objects that they create in order to enhance the objects' visual appeal.

To reconcile strong demand with limited supply, the two publishers have adopted quite different approaches. *Team Fortress 2*'s publisher, Valve, uses rationing: it asks players to use fewer than 800 polygons for hat designs and 8,000 or under for weapons. The problem with rationing is that every design, no matter how superb or worthless, is allocated the same amount of resources. This is not an optimal allocation. The game experience would be better if good designers had more polygons at their disposal and bad ones fewer.

Second Life uses a market mechanism to allocate its supply of primitives. Users buy and sell land on an open market. The land comes with rights to determine how its allotted share of primitives is used. In theory, this ensures that the primitives are used for constructions that yield the maximum net value to *Second Life* and its users. Popular attractions that bring joy to many can charge entrance fees or sell souvenirs to pay for land costs. Unpopular plots will be sold or redeveloped as owners seek better ways to invest their capital. Even when primitives are wasted on unattractive corporate projects done for the sake of publicity, the companies compensate *Second Life* for this by paying the market price for the land. In practice, *Second Life*'s virtual economy implementation is not perfect, but it illustrates the idea of using a market to get more bang for buck out of scarce computing resources.

Besides computing resources, another naturally scarce resource is user attention. This becomes apparent as soon as users have created a large amount of content, so that it becomes difficult for anyone to find the good stuff from among all the substandard contributions. Markets and other virtual economy design elements can be applied to separate the wheat from the chaff.

Attention: Attracting and retaining users

Giving away content for free   Once a digital publisher has a content strategy, whether based on user contributions or professionally created content, it needs to find some users. The marketing of digital content is very much shaped by the fact that it is a so-called experience good: consumers cannot fully assess its value without actually experiencing the product. It is not enough to simply list the specifications of the product in a brochure, as with a hardware component. To dispel the feeling of buying a pig in a poke, you have to let the consumer sample a part of the content.

Free sampling of digital content is not a new thing, but it has become increasingly important. In the 1990s, PC game publishers distributed one-level demos of their games on floppy disks bundled with gaming magazines. In the 2000s, it became standard practice for online game publishers to provide a free "open beta" version of the game for a period of several weeks before the game's commercial launch. Today the majority of new games on platforms ranging from mobile to online are following the so-called freemium, or "free-to-play" (F2P) model, which means that their core features can be accessed for free indefinitely.

This trend toward providing a larger proportion of content for free is the result of two major drivers: intensifying competition and the increasingly social nature of digital content consumption. Advances in digital distribution dramatically lower the entry barrier for new game publishers. This has resulted in an exploding supply of games and digital entertainment on many platforms. Especially smaller publishers with less money to burn on marketing must offer core parts of their content for free to attract users' attention. At the same time, the widespread adoption of Internet access, social networking, and connected mobile devices means that consumers increasingly expect their digital experiences to be social. Building a critical mass of users that provides a social experience is easiest to achieve through free access. The shift toward free is not limited to games: publishers of books, music, movies, and many other products are taking similar steps.[3]

But the more content a publisher gives away for free to attract users, the less content it has left to sell, a trade-off illustrated in figure 1.1. The diagonal line is the publisher's content budget line. It shows the publisher's range of choices, from giving 0 percent of the content for free (resulting in zero users) all the way to giving 100 percent of the content for free (resulting in zero revenues). Watching ads is a type of payment, so in our analysis, even purely ad-driven digital platforms are not considered 100 percent free. Point A represents a particular choice on this continuum, resulting in total revenues that equal the area of the rectangle it defines.[4]

3. The current editor of *Wired* magazine, Chris Anderson, has written on the declining prices of goods in the digital age. His book, *Free* (2010), suggests to business leaders that giving products away may be the best (or only) route to profit.
4. Mathematically inclined readers will realize that the point that yields the greatest revenues is determined by the slope and intersect of the diagonal. These depend on factors such as target audience and revenue model, and in reality the line may well be curved rather than straight. This model is thus more illustrative than analytical.

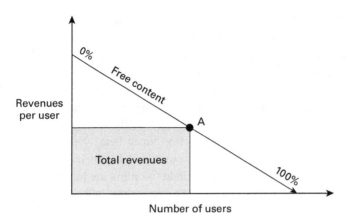

Figure 1.1
Content publisher's revenue-maximization problem

A particularly powerful way to separate free and paid content in a service is to use a virtual economy. Virtual economy features provide many ways of adjusting the balance toward an optimal position. One common solution in games is to create two virtual currencies: a "soft currency" that can be obtained for free and a "hard currency" that needs to be purchased for real money, along with two corresponding marketplaces. The available content is turned into virtual goods—virtual items, characters, area unlocks, replays, and so on—and distributed between the two marketplaces.

Rewarding users for referrals and loyalty   Providing access to content for free is only the first step in marketing digital content. Publishers still need to get the word out about this free content to potential users. Traditional advertising is one method, but in many segments and product categories, word-of-mouth marketing through social media is even more important. For example, so-called social games use every opportunity to ask players to invite their friends to the game. Many games are naturally more fun to play with friends, so players have an implicit incentive to comply. But many publishers also provide explicit rewards for referrals, especially free virtual goods or currency. A more subtle way to incentivize referrals is to build the game in such a way that progress is faster when playing with friends. Whichever the method, virtual economy design is usually the key to implementing it.

Virtual rewards and the structure of the economy as a whole are also commonly used to incentivize other desirable user behaviors, such as daily logins and participation in the user community. These incentives are aimed at improving the stickiness or retention rate of the service. Attracting lots of new users helps little if none of them come back a second time and turn into regulars.

Locking users in   The final aspect of retaining users is minimizing their likelihood o. defecting to a competing service. Bestowing users virtual goods that are difficult or costly to obtain can make them feel invested in a service. The prospect of losing this investment and having to start from scratch is a significant deterrent against defection. At the same time, clever virtual economy design can also be used to lower the switching cost for users coming in from a competing service.

Monetizing

Price discrimination   Once a publisher has created a set of content and found users who want to consume it, the only question that remains is how to make money from the equation. Until recently, the main revenue models for digital content were physical retail, digital retail, subscriptions, and advertising. All of these models can and are being used to monetize services that contain a virtual economy. But virtual economies also add an entirely new model to this repertoire: the selling of virtual goods and currencies for real money. This model is also known as the micropayments or in-app purchases model, depending on the platform and the type of content.

The virtual goods revenue model has one distinct advantage over the earlier models: it makes it possible to charge very different amounts of money from different users depending on their willingness to pay. This typically happens through consumer self-selection. The publisher provides a wide range of payment options, from using the service for free to paying for any quantity and combination of virtual goods and value-added services. Based on factors such as their personal value for time and money and their self-identification as a certain type of consumer, users then spend different sums. Some pay little or nothing; in a flat fee model, most of them would not have become customers at all. Some pay a lot—even orders of magnitude more than what they would have paid as a flat fee. When this price discrimination succeeds, it results in total revenues that are much greater than in a flat fee model. This is illustrated in in figure 1.2.

Managing the rate of content delivery   Regardless of the revenue model used, when the publisher successfully sells some content to a user, it has to deliver it. It needs to deliver enough content to keep the customer happy—but not more content than is necessary. Remember that content is a consumable good, so each piece of content delivered to the user is one piece of content less that can be sold to them in the future. The right amount of content is the amount that the publisher promised to the user. That tends to vary significantly between revenue models.

Physical retail is slow and expensive, so when a publisher uses physical retail, it is most economical for it to sell as much content as possible in a single package. A whole year's worth of game development effort is packed into a box with a $60 sticker and

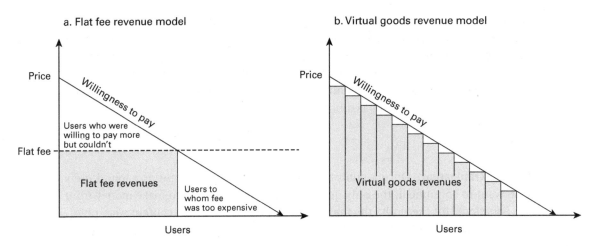

Figure 1.2
Willingness to pay and total revenues. a. Flat fee revenue model. b. Virtual goods revenue model.

released as an AAA title with a big marketing campaign.[5] The result typically provides around fifteen to twenty-five hours of intense, no-holds-barred gameplay.

Digital distribution, a more recent innovation, is much faster and has fewer overheads. Updates can be issued over the Net and users can be billed by credit card. This makes it feasible to sell a year's worth of development effort gradually. This can mean turning the content into a subscription service, like classic MMO games, or it can mean monetization through virtual goods sales or advertising. In either case, the publisher is charging for the content in small bits, and consequently, the content must also be delivered in small bits. It will not do to just throw all of its painstakingly developed assets at the player within the first fifteen hours of play, as retail games do. If it does do that in a subscription service, what content will it give the users next month, and the month after that? In a subscription service, content must be stretched out over time—not too thinly, lest users find the service too boring and quit, but not too generously either, lest the publisher run out of content before recouping development costs. In games, stretching out content is usually accomplished by making it repetitive, like having to accumulate a certain number of coins in one area before being able to proceed to the next one.

Virtual economy features can be a great tool for managing the rate of content delivery. Parameters like prices, taxes, productivity, efficiency, and depreciation directly influence how quickly players are able to get things done and progress through content.

5. The term *AAA* is used in the game industry to loosely refer to big budget games released by established publishers for major platforms such as consoles. Here we use it to mean especially games that are mostly single player and sold as packaged goods.

Some of them are also easy to control in a finely grained manner. The flip side is that unexpected interactions and loopholes in economic design sometimes allow users to advance much faster than the designers anticipated.

In services that rely on virtual goods sales as their main revenue model, managing the rate of content delivery is even more important and interesting. Now the publisher needs to maintain a fine balance between spooning out just enough free content to keep users coming back, and yet little enough to keep them hungry for the additional content that could be obtained by virtual goods purchases. In practice, this tends to lead to content that is stretched very thinly indeed. In the time that it takes a user to harvest a single pumpkin crop in a free Facebook game, they will have saved the entire world twice in a typical AAA title. (The business advantages of this incremental delivery schedule are discussed in box 1.2).

When a user does decide to splurge on virtual goods in a F2P game, the economy must be designed so that the appropriate amount of content is released promptly. If users so wished, in theory they should be able to buy and experience the entire content of the game in a single session, provided they would be prepared to pay for it a sum that corresponds to their entire expected lifetime value to the publisher. In practice, in a multiplayer title, designers also need to consider what this would mean to other players' game experience.

The content delivery schedules of different game categories associated with the revenue models discussed here (retail, subscription, virtual goods) are illustrated in figure 1.3. In the case of F2P games, the graph depicts content delivery to a player who is not paying anything.

Managing the rate of content delivery does have a further, nobler purpose beyond maximizing publisher revenues. As players, we are naturally eager to see what's behind the next corner as fast as possible. But if you rushed through all the vistas of a game in an hour, how much of an impression would they leave on you? Economists would say that the consumption of game content has a diminishing marginal utility: the more of it you experience in one sitting, the less impact each increment has on you. This means that the total amount of entertainment we obtain from a given set of content is greater if we stop and smell the flowers once in a while. A good game designer will therefore always put some speed bumps on the players' path, regardless of the revenue model.

The objectives of virtual economy design

Summarizing, any virtual economy–related feature built into a multiplayer game, virtual environment, or other digital service must aim to contribute to at least one of these objectives:

1. *Creating content.* Virtual economy features can form part of interesting single-player content or act as a framework for the generation of user-created content. Both usually involve introducing artificially scarce resources into the economy that create challenge

Box 1.2
The economics of free-to-play game development

The virtual goods revenue model allows content to be sold continuously in small increments. F2P publishers that are able to structure their development process around this model can realize two significant economic advantages: reduced working capital requirements and reduced risk.

Consider the following example. An AAA retail title and a similarly sized F2P digital title both earn $11 million on a development budget of $10 million. The AAA publisher had to invest the whole $10 million upfront, before the product hit the stores, so its return on investment is only 10 percent. In contrast, the F2P publisher was able to launch the product with only a small part of the content finished. New content was added throughout the year, its development funded by sales from the already published contents. Although the total development cost added up to the same $10 million, the maximum amount of capital tied up at any point was only $1 million, resulting in a whopping 100 percent return on investment.

Because of the total upfront commitment, the AAA publisher also faced a huge financial risk in case the game failed to sell. Many game studios have met their demise because of a single unsuccessful AAA title. F2P is less risky: if the F2P title had failed to gain traction after launch, the publisher could have cut its losses at any point by simply canceling further development.

This analysis is of course an idealization that glosses over many real-world factors. One such factor is that many consumers prefer to buy content as a product rather than as a service residing in the cloud. Yet so strong are the economics in favor of F2P and games-as-a-service that this is the direction to which the game industry and other digital industries are heading. Why now? Why not ten years ago? The digital distribution and billing infrastructure that F2P requires was essentially in place over a decade ago. What was missing was the virtual economics know-how. Except for a few pioneers like Matt Mihaly of Iron Realms Entertainment and Sampo Karjalainen, Sulka Haro, and others at Sulake Corporation, Western developers had not yet discovered that virtual goods and currencies could be sold for real money, let alone that this could be consistent with a good game experience. Virtual economics is an innovation, an enabling technology that makes F2P games possible, much in the same way as broadband makes digital retail possible.

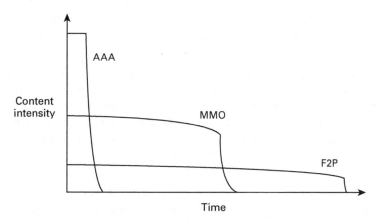

Figure 1.3
Rate of content delivery over time in different game categories

and competition. Virtual economy features can also be used to provide incentives for users and third-party developers to contribute new content. All digital services rely to some extent on naturally scarce computing resources and user attention. Virtual economy features, especially suitably defined virtual property rights and markets, can be used to ensure that these resources are put to the most valuable uses possible.

2. *Attention: attracting and retaining users.* Virtual economy features can be used to give out some content for free in order to attract users while reserving other content for paying users. A typical way to achieve this is by creating two currencies: one that can be earned for free and another that must be purchased. Virtual goods and currencies can also be used to reward users for referrals and loyalty. Virtual goods by their very nature also tend to create lock-in, where users are discouraged from switching to a competing service because in doing so, they would lose the time and money invested in their virtual possessions on the present platform.

3. *Monetizing.* The most obvious way in which virtual economy features can contribute to monetization is through the sales of virtual goods and currencies for real money. Compared to other revenue models, this model has the advantage of supporting price discrimination: charging users according to their willingness to pay. But even in games and services that use some other revenue model, the virtual economy can contribute to revenues by regulating the rate at which users gain access to content. In a subscription game, content needs to be dispensed relatively rapidly in order to keep paying subscribers attracted. In a purely advertising-supported service, content can be dispensed at a slower pace to keep people hooked for the longest possible time.

Now that we have examined the objectives of virtual economy design in detail, let us briefly return to the question raised earlier in this chapter. How do the goals of virtual economy design differ from the goals of conventional economic design? Although both schools are based on the same models of human behavior, conventional economics focuses on only one of the points in the list: naturally scarce resources and how they can be allocated efficiently. Conventional economics is typically not concerned with artificially scarce resources created for the sake of attention or on the notion of the economy itself as consumable game content. Thus the simultaneous ascending auction, a game created by conventional economists, is great for allocating naturally scarce resources such as radio frequencies, but it generates little excitement, fun, or loyalty. The textbook economist, asked to analyze *EVE Online*, mistook the artificial scarcities and inefficiencies of *EVE*'s economy for natural ones. Instead of analyzing them as content, the textbook economist analyzed them as costs and concluded that they should be removed—taking away most of what was attractive in the economy in the first place.

Economics as an organized discipline developed out of studies of agriculture, manufacturing, and trade. Its development has been shaped by the need to find solutions to real human tragedies such as famine and unemployment. But today, at least in the world of online games and digital services, the scarcest resources are no longer food and shelter but human attention. In the pursuit of this resource, even the economy itself needs to be fashioned into a consumable good.

Overview of this book

How do you go about designing a virtual economy in practice? The array of questions and possibilities is vast. Some virtual economies mimic the physical world in appearance, while some are so deeply embedded into digital services that we barely see them for what they are. Every virtual item and currency unit is somehow produced or issued: bought for real money, earned as a reward, created through gameplay, or even designed from scratch by a user. Some virtual goods can be traded between users, while some can be purchased only from the publisher. Some exchanges take place using a virtual currency, and sometimes real money is used. Many virtual goods change hands outside markets, as gifts or even through theft. Some virtual goods are consumed when used, some have a limited lifetime, and others never expire. In this book, we spell out all these choices in a structured manner, explain the implications of the different alternatives, and provide guidance for choosing among them. To do this, we need to introduce a range of elementary concepts and theories from economics. As a result, the book can also double as a basic introduction to economics for digital natives who are not economics students—a sort of Economics for Orcs.

Economists recognize a handful of fundamental concepts or building blocks that any economy is made up of. One is economic agents: the people who populate the economy. They own things and make decisions. Another building block is goods. Without goods, there is no economy, just a conversation club. A third building block is production. Other important building blocks are markets, institutions, and money. A virtual economy is essentially a combination of these building blocks, configured in a specific way. The rest of this book is loosely arranged around these building blocks. Under each topic, we introduce the basics of the relevant economic theory as well as the practical design issues that digital developers face, and show how the theory can be used to inform decisions and analyze design. Toward the end of the book, we also cover topics related to the management of a running virtual economy. The topics covered in each chapter are briefly introduced below.

In chapter 2, we focus on economic agents. We introduce the rational choice model of how economic agents make decisions and discuss other ways in which human behavior can be modeled. We consider what types of agents there can be in a virtual economy and conclude that a typical virtual economy contains only two types of agents: users and the publisher. Less frequently appearing agents are advertisers and third-party developers.

In chapter 3, we focus on goods. We explain the differences among material goods, information goods, and virtual goods. We dip into social sciences and cultural studies to introduce a broad range of reasons that people can place such high value in intangible virtual goods and review some prominent examples of such high-valued goods.

Chapters 4, 5, 6, and 7 are devoted to markets, the defining institution of modern economics and an important building block in virtual economies as well. In chapter 4, we introduce the basic concepts of supply, demand, and market equilibrium in a competitive market and show how they can be applied in a virtual economy setting. In chapter 5, we examine how the basic competitive market can be bent into different shapes through regulation in order to pursue design goals like fun and monetization. In chapter 6, we focus on market power: the ability to dictate prices. We examine different strategies that publishers can use to develop market power and set the prices of their virtual goods in profitable ways. In chapter 7, we examine the concrete mechanisms through which buyers and sellers on a market do business, like shops, auctions, and bourses. We then finish our series on markets with examples of how users can sometimes circumvent our market design decisions.

Chapter 8 focuses on unanticipated behaviors in virtual economies: how things do not always go as the designer intended. We introduce the economic concept of externalities: costs or benefits that a transaction causes on a third party. We use this concept to examine a phenomenon called secondary market trading, where users trade virtual goods for real money without the publisher's sanction. We analyze the consequences of secondary market trading and present various approaches to dealing with it based on the theory of externalities.

In chapter 9, we examine various nonmarket flows of wealth in an economy, including corporations, crime, and charity. We introduce the concept of institutions:

self-enforcing social formations like companies, guilds, and justice systems that form a powerful counterbalance to markets. We consider how virtual economy designers can promote the growth of institutions and use them to achieve design goals.

In chapter 10, we focus on money. We explain what money is, what it is used for, and the different types of money. We examine the attributes and affordances of good money and show how to design money that works well in a virtual economy. We also begin to discuss some of the macroeconomic aspects of money.

Chapters 11, 12, and 13 are devoted to macroeconomic design and management of a virtual economy. In chapter 11, we introduce the very important concepts of faucets and sinks: features that add new goods and currency into circulation and features that remove them from circulation. We show how they can be combined with other building blocks like markets and institutions to create a complete virtual macroeconomy. Chapter 12 focuses on how to manage a virtual macroeconomy. We introduce economic indicators that can be used to monitor the economy and discuss policy levers that can be used to adjust it toward desired directions. In chapter 13, we look at policy-making in a virtual economy: how to aggregate user interests that inform policy, how to implement policy, and how to assess the effects.

In chapter 14, we finish the book by considering whether there are any learnings in virtual economies that we could take to the real economy, to help us deal with the crises now besieging the global economy from every side.

Although many of the chapters build on earlier ones, it is not necessary to read the book in a strictly linear order. If you are already familiar with games and digital services and simply want a crash course in elementary microeconomics with highly unusual examples, read chapters 2, 4, 5, 6, and 8. If you are already well versed in economics and wish to learn more about virtual economies, start from chapters 3, 8, 10, and 11. If you are simply looking for quick design inspiration, check out chapters 3, 7, and 9.

2 Theories of Human Behavior

Although economic discussions focus heavily on such inanimate things as goods and money, economics is fundamentally a social science: a science that studies the behavior of people. All economic theories, even if on the surface they talk about entities like markets and supply curves, are essentially theories about how people behave in interaction with each other in different situations. In this chapter, we introduce the fundamentals of how economists as well as some other social scientists think about human behavior. In later chapters, we use these ideas to understand how larger formations like markets and entire virtual economies work.

The cornerstone of most economic theories is a model of how people make decisions, known as *rational choice*. It posits that in every decision-making situation, people try to pick the best alternative in light of their preferences. In this chapter, we present a simple rendition of the rational choice model and show how it can be used to predict people's behavior in simple decision-making situations. Along the way, we lay out a few of the most basic concepts used in economic analysis.

The rational choice model is not the ultimate theory of human behavior. Economists often need to amend it with additional rules and caveats to make it match better with reality. Other scholars have developed completely different models of human behavior that can replace and complement rational choice in different situations. For example, game scholars have developed theories of why we play games. We also discuss these theories (see box 2.1).

Rational choice

The core of the rational choice model is the idea of preferences: that people prefer some things over other things. For example, someone might prefer winberries[1] over strawberries and strawberries over smallpox. When presented with a choice, people choose the

1. Winberry, also known as bilberry, is a dark blue fruit that grows in the wild in the northern and mountainous parts of Europe. It is often confused with blueberry, its less fragrant cousin.

Box 2.1
Theories and models

In economics, a *model* of human behavior is simply a set of rules that state how a person is expected to act in response to a given situation. A model can be expressed in plain English, as, "When presented with two equivalent job opportunities, a person chooses the one that pays more," or it can be presented in mathematical notation, or in the form of a graph. A model can focus on a very specific situation, like choosing a job, or it can be very general, like the rational choice model that is in principle intended to apply to all human decision-making situations. Models do not aim to be 100 percent accurate descriptions of reality. Instead, they try to capture only the most important factors influencing behavior and to leave out all the finer details. After all, they're called "models," not "replicas." The more complex a model is, the more accurate it can be, but the harder it is for us to glean useful insights from it. Of course, even a simple model that focuses on the wrong things is useless. How accurate a model is often depends on the context.

The word *theory* is often used interchangeably with *model*, but it can also denote a larger concept: a set of interlocking models that together explain some larger object. For example, microeconomic theory combines the rational choice model with other models to produce a sweeping account of how entire firms, industries, and markets work.

---

best alternative in light of their preferences. In an ice cream shop offering a free sample of one of the above three flavors, our person would go for winberry. Simple—but from this incredibly simple starting point, we can derive almost all the fundamental theories in microeconomics.

Utility and marginal effect

Utility is a measure of how preferable something is in relation to everything else. When something has a given utility to us, it simply means that we prefer the thing over everything that has a lower utility to us. Using the example, our person's utility for winberries could be 3, strawberries 2, and smallpox 1. Utility is not really a measure of usefulness, just another way of talking about preferences, regardless of whether we prefer something for its usefulness, flavor, or some other reason. Utility, like preferences, is personal: one good has a different utility for two different people.

What if our person—let's say they're a student—was offered another free sample of ice cream. Would they still go for winberry? How about a third time? At some point they would probably grow tired of its aromatic flavor and decide to try plain strawberry instead. Each additional portion of just about anything consumed on the same sitting tends to be less preferable than the previous one. This effect is known as *diminishing marginal utility*. Let's break this concept down into parts.

The word *margin* typically means something like the edge of a page or a profit margin. In economic analysis, *margin* has a precise technical meaning: it means an increment, an addition, an extra. If a person takes 100 actions and each action has an effect, the effect of each action taken is the *marginal effect* of that action. So when we say that winberry ice cream has a diminishing marginal utility, we simply mean that each additional portion of it is less preferable than the previous one (see box 2.2).

Graphs

Economists frequently illustrate and analyze relationships using graphs. Let's get acquainted with graphs by plotting our winberry ice cream eating situation on one.

With a picture like figure 2.1, what we are saying is that the size of Y depends on the size of X. In this particular diagram, the picture says that as values of X (portions eaten) get larger, the associated values of Y (marginal utility) get smaller. It simply repeats what we said earlier: that the more portions our student eats, the less utility they obtain from each portion.

Now let's draw another graph depicting the same situation, this time using total utility as the *y*-axis. While marginal utility is the utility of each individual portion, total utility is the sum of the utilities of all the portions. The total utility of winberry ice cream eating is depicted in figure 2.2. The figure shows that the first portions cause our student's total utility to go up fast, but subsequent portions move it up less and less as they grow tired of the stuff.

These two graphs are mathematically linked to each other by the conceptual relationship between the total and the marginal. That means we can derive each graph from the other. A little math would show that the points on the second graph can be derived from the area that falls under the points in the first graph. The points on the first graph can be derived from the slopes of the second graph. They are just different ways of looking at the same data.

Often economic analysis requires the reader to jump from one graph to another, which is to say, to switch focus from one set of relationships to another or from one perspective to another. Also, it will be common to put multiple lines on a single graph as a way to illustrate how forces operate with one another. The next section walks through that sort of exercise.

Predicting behavior

What if our student had to pay for the ice cream? Would they buy it? The choice of whether to buy something can be rephrased as a choice between two alternatives: ice cream versus the best alternative use a person has for that money right now. The alternative use for money could be another purchase, or it could simply be saving the money for later use. As long as the ice cream is more preferable to our student than

Box 2.2
Marginal analysis

Suppose a company is selling ships in order to make money. The company has sold 3 ships, and made $300 million. It is commonly understood that the *total* revenue is $300 million and that the *average* revenue per ship is $100 million. What economists add to this picture is not so common, and this is the *added* revenue of each ship sold—the *marginal revenue per ship*. Suppose the first ship was sold for $130 million, the second for $90 million, and the third for $80 million. Then we say that the marginal revenue per ship looks like this:

Ship	Marginal Revenue per Ship
1	$130 million
2	$90 million
3	$80 million

Social scientists' notion of *margin* refers to the additional effect of an action, as in, "The marginal effect of the second ship was to earn an additional $90 million in revenue."

Economists often analyze marginal effects rather than totals or averages. The reason is simple: marginal analysis tells you what to do. Our company in the example must decide, ship by ship, whether to continue producing and selling. The CEO may have woken up this morning and said, "This company will be profitable." But this is a *global* commitment or aspiration, not a decision. The actual decision to sell happens in the moment, *locally* in terms of time and space. With each sale, the company must decide to build and sell another ship, or not. The decision then comes down to benefits and costs. The CEO must ask, "How much more money will we make if we sell another ship? And how much more money will building that ship cost us?" If the local cost—the marginal cost, the cost of building an additional ship—is greater than the local benefit—the marginal revenue, the money to be made from selling another ship—then the company should stop production. In essence, marginal analysis is how the CEO takes the company's global goals—to make money—and turns them into practical decisions: "If this particular ship does not make money, don't build it."

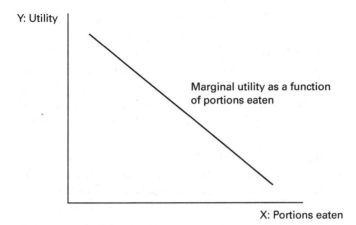

Figure 2.1
Marginal utility of eating portions of winberry ice cream

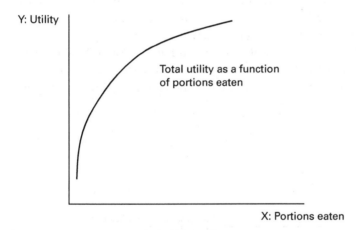

Figure 2.2
Total utility from eating portions of winberry ice cream

the best alternative use they can think of, the rational choice model predicts that they will go for the ice cream. But the benefit that they get from the ice cream is now partly offset by the lost opportunity of spending the money on something else. This is known as an *opportunity cost*. Even actions that don't cost any money have an opportunity cost because the lost time could have been spent on some other activity, possibly one that is fun or profitable. This explains why we don't rush to take every "free" offer and promotion thrown at us. They're not really free: they cost us other opportunities. Only if the benefits outweigh the costs will we take an offer.

Now we are ready to take on the most important question that the rational choice model can answer: How many portions of ice cream will our student buy and eat? To answer this question, we need all the concepts and tools already introduced: marginal utility, graphical analysis, and opportunity cost. We start with the opportunity cost. Let's say one portion of ice cream costs $3. The opportunity cost of eating one portion is then "the best alternative use the student has for $3." We can mark this simply as $3. If they buy and eat another portion, the price, and therefore the opportunity cost, are still the same $3. The same is true for the third portion; this shop offers no bulk discounts. We can thus say that the *marginal cost* of eating ice cream is a constant $3. Figure 2.3 shows the marginal cost of eating ice cream as a graph.

Because the marginal cost is constant, it shows up in figure 2.3 as a flat line. Note that the name of the *y*-axis is Utility rather than Cost. This is because an opportunity cost is really just lost utility. Both can be measured on the same axis. Now we'll do just

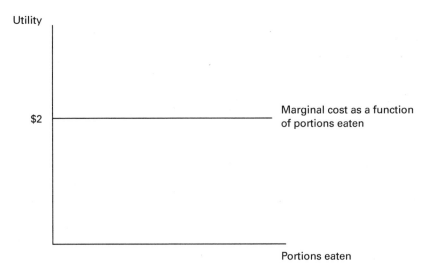

Figure 2.3
Marginal cost of eating ice cream

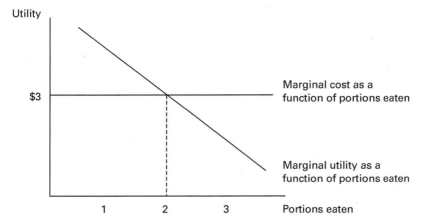

Figure 2.4
Marginal utility and marginal cost of eating ice cream

that and add the marginal utility of eating ice cream, first presented in figure 2.1, to the same diagram. The result of this combination is shown in figure 2.4.

In figure 2.4, the flat line of marginal cost intersects with the downward-sloping marginal utility line at a point where portions eaten equals 2. This value—two portions of ice cream—is our first example of an *equilibrium point*, a place where opposing forces in a system balance one another so that the system comes to rest. The two forces in this case are our student's desire to eat ice cream balanced against their desire to save money for other purposes. Each time they eat a portion, two things happen: they get some utility out of it, and they have to pay for it. These two effects are shown in the marginal benefit and the marginal cost curves.

To see why 2 is the balance point, consider some number of portions fewer than 2. Consider the first portion. When the student eats the first portion, the marginal utility curve shows that its contribution to their well-being is above $3. This means that they obtain a net benefit from eating this portion—the benefits exceed the costs. It was a good idea to eat it. Because benefits exceed costs here, the net power of the forces in play is pushing the student's consumption upward. Portion 1 is not an equilibrium; they can get more bang for their buck by eating more.

Now consider a number of portions greater than 2, such as 3. The marginal utility curve tells us that the third portion, if eaten, would contribute added utility worth less than $3. This means that the student would incur a net loss from eating this portion. The third portion does not taste bad—they would still enjoy it, it would taste good, and they would get some marginal benefit out of it. The point is that this third portion is no longer so good as to be worth paying $3 for. The benefit it provides is worth less than the $3 it costs. Because costs exceed benefits here, the net power of the forces at play is pushing his consumption downward. Portion 3 would not be an equilibrium; the student would get more bang for their buck by eating less.

So the first portion was worth eating and the third was not. What about the second? The second portion is where the marginal benefits equal the marginal costs, and this, it turns out, is the optimal amount to eat. If our student eats more than 2, even one ounce more, they will be eating a bit of ice cream whose marginal cost exceeds its marginal benefit. If our student eats one ounce less ice cream, they will be failing to eat a piece of ice cream whose benefit exceed its cost. It is foolish to do something when the cost to you is greater than the benefit; it is just as foolish to *not* do something when the benefit to you exceeds the cost. Therefore the amount of ice cream to eat, if you are not being foolish, is 2. The forces of desire for food and reluctance to pay exactly balance one another when our student eats 2 portions.

At this balance point, we say that the system is in equilibrium. We predict that a normally reasonable person in this situation would choose to eat exactly two portions of ice cream, no more and no less. Moreover, we can also predict that if the price of ice cream were to rise, lifting the marginal cost line to a higher level, the predicted ice cream consumption would fall. Why? Because when you shift the marginal cost line up, it intersects with the marginal utility curve at a point farther to the left, that is, at a lower number of portions. There would be a new equilibrium of the system, something less than two. Thus, we predict that raising the price of ice cream would cause its consumption to fall.

Similarly, if there was a change to the ice cream's recipe that made it taste even better than before, we would shift the marginal utility line upward because each portion now gives our scholar more joy than it gave before. By shifting the marginal utility curve up, we move the intersection of the two curves to the right. Thus, we would predict that consumption rises. (For a real example of such an outcome in a virtual economy, see box 2.3.)

Social scientists use this kind of *marginal analysis* in all kinds of decision-making contexts to find equilibria, make predictions about outcomes, and calculate the winners and losers from social change. Our aim is to teach virtual economy designers to use it in their design decisions.[2]

Agents in a virtual economy

Before we continue to more elaborate models of human behavior, let's stop for a moment to talk about the first building block of a virtual economy: *agents*. In economic

2. To dig deeper into the topics covered in this chapter so far, rational choice and marginal analysis, consult a standard microeconomics textbook, such as Mankiw (2011) or McConnell, Brue, and Flynn (2011). While it may be going too far to say that all economics textbooks are the same, it is true that the books are largely homogeneous. Most authors explain the same things in the same way, sometimes in the same order. Moreover, the books change very little from year to year.

Box 2.3

Consumption of virtual missiles in *EVE Online*

In *EVE Online*, owners of missile-firing battleships have a choice: they can carry either torpedoes or cruise missiles. For a long time, the two were approximately equally popular. In December 2007, the developers changed the torpedoes' attributes, making them more powerful but decreasing their range. Players reacted to this immediately. Most people started to prefer cruise missiles to torpedoes. As a result, the demand for cruise missile launchers shot up as the demand for torpedo launchers sank. This is illustrated in figure 2.5, which shows the market prices of these two weapons over a period of two years. On the day the change was made, the price of cruise launchers doubled, while the price of torpedo launchers fell 80 percent. Within a couple of months, the prices had stabilized in a new equilibrium.

In terms of volume, the average number of cruise launchers sold per day increased from around 1,000 units before the change to 1,800 units immediately after the change, to over 3,000 units by late 2008. The daily sales of torpedo launchers fell from around 1,000 units before the change to fewer than half that immediately after the change. It then slowly rebounded to approximately 1,500 units per day by the end of 2008 as the economy grew. The players' reaction to the change revealed their preference clearly: most prefer to fire at their enemies from a distance!

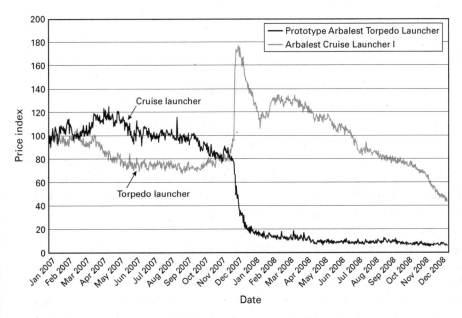

Figure 2.5

Price of missile launchers over time

parlance, a decision maker in a rational choice model or any other model is called an agent. In the examples, our agent was an individual person, but an agent can also be a household, a company, or any other decision-making unit whose behavior we want to model. In general, agents are the actors who populate an economy.

Who populates your virtual economy? What kind of agents does it host? Answering that question is the first step in designing a virtual economy. The most common answer is simply "users," who dynamically step into such roles as "producer" and "consumer," for example, depending on situation. Many virtual economies also involve the publisher in the role of an agent that sells things at fixed prices. The publisher is often represented in this role by computer-controlled merchant characters, traditionally known as NPCs (from nonplayer character).

There are also less common agent types that appear in some virtual economies. For example, digital games distribution network WildTangent's economy includes advertisers, who can buy virtual coins and give them to players in exchange for watching ads. The Facebook credit economy has consumer accounts as well as third-party developer accounts. Online hangout *IMVU* has normal users as well as content creators, who can create and sell new virtual goods. Enumerating the different agent types that will appear in the economy is important because we often want to provide a different set of features to different types of agents. In chapter 5, which deals with designing markets, we show how to give different agents different roles in the market. Another reason that agent types matter is analysis: different types of agents may need to be modeled differently, as their options, incentives, and decision-making processes may differ.

Amendments and alternatives to rational choice

It is possible to find many situations where people's behavior deviates from the predictions made by the rational choice model. Such behavior is sometimes termed "irrational." The words *rational* and *irrational* as used in economics should be understood as labels—not as value judgments concerning the soundness of a behavior. Sometimes behavior that fits well within the rational model leads to absurd outcomes, like the collective destruction of our natural environment.

Individual occurrences of irrational behavior are not a concern to the validity of our rational choice model because they have little impact on the equilibria of markets and other institutions. Even if they occur frequently, random deviations from rationality balance each other out in such a way that the general tendency of our predictions is still right. However, it is possible to identify various situations where people systematically behave contrary to the predictions of rational choice. We next describe some circumstances where this occurs and then introduce the main theories used to account for them.

One area where people consistently make nonrational decisions is choice over time.[3] People usually discount the future to some extent; it is better to have an apple today than in a year's time, and so one should pay $1 for the apple now but only 75 cents for the apple next year. This makes perfect sense. Yet individual people, when given choices to take prizes now or later, often reveal inconsistent attitudes about the future. They will, for example, change the extent to which they discount future effects if one frames the situation as an acceleration or a delay. It should not matter that the $100 in a year is going to arrive "next year rather than ten years from now" versus "next year rather than next month." In both cases, the money will arrive *next year*. If a person is asked to give up something now in return for that future payment, the amount they would be willing to give up should not change just because they are told that the payment's timing was once different. And yet it does. A payment accelerated is treated as being worth more, a delayed payment worth less.

Another violation is the irrelevant alternatives paradox. Say, we give a person a choice between a chicken sandwich and a cheeseburger and observe that they choose the chicken. Now we add the option of eating the sandwich while wearing a blue hat or a red hat. The person's choice of sandwich shouldn't change, but in experimental settings, people will switch choices when an irrelevant choice is added. It makes no sense—which hat one is wearing has nothing to do with the preference for food—and yet our minds do use information about irrelevant alternatives to make choices. One example of actual experimental results is framing. It should not matter in which order candidates appear on a ballot, and yet it does.[4] Another is status quo bias; it should not matter that option A is currently in effect while option B is not. And yet such things do affect choices.

Another class of irrationalities comes under the heading of self-control. There is clearly a conflict between what one part of the mind knows to be best and what another part of the mind chooses to do.[5] The evidence here comes not only from research studies but from the existence of entire market sectors devoted to providing self-oriented behavior modification services. Addiction is certainly a big contributor to economic irrationality (Is the cigarette really so tasty that it's worth $10 a pack?), but any number of other compulsions, fears, and fantastic expectations are served up by

3. Choice over time is an example of an area where economists and psychologists have worked together. By following the references in papers such as Frederick, Loewenstein, and O'Donnel (2002) and others listed in the next few notes, readers can tap into more of the collaborations across these fields.
4. Rubinstein and Salant (2008).
5. Kahneman (2011). Daniel Kahneman is a psychologist who together with his psychologist colleague Amos Tversky was pivotal in launching the behavioral turn in economics. Despite having never taken a single economics course, he won the 2002 Nobel Prize in Economics.

the dark recesses of the mind. Oscar Wilde said, "I can resist anything but temptation." It is obvious that the logical, by our own judgment, is often not the desired course of action. We know a choice will move us away from our own goals, yet we choose it anyway.

Speaking of fear, economists have long known that choices involving risk are plagued by irrationality. As with time choices, we have a sense of what economically rational decisions would be based on mathematical optimization theory, confirmed by the practice of businesses (such as insurance companies) that would fail if they have bad risk models. Repeated studies have shown that people generally do not choose as a prudent insurer would. For example, preference for lotteries should not be affected by the addition of an unrelated lottery to the choice problem, but it often does.[6] Or we should care just as much about a $100 gain as a $100 loss, yet people are very much more concerned about the loss than the gain.[7]

Bounded rationality

In recent decades, economists have started to take these deviations from rationality seriously and seek models that could accommodate them. It's good to know what kind of deviations happen out there, but it's even better if you can provide a rule that predicts when they will occur and in what form. This field of study is called *behavioral economics*.[8] An overarching model frequently used in behavioral economics is bounded rationality: the idea that people's rationality is limited by the information they have, the cognitive limitations of their minds, and the time and effort it takes to arrive at a decision. We briefly introduce these three areas.

People obviously cannot be expected to make correct decisions based on incorrect or incomplete information. Thus, their decisions are based on expected rather than actual outcomes. People also cannot be expected to correctly judge the consequences of their actions in matters on which they lack experience. Thus, for example, complex problems involving risks of highly unlikely events such as plane crashes or winning the lottery are problems for which we are not well prepared. Problems that extend many years into the future are difficult; we experience only one lifetime.

People are not computers. Our cognitive apparatus works in complex ways. Many deviations from rationality can be traced to a cognitive bias in our brain that systematically favors one type of choice over another. Using experiments and observations, behavioral economists and cognitive scientists have documented a large variety of such

6. Allais (1953).

7. Kahneman and Tversky (1984).

8. Behavioral economics represents an exciting new direction for economics. To dig deeper into behavioral economics, see Ariely (2009) for an accessible introduction and Akerlof and Shiller (2009) on implications to macroeconomics. Hamari (2011) examines the use of behavioral economics in game design.

biases in our decision making, like how potential losses seem greater than potential gains of equal value. They seek to explain why these biases exist by building models of how the mind works. One particularly important cognitive bias is *framing*: the observation that people react to a choice differently based on how it is framed. For example, a treatment to a deadly disease that saves the lives of 200 out of 600 people is a much more favored option than a treatment plan that results in the death of 400 out of 600 people, even though both outcomes are actually the same.[9]

People cannot be expected to spend more effort on making a decision that the result itself is worth. Therefore, they do not necessarily optimize their behavior, that is, they do not always seek the best choice. Instead, they may be content with good enough. They set standards of a minimally acceptable outcome and keep working until they get there. This model is known as *satisficing*, from *satisfy* and *suffice*. For example, from a list of options, people tend to favor the first one. Another model that answers the need to reduce the costs of decision making is *heuristics:* the idea that people make decisions based on rules of thumb that they have in store for different situations. One such rule of thumb is to prefer familiar options over unfamiliar ones. As a result, people favor a brand they have seen in advertisements despite knowing nothing about whether the product is actually superior.

Evolutionary psychology

The bounded rationality approach takes rational choice as the baseline theory and builds elaborations on top of it. Other scientists model human behavior on entirely different foundations. Evolutionary psychologists contend that since our minds are the result of evolution, our behavioral patterns must also derive from natural selection to some extent. They posit that we have evolved to make decisions that keep us alive and maximize our chances of propagating our genes. Many times this results in behavior that is consistent with the rational choice model, like preferring fresh food over rotten food. But when it comes to things like dealing with loss, natural selection may have favored playing it extra safe, leading us to have what appears as a cognitive bias from the rational choice perspective.

The heuristics described in the previous section can be understood as behavioral strategies that have evolved through natural selection to provide us with quick decision-making ability. When we encounter a situation, we reach into our heuristics toolbox, searching for analog situations and tools that suit those situations. Often we find the tool that works perfectly. The dynamic of directed motion tool was not evolved to park cars but rather to steer the human body. Long ago it was extended so that it could

9. Tversky and Kahneman (1981). Although the concept framing has entered economic analysis only relatively recently, it has a long history in sociology, linguistic analysis, and cultural analysis; for example, see Bauman (1975).

steer a human body holding a spear or a log or paddling a boat. When we began to drive, this tool popped up, and in practice it works quite well.

Other tools in evolution's toolbox have not worked out so well in the modern context. We have a heuristic insisting to us that when we see salty, fatty food, we should eat it. Today that choice is directly counter to our selection prospects. This mismatch between prehistoric heuristics and postindustrial contexts can be one source of systematic irrationality.[10]

Social psychology

All of the models presented thus far assume that people make decisions as individuals. This is not entirely accurate. People obviously influence each other's decisions when they interact on markets, in companies, and so on. This is what the rest of this book is largely about. But social scientists who study close interactions between people have observed a number of more subtle ways in which people influence others' decisions—at cognitive, unconscious levels. One such way is *conformity*, the tendency to act and think like other members of a group. Another way is *social proof*, the tendency to assume that actions of others reflect the best behavior in a given situation. Thus, if presented a choice between two very similar links, we tend to follow the one with more Facebook likes, even if we know nothing about the likers' preferences. It is often possible to provide plausible evolutionary justifications for social psychological effects. In a hostile prehistoric jungle, it doesn't matter what you personally think is the best path; the correct path is whatever the rest of the band takes.

Theory of play

The theories that we have discussed thus far are general theories of human decision making. To finish off the chapter, let's look at one very specific area of theorizing about human behavior that is relevant to virtual economies: play and games. Why do people play? Rational choice says that people do things because they prefer them over other things. But why do they prefer play over other things? That rational choice cannot explain. The intuitive answer is that play is preferable because it's fun. Why, then, is play fun? Examining these questions will provide background for our quest to design good virtual economies.

The nature of play and games has intrigued philosophers since ancient times. Today it is examined in the vibrant academic field of game studies. It is outside the scope of this book to review all the interesting theories about play and games that issue from this field, but we pick up a few relevant insights. Some game scholars focus on rules, manifested as both formal game mechanics and emergent rules of free play. A key

---

10. Rubin and Capra (2011).

insight from this area is that people like to overcome challenges. Games are a lot about presenting people with artificial challenges to overcome. Another fact is that people like rewards, even virtual ones. These mechanics work best in combination. A game about picking up gold is mildly entertaining, as is a game about running away from a dragon. A game about picking up gold that's being guarded by a dragon—now *that's* fun. Other game scholars focus on the narrative elements of games and play: what kind of story the game embodies, how is it conveyed, how meaning is constructed from the game elements by the players themselves, and so on. From this perspective, it's the story that makes the game fun.[11]

Outside of game studies, play is examined by biologists and behavioral scientists who study play in animals. They approach play from an evolutionary perspective, asking, What function does play have? It wastes energy and exposes young animals to danger, so it must have some useful function to have survived natural selection, says their theory. Such functions have been surprisingly difficult to identify, but for many animals, there is now evidence that play is indeed beneficial to survival and procreation. One of its proposed functions is training: practicing essential skills like fighting and running in a safe context.

Let's go out on a limb and analyze human play from an evolutionary standpoint. Artificial challenges, especially ones followed by an artificial reward, are easily cast as training. The fun and pleasure derived from games would thus be evolution's way of rewarding us for training and encouraging us to do more of it. How about narratives? What would be their function? Many game narratives seem to have at least a metaphorical relationship to actual survival-relevant situations. The game about gold and dragons clearly relates to the challenges of finding food in a dangerous environment; throw in a princess, and you have the mating problem as well. Perhaps good narratives make training more immersive and therefore more "realistic," thus increasing the evolutionary rewards.

If we accept this evolutionary interpretation, then video games are like safer sex: they fool our genes into giving us mental rewards without advancing the gene's cause much at all. Here we refer to the fact that "training" with video games does nothing to train our physique, although especially purpose-designed learning games can train our mental faculties. But even from a functional perspective, are digital games just training? In a world of 2 billion Internet users, where video games connect entire generations, distant lovers meet in online worlds, and some people earn their living

11. On the rules approach, see Aarseth (1997) and Eskelinen (2004). On the narrative approach, see Murray (1997) and Atkins (2003). For more recent analyses that combine both approaches, see Juul (2005) and Bogost (2006). All of these authors are scholars hailing from literature and film studies backgrounds, united by a belief that digital games have become significant cultural objects that require critical scrutiny.

in a fantasy game, are games just training, or the real thing that one should train for? We will return to this idea at the end of the book. Now, let's start talking about virtual economies.

Why are virtual economies fun?

Virtual economies have been a core feature of multiplayer digital spaces almost from the beginning. Even before computers, games about the economy have long been popular. The best-selling board game in the world is Monopoly, a rather vicious game about destroying economic opponents.[12]

The popularity of economics in games is something of a mystery when one considers that most students (we speak from personal experience) think that economics is among the most boring topics anyone could study. Even business is better, despite being quite entwined with economics, because in a business course, at least students are learning how to make money for themselves. Economics, by contrast, is about money and markets in a general sense, about businesses that the student is not expected to own someday, about hypothetical choices in dry and abstract settings. Moreover, the lessons of economics are depressing: no free lunch, profits are fleeting, you get what you pay for, caveat emptor, the government is powerless. Carlyle famously named economics "the dismal science." How can a subject so dismal, so frustrating, and so boring lead to good game play?

The question has not been subjected to much research, but an answer may be sketched as follows. The science of economics focuses not on the practice of economic choice but on the analysis of optimal outcomes and predictions of behavior. Such knowledge is absolutely essential to the understanding of how an economy works and of course is critical for anyone trying to design an economy. But this knowledge is not essential to *being* in an economy and acting within it. In the same way, acoustic theory is not at all like playing a musical instrument. True, if you want to design musical instruments, it is probably a good idea to study acoustic theory, but this knowledge is not necessary to play. And the joy is in the playing. The joy of the economy comes from being an economic actor.

12. Along with most other game designers, we find that Monopoly is actually not a good economics game. It depicts the economy incorrectly as a winner-take-all situation. If that were so, there would be no economic growth, and we would all be living in caves to this day. Moreover, only one man would own all the caves and everyone in them. Obviously that's not how the economy works in the real world. Contemporary economics board games such as Power Grid and Settlers of Catan do a much better job of depicting the economy realistically. In such games, the market allows everyone to gain from trade. Everyone's share of the pie grows because the pie gets bigger, and "victory" just means that one person, through skillful play, gained somewhat more than the others.

We said above that fun is probably derived from being in challenging states that have a metaphorical relationship to survival yet are completely safe. It is indisputable that the actions of an economic agent have long been part of humanity's behavioral repertoire. If bees and pigeons pay attention to the economic consequences of risk, the risk assessment system in the brain must be quite old indeed. Managing a household, as beavers and birds do too, must also be a very old economic activity system in the brain. Trading with others is a relatively late addition to the toolbox of economic heuristics, but it too has been around for thousands and thousands of years. So has food storage. Mistakes in any of these areas could have been deadly for early hominids: bad risks, poor resource management, and foolish trades are a sure road to starvation and death. It is safe to say that economic choices have long had survival relevance for us.

Economy games are fun because they allow us to practice these heuristics in circumstances that are safe. In doing so, we are mastering a complex set of problems in complete autonomy, though we do need to trade and compete and compare with other people. Economy games, in other words, not only satisfy the requirements for fun; they also meet the requirements for intrinsic motivation very well.

We would venture to suggest, based on these thoughts but also the near universal presence of economies in games, that economic simulation is second only to combat simulation in its ability to produce fun and other pleasurable sensations.

3   Goods: Material, Digital, Virtual

In the previous chapter, we looked at economic agents and how they make decisions. We showed how to predict the consumption of ice cream using the rational choice model. The same model can be used to predict consumption in a virtual economy, but the goods available in a virtual economy are very different from ice cream. In this chapter, we ask, "What exactly are virtual goods, and why are people attracted to them?" This will help us both understand user behavior and design effective virtual goods, the second building block of any virtual economy.

Types of goods

In the widest economic sense of the word, a good can be anything at all that has some value to someone: a tangible product, a service, a piece of digital content, clean air. Much of economic analysis focuses on a subset of goods known as excludable goods, which are essentially goods that can be effectively owned by someone, like tangible products. Gravity is highly useful, but it falls outside the scope of economics because it is freely available to everyone.

Information goods

When we think of digital goods, we usually think of digital information goods, like mp3 files, software packages, and e-books. An information good is defined as a good whose value is based on the information it contains. This can be anything from music, film, and software to news, facts, and poetry. Information goods need not be digital; they can also be physical. For example, DVDs, books, magazines, and newspapers are physical information goods. Regardless of the medium, people value information goods because of the information they contain. The actual material into which the information is encoded usually has little value. Wipe away the contents, and a DVD is just a worthless piece of plastic.

Information tends to be *nonrivalrous* and *nonexcludable* (box 3.1).[1] If I read something interesting in a book, I can share that information with my colleague over tea and keep the information myself too (nonrivalrous). There is little the publisher can do to stop me from sharing it (nonexcludable). Digital information is even more nonexcludable: I can share a perfect copy of the contents of an e-book with my colleague and still retain it myself too. This is called digital abundance, and it seriously disrupts the publishing industry's conventional business model of selling copies of information. What's more, digital abundance negates huge swaths of economic theory that are predicated on the assumption that goods are scarce. A whole subfield of economics focuses on the complications and consequences of information.[2]

Virtual goods

Not all digital goods are information goods. Unique contact numbers in ICQ and virtual cars in online racing games are examples of digital goods that derive their value not from information but from *function*—either a tangible use in a given digital environment or a psychological or social function, such as standing out in a crowd. To set these goods apart from digital information goods, we call them *virtual goods*. The remarkable thing about virtual goods is that although they are digital, they can easily be made rivalrous and excludable.[3] A virtual car in an online game cannot be copied without the publisher's cooperation. You can take a screenshot of it and send it to your friend, but the result is comparable to a photograph of an actual car—just an image that bears none of the functionality of the original. From a consumer's perspective, virtual goods are therefore closer to material goods than to what we conventionally

1. Some special types of information are rivalrous. For example, if I know that Apple stock will rise tomorrow, that information can be very valuable to me if I don't share it. I can buy Apple stock tonight and make a profit when the price rises. But if I share my information, other people will buy the stock and cause its price to go up before I've had a chance to buy it myself. Sharing the information makes it less valuable. In marketing, the process is reversed. Suppose I know how to fix computers better than anyone else in the world. If I don't share that information, no one asks me to fix their computers. I gain nothing. If I share it, lots of people ask for my help and I make a lot of money. The information is more valuable to me the farther it spreads.
2. For an accessible introduction to information economics and its managerial implications, see Shapiro and Varian's *Information Rules* (1999). Carl Shapiro and Hal Varian are traditional microeconomists who just before the dot-com bust pointed out in their book that the Internet represented nothing qualitatively new in terms of economics. Things that seemed extraordinary were simply the playing out of information economics in novel circumstances. This insight, with which we largely agree, motivates our approach to the subject matter as well. Virtual economy analysis does not reinvent economics, but it does apply economics to a new situation.
3. The rivalrousness of virtual goods and its implications from a property law perspective was first analyzed by law professor Joshua Fairfield (2005).

Box 3.1

Excludability and rivalrousness

Two important economic characteristics of goods are *excludability* and *rivalrousness*. A good is said to be *excludable* when it is possible to prevent people from using it and nonexcludable when it is not possible to do so. For example, a tuna steak is excludable because its owner can prevent you from eating it. But a tuna fishery in the high seas is not excludable because anyone can enter and use it. A good is said to be *rivalrous* when one person's use of the good diminishes others' ability to do so and nonrivalrous when multiple people can use the same good without loss of value. A tuna steak is absolutely rivalrous because one person's eating it will prevent others from doing so. A tuna fishery is nonrivalrous up to the point that the number of fish caught is sustainable, after which it turns into a rivalrous resource. Most nonrivalrous goods are so only up to a certain level of use. These two dimensions can be used place goods into four categories:

	Rivalrous	Nonrivalrous
Excludable	**Private goods** fish steak, virtual item	**Club goods** movie theater (below capacity), website
Nonexcludable	**Common goods** fishery (overfished), clean air	**Public goods** lighthouse, information

Excludability and rivalrousness are closely connected with scarcity—the situation where there is not enough supply to meet all possible desire. Rivalrous goods (whether naturally or by design) are usually scarce unless there happens to be very little desire or lots of supply for the good. Absolutely nonrivalrous goods like gravity cannot be naturally scarce, as they can by definition be used by any number of people. But excludable nonrivalrous goods can be made artificially scarce by limiting access to them. Thus, for example, a website that could in principle be viewed by any number of people is turned into an artificially scarce club good with the addition of a paywall.

think of as digital goods. From the producer's perspective, virtual goods are still digital goods: their marginal costs of production are essentially zero. In this sense, virtual goods represent the best of both worlds: exclusive objects that cost nothing to produce!

Besides virtual goods, any digital service will obviously also need to include other assets, like user interface elements, background graphics, and virtual landscapes. These are also goods, but they are club goods that are available to every user rather than private goods owned by particular users. As such, they mostly fall outside virtual economy design and belong instead to general game design and user experience design. We will, however, discuss matters of interface design and level design when they relate to markets (chapter 7) and economic institutions (chapters 9 and 10).

From the perspective of economic analysis, virtual goods bring us back to the familiar territory of scarcity. We can use the same decision-making model introduced in the previous chapter to predict agents' behaviors in relation to virtual goods, and that we will do in the next chapter. But first, let's spend the rest of this chapter examining in detail a question that must be on the minds of at least those readers who are not personally familiar with virtual goods: What on earth makes them so attractive to some people?

What makes virtual goods valuable?

When we first started talking about real-money trade of virtual goods at academic conferences and technology industry events around ten years ago, the most common question from the audience was this: Are these people crazy? Isn't it irrational to spend money on virtual game items?

Economic theory doesn't think so. As we explained in chapter 2, the rational choice model posits that each individual has a personal set of preferences that he or she tries to satisfy through his or her choices. In other words, if you really like virtual game items, then it is perfectly rational if you choose to spend money on them. It would be irrational to spend money on something that you find less interesting just because your preference is a bit out of the ordinary. Economic value is completely subjective: something is worth whatever someone is willing to pay for it. Whether the object is a virtual castle or a pair of jeans is irrelevant. Of course, this theory doesn't say anything about where the preferences come from. *Each unto their own,* it simply says. Maybe you have to be crazy to come to prefer virtual items, even if you then pursue that preference with rational consistency. Is that so?

Economists' models don't address the question of where preferences come from. They consider preferences an *exogenous variable:* something that you feed into the model from the outside. Other social scientists have shown more interest in this question. Sociologists, anthropologists, and psychologists have documented a variety of social and mental processes that lead humans to desire one thing or the other. We and other scholars who have examined virtual consumption have found that these same processes can be found generating tastes and desires in virtual environments. In the following sections, we provide a brief summary of these processes, discussing each process on a general level as well as giving examples of its functioning in a virtual environment. This will help analysts understand why some virtual goods are as popular as they are and assist virtual economy designers in developing virtual goods offerings that are as attractive as possible in as many ways as possible.

Because what we are about to cover is a wide body of knowledge with many streams, we must necessarily be selective. We highlight three areas: uses of goods as social markers, personal and emotional significance of goods, and usefulness of goods for catering to basic needs and problems. We start with more intangible desires and deal with the tangible uses of goods last.

Goods are used as social markers

Sometimes we desire goods because of their social value, whether we admit it or not. Sociologists and anthropologists have observed a wide variety of roles that goods play in human relationships. Through possession and display, goods are used to establish social status, express social identity, and indicate loyalty and membership in groups. Through gift giving, lending, and other exchanges, goods are used to build goodwill between people, strengthen relationships, and fulfill social obligations. In modern consumer culture, almost any social encounter, from school and workplace to meeting friends and family, let alone dating, involves the judicious selection, use, and exchange of goods for social purposes. Let's look at each of these uses in a little more detail.

Goods signal social status
Most people are familiar with the notion of status goods: highly expensive or otherwise difficult-to-obtain objects that do not necessarily have much other virtue than their exclusivity. Their value lies in the fact that they set their owners visibly apart from nonowners and can thus be used to signal wealth, achievement, and social position. Economist and economic sociologist Thorstein Veblen, who wrote about conspicuous consumption in nineteenth-century America, observed that the more useless an object is, the more valuable it is for signaling purposes, because it sends the message that the owner does not have to care about productive work.[4] Thus, a 3-carat diamond is an excellent status good, while a backhoe loader is not, even though both cost about the same (see box 3.2 for a virtual example).

Few goods are purely status goods, but many goods can contain a degree of status value. Knowing this, marketers often offer products in two versions: a no-frills version that does the job and a more expensive premium version that can also be used

---

4. Veblen (1899).

Box 3.2
I am rich: The $1,000 iPhone app

In 2008, a German developer released I Am Rich, an iPhone app that had no functionality at all except to display a glowing red gem and an icon that displayed a short platitude when it was touched. The lack of functionality didn't matter. The important feature of the app was not its content but its price: $999.99, the maximum allowable price tag in Apple's App Store.

Economic theory posits that the price of a good reflects its supply and its utility to consumers—that price follows from utility. But in the case of this app, the formula was turned upside down: the utility of the app resulted from its price. As its name suggests, the whole point of the app was to flaunt its owner's wealth. Spending such an outrageous sum on a useless app was certainly a strong statement, regardless of whether you would consider it a smart one.

The app sold eight copies before Apple pulled it from the market the very next day after its release. As a result, the eight existing copies are now almost unique virtual status items, further enhancing their social value. Similar apps have subsequently been released for other mobile platforms.

for signaling. Seeking status and social recognition is something we humans as social animals are naturally predisposed to do. Different people do it in different ways; a PhD degree is a form of status good too. Many status goods are not universally recognized, instead affording status only within a specific group or community. For example, among a group of teenagers, the latest sneakers might be the thing. Among cigar aficionados, it might be a box of genuine hand-rolled Cubans. In a virtual community, status goods take the form of virtual items and currencies. A rare and hard-to-get virtual item distinguishes its owner from the rest just as clearly as a physical status good does in face-to-face settings.

In virtual settings, it is often something entirely different from gold and treasure that obtains status value. Consider the following example. In the massively multiplayer online game *Ultima Online*, gold was not scarce at all. Because of bugs, it at one point existed in such abundance that it lost all its value. Instead, one of the most highly valued substances in the system came to be something brown and decidedly nonshiny. When they created the game world, the developers had placed a handful of horse dung in the stables, presumably in order to enhance the atmosphere. But because they did not provide virtual horses with the ability to produce any more of the substance, its supply was absolutely limited. Players noticed this and quickly grabbed the rare nuggets as souvenirs. A professional virtual goods dealer estimated that at one point, there existed only a single lump of horse dung per 30,000 players. According to the dealer, "Owning one of these was a status symbol, akin to owning a diamond in the real world."[5] The lucky owners would proudly display the cakes at prominent spots inside their castles and be the envy of the social circles. Nuggets were also traded between players for the equivalent of hundreds of dollars in in-game money.

This story illustrates how artificial scarcity allows virtual items to create social distinctions between haves and have-nots in the same manner as physical status goods do. But scarcity is not always guaranteed to last. During the past decade or two, diamonds, PhD degrees, and sneakers have all seen their symbolic value diminish rapidly as increasing affluence and new production techniques have made them more widely available. When this democratization of access progresses far enough, a status good can turn into an ordinary or even a vulgar good. This category shift has happened to countless goods throughout history. Clothes, foods, and household items that once used to symbolize privilege have fallen from grace. In virtual settings, it is even more common. In the online hangout *Habbo*, a rare virtual turntable, once considered one of the system's most prestigious items, was suddenly reissued as part of a campaign. As a result, it plummeted in value in terms of both exchange value and prestige.[6]

Widening access does not mean the end of goods as markers of social distinctions. One process that tends to follow from it is that although elites are forced to abandon their former status goods, they soon find or invent new hard-to-get status goods. As soon as the new status goods become equally common, they are similarly abandoned. This results in an endless game of cat and mouse, a constant quest for ever more exclusive consumption items. Many vendors of virtual as well as material goods exploit this cycle to sell products.

Goods express identity and membership

Another process that tends to follow from the democratization of access to goods is that social status starts to be associated not with goods as such, but with the ability to select very particular varieties and combinations of goods. In other words, status comes to hinge not so much on financial capital as on cultural capital—access to information on what particular style is currently in.[7] For example, among increasingly affluent teenagers, simply having expensive new sneakers is no longer a big deal; the sneakers must be of the correct brand and design as well. This process too is cyclical. As soon as the information spreads sufficiently and the style is popularized, the cultural elite adopts a new style. This results in an endless cycle of fashions, particularly visible in dress but present in almost all areas of consumption.[8]

5. Lehdonvirta (2009a).
6. Lehdonvirta, Wilska, and Johnson (2009).
7. Bourdieu (1984). Pierre Bourdieu was an influential French sociologist and anthropologist who developed the idea of social and cultural capital.
8. This so-called trickle-down model of fashion was introduced by Georg Simmel (1957), an early German sociologist.

Who is the "cultural elite" who gets to set the style? In 1930s Britain, it was the Prince of Wales. But in today's pluralistic society, fashion is incredibly fragmented.[9] A multitude of little cultural elites sets trends in particular social groups and communities: celebrities, artists, designers, scriptwriters, journalists, bloggers, successful Silicon Valley entrepreneurs, popular kids at school, and so on. In digital environments, users often draw inspiration from real-world styles and celebrities when choosing decorations for their profiles and avatars. But trends can also be set in motion by local virtual celebrities, particularly well-known users. Sometimes popular administrators are also emulated like celebrities inside their own service.

In this fragmented world, goods are used not only to play the status game but also to indicate which of the multitude of playing fields you subscribe to in the first place.[10] Are you a career woman, a socially conscious university student, a goth, a Swede, a fan of Japanese anime? To some extent, everyone defines themselves through real and imaginary groups that they see themselves as part of, and they adopt the behaviors and attitudes associated with those groups. This is called social identity. It's a fundamental part of human psychology. In a consumer society, a major way to act out group affiliations is to adopt the goods and consumption patterns of those groups, as when lawyers dress up in business attire or fans buy band merchandise. In a consumer society, you almost literally buy into an identity. Knowledge of the correct things to buy wins you social capital within that group.

In virtual environments, people use goods and styles to express membership in both in-game and out-of-game groups. For example, almost any virtual hangout for teenagers will have avatars dressed as goths and emos, but also as members of quirky local formations, like "horse girls" and "Egyptian mafia" in *Habbo*.[11] Virtual goods designers embed references to popular cultural phenomena into their products, both mainstream culture and Internet culture, to boost sales. They can also obtain licenses to popular franchises like a vampire TV series to sell virtual fan merchandise. The flip side of social identity is that we also define ourselves by what groups we don't want to be seen as part of. For example, some macho men will go out of their way to avoid goods and consumption styles that they think might be perceived as gay. This applies to virtual goods as well.[12]

In a pluralist consumer society, anyone bold enough can in principle start a style by creatively combining goods in a manner that goes outside the boundaries of any of the

9. Featherstone (1991). Mike Featherstone is a British sociologist who writes about consumer culture.
10. Bourdieu (1998).
11. Lehdonvirta et al. (2009).
12. Malaby (2006) provides a model of how users develop and convert capital between its economic, cultural and social forms within and between worlds. Thomas Malaby is an anthropologist who focuses on games and game-like processes.

existing recognized styles. This can be done as an attempt to construct an entirely new type of identity to replace the mainstream identities offered by the society, which are seen as coercive or unequal. For example, in the 1960s, many women eschewed skirts to show their rejection of the roles traditionally offered to women and began wearing pants instead (similar attempts by men to expand into skirts have so far failed to obtain critical mass). In the 1970s, punks adopted crude, shocking, self-made styles in order to renounce the role of obedient consumer and establish new identities supposedly rooted in more authentic values. In the 1980s, menacing hip-hop styles evolved as a symbol of resistance against racial injustices.[13]

Despite this strong political dimension of style, perhaps the most influential factor behind new trends today are, after all, economic interests. Vendors of material as well as virtual goods constantly collude with cultural elites to manufacture trends to sell products. Even styles that start out as protest and rebellion against this very system can end up being subverted for commercial ends. This has happened to Che Guevara shirts, punk leather jackets, and, most recently, the ghetto styles of the hip-hop movement, which became mass-market fashions for middle-class youth around the world, reversing their meaning from resistance to conformity. Over $200,000 worth of virtual goods branded with the rapper Snoop Dogg have been sold in teenage online hangouts.[14]

Flows of goods create bonds and fulfill obligations

So far we have discussed the social processes related to acquiring and possessing goods: how what you own establishes social status and expresses social identity. But some goods are desirable not because they are nice to own, but because they make great gifts. In this section, we briefly examine the social implications of giving away, lending, and trading goods.

If we drew a map of someone's goods-related transactions over a long period of time, we would probably find that this map not only corresponds with that person's social network but also makes it possible to discern the nature of each link or relationship in the network. The exact significance of different material transactions varies between cultural and social contexts, but some general principles can be given to illustrate the concept. Relationships in which the person always pays for goods are most likely commercial relationships, as with a grocer. Relationships in which the person gives and receives goods without compensation indicate more personal relationships, as with a relative or friend. Giving a gift to someone creates a social bond, as favors are expected to be repaid.[15]

13. Barnard (2002).
14. Au (2010).
15. Mauss (1990). Marcel Mauss was a French sociologist and anthropologist.

Box 3.3

Cattle trade and virus diffusion in Madagascar

In a recent study, Gaelle Nicolas and an international team of colleagues analyzed cattle illness in Madagascar.[a] They hypothesized that a particular form of trade called *kapsile* might be a causal factor. In a kapsile trade, the herds of two traders are kept close together for some time while terms of the barter are worked out. The research team first built a social network analysis of the spread of the virus. They then built an analysis of cattle movement in general, and finally a picture of kapsile trading. When the virus diagram was intersected with normal cattle trade, there was little overlap. However, when the virus image was intersected with the kapsile image, the overlap was much stronger. This finding was confirmed with statistical analysis. The implication is that where the trade takes place, and how, has implications for much more than the exchange of goods. All kinds of social material passes along trade routes, including illness but also culture, technology, and political influence.

a. Nicolas et al. (2013).

The total value of exchanges within a relationship in many cases reflects that relationship's level of intimacy, as over time we tend to give the greatest quantity and quality of gifts to our loved ones. The net direction of the gift flow moreover reflects the transactors' relative age or social status, as it is typical for children to receive more from their parents and older relatives than they themselves give back. Between peers, such as neighbors and colleagues, transactors often take care to return favors with goods of approximately equal value, such as taking turns to buy beers, in order to avoid complicating the relationship with uncomfortable feelings of indebtedness. Interest-free loans are similar to gifts. When you borrow a lawn mower from your neighbor, even after you return the object itself, a small debt lingers from its use.

As we can see, flows of goods in society follow the general contours of social relationships. Why is this? One reason is that people actively use gifts, loans, and trades to attempt to shape the relationships that make up their social network. The most obvious example is when someone showers another person with goods as an intentional attempt to win his or her favor. (For an example of unintentional effects, see box 3.3.) Another reason is that social networks structure people's material transactions whether they like it or not. Many times we give gifts because of social obligation rather than our own volition, as with a birthday present to a disliked boss or relative. In such cases, it is our social landscape—over which we have only partial influence—that determines the directions our goods flow to, rather than our own free will.[16]

16. Granovetter (1985). Mark Granovetter is an American economic sociologist known for his work on social networks and how they shape the economy.

Goods provide personal meaning and pleasure

One more class of intangible desires for goods can be found inside the buyer's mind. Sociologists and psychologists who study this hedonic aspect of consumption focus not on how goods structure relationships with other people, but on how people derive aesthetic pleasure from goods, form emotional bonds with them, and use them as raw material for their private fancies and daydreams.

We all have goods that have some special personal significance to us: an engagement ring, a baby toy, a fencing trophy, and so on. Their significance comes from the fact that they are linked with some significant persons and moments in our past. They are souvenirs picked up from the journey of life. Similar mementos, usually but not always of lesser import, can also be found in virtual environments. One item serves as a memory of a past virtual crush, while another commemorates a particularly victorious play session.

Some other goods are personally meaningful not because they recall what was, but because they recall what could be or could have been: personal fantasies, hopes, regrets, and so on. Whole industries feed our daydreams and insecurities through marketing messages and then offer momentary fulfillment in the form of products that let us be kings and queens for a moment.[17]

Personal meaning and emotional pleasure can also be created from goods through active processing rather than simple passive collecting. In an earlier section, we discussed how people use creative combinations of goods, especially in dress, to construct new identity positions as a sort of rebellion against prevailing order. The hedonic perspective calls attention to how that same kind of creative fashion can also be seen as artistry for its own sake. It doesn't always have to be about social struggle; dressing in creative ways can also simply be a joyful aesthetic project. It can fulfill personal fantasies, help relive cherished memories, and evoke the pleasure of self-expression.[18]

In virtual environments that allow users to put their creativity into play, we frequently see wild, crazy, intriguing works of art produced as an outcome. Often the most interesting constructions are based on the creative repurposing and combination of existing objects, much like in the real world. For example, in *Ultima Online*, users developed several different methods of constructing the resemblance of a piano—an instrument not available in the game—by stacking unrelated objects on top of each other. The recipe for constructing a grand piano makes use of dozens of objects, including chessboards, fancy shirts, and fish steaks. The fruits of such creative effort are naturally also displayed to others, sometimes with considerable pride. The hedonic

17. Bauman and May (2011).
18. Featherstone (1991).

pleasures derived from goods are thus rarely pure without some degree of social posturing involved also.

Finally, collecting is another active and sometimes also quite creative way to enjoy goods. It appeals to an apparently rather basic human drive to accumulate things, but also has creative, aesthetic, and emotional aspects. The collector finds beauty in objects that for others may be nothing but outdated tools or trinkets, develops knowledge about them, curates them in clever and creative ways, and develops an emotional bond with the collection.[19]

Collecting is a popular pursuit in virtual environments that feature a large variety of goods. Perhaps the most extreme example of a virtual collector is a player known as Entity, who has set himself the task of collecting one of each virtual item that exists in the sci-fi universe of *EVE Online*. After steadily accumulating his collection for over nine years, he is now in possession of over 9,000 different items. Needless to say, Entity has consequently become a bit of a virtual celebrity figure. Even though starting a collection is usually motivated by nothing more than personal interest, it often takes on aspects of social status competition among accomplished collectors.

Goods fulfill needs and solve problems

We have already dealt with the intangible uses that humans have for goods and showed that people desire virtual goods for the same kinds of social and hedonic reasons for which they desire material goods. Now we finally discuss the tangible uses of goods—their instrumental usefulness. Surely here, only material goods can deliver and virtual goods are exposed as mere frivolity?

The instrumental usefulness of an object, stripped of intangible social and hedonic considerations, is usually understood to be a measure of its ability to cater to basic human needs. There are many theories of human needs, but the bottom line in all is that humans have certain basic physiological requirements, such as the need for energy and oxygen. Food is useful because it provides energy, while a fishing pole is useful because it overcomes the problem of obtaining more food. Virtual goods do, of course, also have usefulness of a sort. They are useful in overcoming problems presented by the game world, in fulfilling the needs of game characters, and as materials in users' virtual crafting projects.[20] But these are artificial problems created by a designer, not real problems. Virtual goods cannot fulfill real needs; only material goods can. Right?

Before we denounce virtual goods entirely, let us ask just one question: By the same standard, how useful are our everyday material goods? How many material goods in our consumer society have something to do with basic human needs? Isn't it so that

19. Belk (1995).
20. Hamari and Lehdonvirta (2010).

in reality, we buy fishing poles for reasons of leisure rather than survival? Food itself is certainly consumed in great excess over what is required for survival—over two-thirds of U.S. adults are overweight or obese.[21] And the numerous tools and implements in our kitchens and sheds answer to needs created not by nature but by culture—and very often by marketing. All kinds of industries, from personal hygiene products to garden tools, operate by constantly elaborating new needs and offering solutions to them in the form of commercial products.[22]

Sociologists and anthropologists argue that what humans understand as "basic needs" has only a little to do with physiology and much to do with their culture.[23] Many goods and comforts that are today considered necessities did not even exist a hundred years ago. Likewise many necessities of the past are today long forgotten. Even some of the most elementary problems that we face, such as the need to get from home to work in the morning and the need to use a car to do so, exist because of the particular sociotechnical arrangements of our society. They are not imaginary problems, but neither are they simply forced on us by the laws of nature. They are actual problems, but we have brought them on ourselves through the paths we have chosen to pursue. Finland has declared broadband Internet connection a basic right. This illustrates how our understanding of necessity changes over time.

Against this background, the usefulness of virtual goods shows in a different light. Yes, they are artificial goods designed to cater to man-made problems. But so are most other goods that are touted as useful. Consider also that more and more aspects of our lives are conducted through digital media. Isn't it only natural that our little problems and solutions be increasingly digitalized as well? We return to this idea at the end of the book.

The value of virtual goods

We have just outlined a variety of mental and social processes that cause humans to need, want, and desire goods. The same processes and institutions could be found operating in both physical and virtual contexts, as well as spanning the two, as when Snoop Dogg sells virtual bling bling. So the answer to the question, "Why do people desire virtual goods?" is, "For all the same reasons as they desire physical goods!"

Where economic theory introduced in chapter 2 tells us how people prioritize their desires to make choices, the theories reviewed in this chapter tell us where the desires come from in the first place. If you are a designer, this is handy because you can attempt to leverage these processes to create desirable goods. If you are approaching

---

21. Flegal et al. (2010).
22. Bauman and May (2001).
23. For example, Belk (2004), Barnard (2002), and Douglas and Isherwood (1978).

Table 3.1

Uses of goods and corresponding virtual goods attributes

Functional: Goods fulfill needs and solve problems.
- Goods can fulfill needs.
- Goods can help solve problems and overcome challenges.

Attributes of valuable virtual goods: performance ("stats"), functionality ("abilities")

Hedonic: Goods provide personal meaning and pleasure.
- Goods can provide aesthetic pleasures.
- Goods can be souvenirs from important life events.
- Goods can evoke daydreams and address insecurities.
- Goods can be used as building blocks in creative self-expression.
- Goods can be collected.

Attributes of valuable virtual goods: visual appeal, sound effects, provenance and history, fictional background story, customizability

Social: Goods are used as social markers.
- Exclusive goods provide social status.
- Goods that are in fashion provide social status.
- Goods can be used to express membership in groups and subcultures.
- Goods can be used to establish and reject identities.
- Exchange strengthens social bonds.
- Gifts create and fulfill obligations.

Attributes of valuable virtual goods: rarity, price, cultural references, licenses

virtual economies with analysis in mind, this is handy because it helps you analyze what makes a given virtual good so popular.

The different functional, hedonic, and social uses of goods identified in this chapter are summarized in table 3.1, along with attributes that are associated with virtual goods aimed at fulfilling these uses. In practice, many of the attributes associated with hedonic items can also contribute to social uses, and vice versa.

What kind of virtual goods should designers emphasize? This depends on many factors, such as intended audience, platform, user-to-user interaction mechanics and revenue model. Figure 3.1 shows an analysis of premium virtual goods catalogues in PC free-to-play, mobile, and social games. It shows the shares of items having functional versus hedonic and social uses. Because of the practical difficulty of distinguishing between hedonic and social uses, they have in this analysis been combined into a single category, vanity. The analysis is based on manually collected data on over 10,500 virtual items from Facebook, iOS, and PC free-to-play games.[24] The overall pattern is unsurprising: in social online hangouts, we tend to find more vanity items, whereas in competitive PC games, we tend to find more functional items. However, comparing group averages masks the immense variation among titles within each group. This is

24. Lehdonvirta and Joas (2012a, 2012b, 2013). These are market analysis reports rather than scholarly publications.

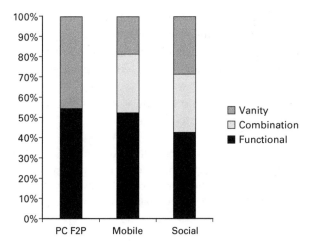

Figure 3.1
Shares of functional goods versus vanity goods on different gaming platforms

especially so in social games. Despite the name, many of them are quite lonely affairs, featuring no social items at all.

Positional goods

In table 3.1, we also list some attributes associated with virtual goods that perform each of the uses well and are therefore highly valued by users. For example, high "stats" and "abilities" make functional game items more valuable. Visual appeal and shared history with an item make for valuable hedonic items. Rarity and exclusivity are the hallmarks of highly valued status items. The thing to note here is that many of these attributes are *positional* attributes: what matters is not so much the absolute value of the attribute, but its value in relation to other items. So, for example, in a player-versus-player combat game, how thick your armor is in absolute terms matters far less than how thick it is compared to every other player. In a social hangout, how exclusive your hat is matters less than how exclusive it is compared to other people's status items. Goods that are valued based not on their absolute qualities but on their ranking in relation to similar items (substitutes) are called *positional goods*.

Positional virtual goods have two major implications for design. The first is that designing the most valuable virtual goods line-up possible is not simply a matter of maxing out all the attributes of every item. If you did that, then all the goods would be on the same rank and none of them would be valuable. Instead, designing a valuable line-up involves designing constellations of goods consisting of good items as well as mediocre and outright poor items that serve as counterpoints to the good items. The second implication is that the value of one virtual good is easily adversely affected by the introduction of a new substitute good that ranks higher. Done carelessly, this can cause great unintended anguish among users. Done cautiously, it can be used to the publishers' advantage in controlling the amount of value in circulation. We examine the macroeconomic implications of positionality more in chapters 11 (planned obsolescence) and 12 (MUDflation).

Now we continue with microeconomic theory and introduce the institution that defines modern mainstream economics: the competitive market.[25]

25. To dig deeper into the main topics of this chapter, social scientific theories of consumption and consumer behavior, see the accessible and wide-ranging introduction by Gabriel and Lang (1995), the sociological perspective by Lury (2011), or the fashion focused analysis by Barnard (2002). For a more detailed application of these theories to virtual goods, see Lehdonvirta (2009b).

4 Supply and Demand

This chapter begins a four-chapter series in which we focus exclusively on markets, the iconic institutions of modern capitalist economies. In game parlance, the word *market* usually refers to a centralized marketplace, like an auction house in *World of Warcraft*. In economics, the word has a slightly different, wider meaning. It encompasses all trade for a given good and its substitutes within a given region, regardless of whether that trade takes place through auctions or other means. In this chapter, we focus on the basic model of a free market, known as perfect competition. The closest real-life counterpart of this theoretical model is a busy player-to-player marketplace with lots of buyers and sellers, like an auction house or an unsanctioned real-money trading site.

Designers don't really create a market. All they do, whether intentionally or not, is create the conditions for a market to emerge. The two basic conditions are that two different persons each have something that the other person values more than they themselves do and there is some means for them to conduct an exchange. There are also other conditions for a perfectly competitive market, which we discuss below. Whenever these conditions are met, a market will push itself into being—not *may*, but *will*. For example, if one person has time to play games but lacks money and another person lacks time but wants a well-played game character, sooner or later they will discover each other, and a real-money market for game characters is born. It is very hard for designers to fight against market pressures; addressing the conditions that lead to their emergence in the first place is far more effective.[1]

Most of the time, designers create the conditions for a market intentionally. They may do so for a number of reasons: to earn revenues from transaction taxes, create a

---

1. In practice, it is often not possible to completely eliminate the conditions that lead to the emergence of an unwanted market without compromising some crucial aspect of the design, such as the ability to spend time to earn rewards in MMO games. In such cases, the only options are to attempt to curtail the market or alleviate its negative effects. These options are discussed in chapter 8, which focuses on unsanctioned real-money markets.

system that rewards user-created content, or simply provide something fun for players to do. Markets are a crucial building block in most virtual economies. For example, MMO games typically contain crafting mechanisms that allow players to produce items and then sell them to other players. But once market forces are unleashed, the designer must take care to channel them so as to avoid collateral damage. For example, a designer who intends that the first moments of a new user will be solitary must take care that no experienced users can gain from buying a new user's inventory and selling it to others. Otherwise new users will be bombarded with trade requests.

In this chapter, we build a model of a perfectly competitive market that emerges from the interaction of supply and demand. We show how market supply is made up of numerous individual suppliers pursuing their self-interest and how market demand similarly consists of numerous consumers. We will show how this model of perfect competition can be used to predict changes in prices and trade volumes in response to events such as patches, and finish with a discussion on the advantages of competitive markets in a virtual economy.

Supply

In chapter 2, we introduced the basic theory of how an individual agent makes consumption decisions. Now we introduce the corresponding theory of how an individual agent makes production decisions. To illustrate the theory, we will be talking about a person who produces apples. Whether these are real apples or virtual apples makes no difference to the theory, but what we have in mind here is an apple-crafting system in an online game.

So we start with a single person who has the ability to produce apples. She makes one apple for herself and eats it. Now she considers, "What if I make another apple?" It would be of no use to her, for she has already eaten. But the question is, can she get something in exchange that *is* of use to her, such as coin, for the apple?

The supply problem

The supplier has a simple decision to make: Given prevailing prices, how much of the item will I make and try to sell?

At first thought, we might also insist that the supplier can choose what price to charge. Yes and no. Yes, someone trying to sell something can charge as much or as little as she wants. I have a cashew nut in my hand, and I can announce to the world that I will part with it for $1 million. No one will buy it, of course, so in fact, I cannot charge whatever I wish. I can only charge as much as the prevailing price for such things. In a competitive market, it is assumed that many people stand ready to sell an item. If I try to charge more than the prevailing price, I will not sell my items: buyers will simply find the next seller and purchase from her. I can always charge less than the prevailing price if I wish, but that makes no sense. Thus, we assume that suppliers in the end face only one decision: Given the prevailing price, how many items will I make and try to sell?

The answer depends on the cost of making the item. Now, in many contexts, people enjoy making and selling things. We might even suppose that a person likes the work so much that it does not "cost" them anything to do it. This is the fun of virtual economies that we discussed at the end of chapter 2. Let's set that aside for a moment, however; we will address it later in this chapter. For now, let's assume that the work itself is not fun at all and is in fact costly to do. This means that the only reason a supplier might make this good and sell it is that they can earn money doing so. Also, recall that we are speaking here only of production for sale on a market; we assume that our supplier has made all of the good that they need for their own use and is now considering whether to make more just for sale.

If the supplier gets no inherent joy from producing and is acting according to the rational choice model introduced in chapter 2, they would make their production decisions coldly by comparing the benefits and costs of making the item. As we saw in chapter 2, the way to do this is to apply not global reasoning ("I want to make as many items as I can without losing money") but rather marginal reasoning ("I want to make another item if the benefit I get for it exceeds the cost of making it").

Law of supply

The cost of making something can consist of many components. If our seller was a real-world business, we would talk about the costs of renting factory space, borrowing start-up funds, and paying workers. In virtual economies, however, the more typical case is that the supplier is one person who is devoting time to making something using the technology that the virtual environment affords. Ultimately, then, the virtual economy supplier's cost is their time—or to be more precise, the opportunity cost of their time: the value of the most fun or profitable activity that they could be doing instead of producing things.

So assuming that the price offered per apple is 5 coins, and that the supplier values the time it takes to produce one apple at only 0.5 coins, it makes sense for them to produce a bunch of apples. But here's the thing: the more time they spend on producing apples, the more valuable each minute of their remaining time becomes. When you are devoting only five minutes to virtual apple production, the cost of adding one minute is low, almost zero. Now suppose you are devoting eighteen hours a day to virtual apple production. At that level of time input, you are sacrificing a great many things in order to keep working. You probably have given up much paid employment or school in the offline world; you have given up most offline social relationships; you have given up most gameplay, online and off; you have given up much sleep. Adding an extra minute to your production now is really quite expensive. As tired as you may be, you would have to give up yet another minute of sleep. As bored as you might be from repetitive apple picking, you would have to give up yet another minute of free time. As lonely as you may be, you would have to cut back your social outings by yet another minute. As poor or uneducated as you may be, you would have to give up yet another minute or work or study. At this level, the opportunity cost of your time has become really high. Thus, we say that spending time has an *increasing marginal cost.*

The consequence from increasing marginal costs is simple: if we want to get more apples from our supplier, we have to offer them more money. If we offer them 5 coins per apple, they will put aside enough time to make a certain amount of apples. If we then offer them 10 or 20 or 100 coins per apple, they will decide to make and sell more apples; at 100 coins per apple, maybe they will make not 10 but 50. They do this because we have made apple selling so lucrative that it beats out more of the competing demands on their time. But we cannot expect the supplier to simply give us more apples without offering them more compensation. By the same reasoning, if we suddenly offered them only 2 or 3 coins per apple, we cannot imagine that they would continue to make and sell the same amount. There are other uses of their time, and we have made apple selling less worthwhile. Naturally they shift their attention to some other activity and produce fewer apples for the market.

This is the law of supply: the higher the price, the more of the good that suppliers will bring to the market. The law of supply applies in all economies, regardless of whether they are virtual. In the brick-and-mortar economy, higher selling prices induce companies to hire more talent, borrow more capital, and buy more materials, all in order to increase production. Hiring all of those extra resources is expensive, and indeed, it becomes more and more expensive as the amount of extra resources increases. Now you might protest that this is not true—that for a company, resources actually become cheaper the more you buy them, thanks to so-called economies of scale. The economist's response is that economies of scale do exist for some resources on some scales. But once you exhaust the local talent pool, capital from close sources, and local raw material supplies and have to reach farther or offer higher rates than other businesses to obtain them, costs invariably increase. In other words, there can be some local downhills in the cost curve, but in the big picture, marginal costs always tend to increase.

The supply curve

Thus, we have the law of supply for a single supplier: a person making and selling virtual apples. Now let's assume that they're not alone; there are several suppliers, all of them ready to produce virtual apples that are all roughly the same. If a price of 5 coins per apple is enough to make our original seller bring 10 apples to market, and another seller to bring 12 apples to market, and a third seller 9 apples to market, then the total number of apples supplied to the market at 5 coins per apple is 10 + 12 + 9 = 31. We can thus go from an individual person's incentive to a market condition by adding up.

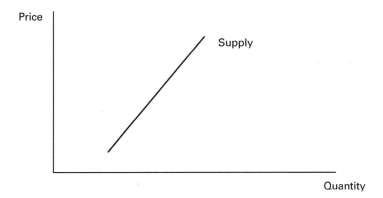

Figure 4.1
Supply curve

We add the amount supplied by each supplier at a given price to arrive at the *market supply* of the good at that price.

The market supply behaves just like individual supply. If the price of apples goes up, every one of our suppliers will bring more apples to market, and the overall market supply will rise. The name for this rule is the *supply curve*. The supply curve is a set of money-good combinations that shows the line between when it is, and is not, in the interest of suppliers to make a good and bring it to market. For example, a point on the supply curve might be {100 coins, 2,500 items}. What this says is that if the price that a supplier can receive for the good is exactly 100 coins, it is worthwhile for all the suppliers together to make exactly 2,500 items, no more and no fewer. According to this rule, the reason the suppliers make 2,500 apples and not 2,499 is that there was one person whose time in making just one more apple was worth the 100 coins. The reason no one makes the 2,501st apple is that there's no one in the market whose time is worth the 100-coin benefit of selling it.

Figure 4.1 shows the supply curve. In general, it need not be a straight line (as shown here), but it does slope upward. The upward slope represents mathematically the law of supply: higher price, more supply (this law is not ironclad, though; see box 4.1).[2]

Demand

Now is a good time to lay out some additional assumptions behind the model of a competitive market we are working toward. A competitive market requires that there be

2. To be precise, this is a short-run supply curve. In the long run, the theory predicts that competition from new suppliers entering the market will tend to flatten the curve into a horizontal line. In practice, the pool of potential entrants is limited to the users in the system, so the supply curve is likely to remain upward sloping even in the long run.

Box 4.1
Backward-bending supply curves: The pitfall of incentive systems

The law of supply is not a law in the sense of the laws of physics, but in the sense of a frequently occurring pattern in human behavior. Though significant deviations from the law are rarely observed, they are very much possible. One major deviation is the backward-bending supply curve: as a price keeps increasing, after a certain point, the quantity produced stops increasing with it and instead turns backward into decline. The explanation for this is that at extremely high price levels, suppliers are earning so much that they don't really need any more money—they start to prefer other things instead, like free time. So when the price increases even more, it serves as no additional incentive to them. Instead, they take it as an opportunity to work less for the same income, and production falls. In practice, though, prices are rarely so high in material economies as to take markets into backward-bending territory.

In virtual economies, where all kinds of extremities are more commonly observed, the backward-bending supply curve can be a real concern. Take a fairly common virtual economy: an online community that incentivizes its users to log in daily by rewarding each login with points that can be redeemed for virtual goods. In effect, this is a market where the publisher is buying logins from users. The law of supply says that the higher the price offered, the more logins will be supplied. To a certain extent, this rule will hold true. But as the publisher keeps increasing the reward, eager to boost its number of daily active users, a point will eventually come where additional rewards start to *reduce* logins. The reason is simple: by now, the reward is so high that only a few logins per week will yield sufficient points to purchase all the goods the user could possibly want. Additional points now reduce rather than increase the incentive to log in frequently.

In a virtual economy, you usually want to run all markets in the normal law of supply land. If a market is in backward-bending territory, it generally means that some balancing is needed.

many buyers and sellers, not just one or a few. Otherwise the market will not be competitive, but a monopoly or an oligopoly. That being said, a competitive market also requires that not everyone can buy the good and not everyone can supply it. Otherwise people would just supply the good for themselves. We want a circumstance in which everyone has something they need and something they can supply. This is called *specialization*. In the brick-and-mortar economy, it tends to arise naturally, as people focus on their strengths and opportunities rather than trying to do absolutely everything for themselves. Both of us are scholars, and we have neighbors who make computer games and play the violin. None of us could possibly provide for more than a tiny fraction of our needs through our own work; we have to trade. In virtual economies, though, sometimes not as much specialization occurs. The farmer-miner-chef-armorer-swordsmith-warrior is a rather independent fellow. If you want to encourage economic interaction that leads to social interaction, you might want to make it harder for people to supply everything for themselves, or increase the returns on specialization.

Let's now look at the demand side of the market—the people who don't supply apples for themselves but may be interested in buying them from others. As above, we will begin with a single person, the apple consumer. The consumer (or "demander") wants apples because they provide some kind of benefits to them. Those benefits can be functional ones determined by the virtual world; perhaps the apples are used to feed horses, which then transport users around the virtual space. Or the apples are inputs to the production of pies, which hungry halflings eat. The benefits could also be mental or social in nature; perhaps apples are valued for their attractive and well-proportioned form. For whatever reason, apples have value to their demanders.

The demand problem

Like the supplier, the demander takes the prevailing price as a given and has a decision to make. Given the prevailing price, how much of the item will I purchase? We already solved this problem in chapter 2 for winberry ice cream. The answer comes from marginal, not absolute, reasoning. The buyer asks, "Should I buy another item at this price?"

To see why this applies to virtual apples just as well as to ice cream, note that whatever the source of value of an item like virtual apples, it is not infinite: there is a price at which the consumer would not buy any apples at all. If the price of apples were 100,000 coins, our consumer would not buy even one; a single apple powers a single horse or a single halfling for a day or less. There are better uses than that for such a huge pile of purchasing power. Horses and halflings can go hungry for a while. Thus, while our consumer would like an apple, they will go without if the price is so high.

If we lower the price, however, eventually we get to the point where the demander would buy one apple. Eventually, at a low enough price, the consumer concludes that the most valuable use for the money at stake is to obtain the benefits the apple provides.

What if we lower the price still further? Eventually we will go low enough that the consumer would buy a second apple. Two pie-fed halflings are better than one! If we continue lowering the price, the demander will buy more and more apples until, when the price is zero, we discover how many apples the consumer wants when they are absolutely free.

Law of demand

Note the relationship between the price and the demands of the consumer: as price falls, the consumer buys more apples. This means that when price rises, the consumer buys fewer apples. This is the *law of demand:* if you want someone to buy more of a thing, you must charge them less per item. When a price is stated, the consumer decides how much they want at that price. They will not buy more simply because you

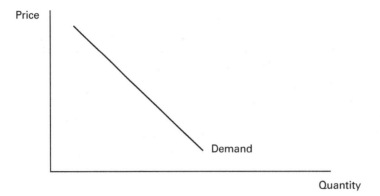

Figure 4.2
Demand curve

urge them to do so. If, however, you make the item cheaper, they will consider buying more of it. If you raise the price, they will almost certainly buy less. Like the law of supply, the law of demand applies in both virtual and physical contexts.

The demand curve

As with supply, we can add together the purchases of different people. If we have 370 consumers and each is willing to buy 10 apples when the price is 8 coins each, then at the price of 8 coins, we can sell a total of 3,700 apples. If we raise the price to 11 Coins, each of these consumers will buy fewer apples, and the total of apples bought will also fall. If we lower the price to 3 coins, our apple consumers will buy more apples. Thus, by adding up the demands of all the consumers in a market at each price point, we get a relationship called the *demand curve*. The demand curve, shown in figure 4.2, has a negative slope, reflecting the operation of the law of demand (but for an exception, see box 4.2).

Equilibrium

We began with single sellers and buyers and a rational model of how they would part with their apples and their coins. We used them to derive general rules at the market level, one saying that the market supplies more when the price is high, the other that the market demands less when the price is high. We gave those two rules a graphical and mathematical expression as the supply and demand curves. They are shown together in figure 4.3.

It is appropriate to put both rules on the same graph because, after all, both express a particular relationship between the price of a good and the quantity of it on the

Box 4.2

Status items and upward-sloping demand curves

> As with the law of supply, the law of demand is not absolute. There are rare situations in which the demand curve can slope upward; in other words, higher prices can paradoxically lead to higher demand. In virtual economies, this situation is most likely encountered with goods that are desired because of their social status value. As discussed in chapter 3, the price of a good can have a big impact on its perceived status value. An otherwise useless item that no one wants to buy can sometimes be turned into a desirable status item just by increasing its price. The result is an upward-sloping demand curve. Goods like this are called Veblen goods. The upward-sloping curve is never limitless, however. At some point, the normal law of demand kicks in and higher prices start to result in lower demand.

market. The supply graph shows how much people will bring to market for different prices. If paid the price P for their wares, the suppliers will bring an amount Q_s. The demand graph shows how much people will buy at different prices. At the same price P, the consumers are willing to buy Q_d.

We are now in a position to discuss concretely the market forces that emerge so powerfully from these conditions. Note that at the price P, the quantity that buyers want to purchase is greater than the quantity suppliers are bringing to the market. The urge to buy exceeds the willingness to sell. People search for the item in the hopes of buying it, but they find no one willing to sell. Those who consider making and selling the item are deterred by the fact that the current price is so low. Everyone who is willing to bring the item to market at that price is doing so already, and yet there are still buyers out there hoping to make a purchase.

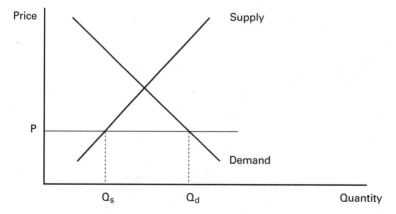

Figure 4.3

Supply and demand

Consider this situation in practical terms, and imagine what sort of social pressures it brings to bear. Consumers are eager to buy, and they therefore urge those who hold the item to give it up. "My halflings need their pies!" cries the apple consumer. "Please make me another apple!" Yet no one can be expected to do more work simply because they are urged to do so. An entirely normal response to the consumer's pleas might be, "I will go back to my orchard and get you another apple, but it will cost you. Pay me more coins for apples, and I will go back to work." Together the apple maker and the apple buyer agree on a new price, something north of P, and the consumer gets his extra apples.

We've just described the case of one consumer and one producer striking a deal at a price higher than the current market price. But if one pair can make such a deal, many others can as well. In the general circumstance where the quantity being desired exceeds the quantity being delivered, the deals that will be struck all share one critical feature: they have a higher price. When demand quantity exceeds supply quantity, price pressure is upward. At prices like price P above, prices are forced upward by the haggling and deal making of the thousands or millions of people in the market.

What happens if the market price is higher, like price P_h in figure 4.4? Here the situation is reversed. At the high price, the quantity supplied, Q_s, is bigger than the quantity demanded, Q_d. There is more supply on the market than the demand can support. Producers have made the decision to make many things based on the high prices. Yet those same high prices cause buyers to stay away. Not all of the buyers stay away, mind you; some are willing to purchase the item even at the high price. Some people care about their halflings and their pies so much that they will pay a great deal to have the necessary apples. But the buyers on the market are too few, and many an apple seller is left with unsold apples in the shop.

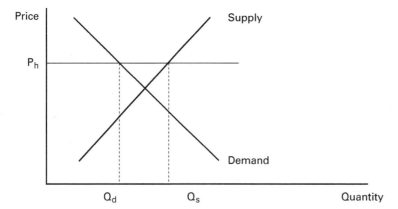

Figure 4.4
High prices

Consider again what this means in practical terms. An apple seller has already sunk their time into making the apples that now sit unsold in the store.[3] The apples are of no use to the seller. They may as well get some coin rather than nothing. It may be that the seller produced the apples on the assumption that they could be sold for 20 coins each, but that now seems impossible. When people come to the shop and buy one or two apples at the price of 20, the seller says, "Aren't your halflings hungrier than that? Why not buy a few more?" But consumers do not respond to mere urging. A consumer might, however, reply, "Let me look at these extra apples, and if you're willing to cut me a break on the price, I might take them." Indeed, if the apples are worth nothing on the shelf, why not then have a great apple sale? Lowering the price would clear the seller's stock of unwanted apples, because, as we have argued, the lower the price of apples, the more buyers. And if one apple seller can lower prices, so can all the others. Thus, the deals now struck between apple sellers and the buyers all share one important feature: lower prices. When supply quantity exceeds demand quantity, price pressure is downward. At prices like price P_h above, prices are forced downward by the haggling and deal making of the thousands or millions of people in the market.

When prices are high, price pressure is downward. When prices are low, price pressure is upward. When does price pressure stop? That is, when does the system come to a rest? Or, more accurately, what is the target price toward which the system is always moving? It is called the *equilibrium price* and is the price at which the quantity supplied and the quantity demanded are equal. This is illustrated in figure 4.5.

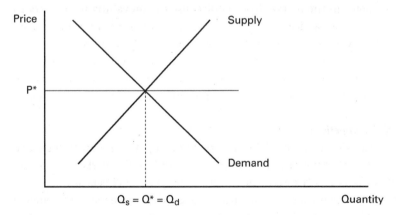

Figure 4.5
Market equilibrium

3. Being virtual apples, they're not going to rot, though their rotting would not change the analysis here. Goods that expire over time are discussed in chapter 11.

At price P*, the amount the sellers bring to market is just matched by the amount that buyers want to purchase. We say that P* "clears the market" in the sense that everything brought there is sold. And while in the real world, because of the fluctuations of circumstance, no market is ever completely at rest, all markets have an anchor price or target price toward which they move constantly, whether rapidly or slowly. Whenever the market price is not at this anchor or target price, pressures build for buyers and sellers to reconsider the prices being paid and received. Demanders are always wondering why they have to pay so much; suppliers are always wondering why they receive so little. When the market produces too few or too little of a good, these thoughts, which are constantly in our minds, bear fruit in tougher terms from one side or the other. The huge retail store with extra televisions in stock is forced to offer them at bargain prices that match what other stores are offering. The sad apartment hunter, seeing that no lodging can be had at any reasonable price, finally knuckles under and pays an arm and a leg for a small apartment. Between them and collectively, these actors push prices up and down. It is neither a whimsical process nor a controlled one.

Now we can see more clearly why P* is a "prevailing price," as we have described it previously. No single person in our apple market was able to dictate P* to anyone else. The price emerged by itself. A person can attempt to strike deals and search for bargains and opportunities, but they cannot force anyone to accept their terms.[4] There are always other people in the market, and any partner in a transaction may always go somewhere else. The apple seller is free to charge 100,000 coins per apple, but they will have no buyers. The apple buyer is free to insist that sellers give them apples for free, but none will. Each actor in the market has a choice: use the prevailing price or try to strike a special deal. The special deals require the agreement of another person and are possible only if the prevailing price is far from the equilibrium. Moreover, any such deals move the market toward that equilibrium, making them special indeed, and rare. And thus, for most of us, at most times, whether dealing virtually or not, we pay the prevailing price for things we buy and receive the prevailing price for things we sell.

Conditions for perfect competition

Now that we have introduced the model of a perfectly competitive market, let's take a step back and review what conditions were necessary for such a market to emerge. The purpose of this exercise is twofold. For designers, it acts as a checklist of features to include in the design when they want to encourage a competitive market to emerge or a checklist of features to avoid when discouraging a market. For economic managers and analysts, it acts as a guideline for determining to what extent the perfect

---

4. Assuming, of course, that there is a norm against coercion and everyone follows it. This is not always the case, especially in virtual economies. See the "Crime" section in chapter 9.

competition model fits the actual market they are looking at. If the conditions are present, the market is most likely fairly competitive and you can be reasonably confident in using the tools provided in the next section to predict how it reacts to changes:

1. *Numbers.* Perfect competition assumes that there are lots of buyers and lots of sellers. How many is "lots"? This question has no firm answer, but the rule is generally that a competitive model is not appropriate if the economic agents can form a group that moves prices up and down by their joint decisions. Such coordination (or conspiracy) is more difficult as the number of conspirators rises. As a result, the number of people required for competition in a given system depends on how easy it is for users to collaborate to manipulate the market.

Institutions certainly matter. If buyers or sellers are able to create large coordinating organizations such as industry associations or trade unions or player guilds and then give all power over buying and selling to the leaders of the organizations, then the right model is not a competitive one but rather some other model, such as a bargaining model among the few leaders of these great associations.

Practically speaking, most noncompetitive models of the market tend to assume that the number of people setting the prices is no more than a handful—certainly fewer than a dozen. Most readers will grasp through intuition or experience that it is rare for three or more human beings of any disposition whatsoever to be unanimous on any question. Indeed, anyone with time in a canoe knows that getting even two people to collaborate is a challenge. Thus, for most practical purposes, you can assume that once there are more than a dozen or so people involved in a virtual economy and no institutions controlling their behavior, the market is fairly competitive.

2. *Specialization.* A second requirement for a competitive market is that the people in the economy have to be different in terms of what they can produce. If everyone can produce everything with equal efficiency, there is no need to trade with anyone, as everyone can just as well satisfy their needs through their own work. But if natural endowments or skills developed through specialization lead some people to be better at some things and others at other things, there will be a natural incentive to trade. Many players seem to find it most satisfying to partially meet their needs through their own work—perhaps reinforcing a sense of autonomy and efficacy—and to partially meet them by shrewd acquisition from markets and other sources.

3. *Free entry.* Competition works only if there are competitors, which means that at any state of the market, it is possible for someone else to enter a given trade on either the demand side or the supply side. By "possible" we mean "technically possible." It may often be the case that no one chooses to enter a given market as a new producer or consumer. Even if no one new enters, however, the possibility that they could is what keeps the market competitive. Thus, there can be no laws or codes or associations that fix a certain number of producers or consumers. Also, entering a

market cannot be so costly that only a few can afford to make the step. If it is very costly and time-consuming to switch from blacksmith to soy farmer, the soy market will not be competitive.

4. *Homogeneity*. The model of perfect competition for a single market assumes that the goods being traded are all exactly the same. This is never true in the real world; each item in a market is slightly different from the others, if only by a tiny bit. If the goods in the market are all roughly the same, then a single competitive market model applies. If the market has goods that differ in a significant way—high-quality and low-quality soybeans, for example—they should be analyzed in two separate markets.[5] In the real world, it can be hard to decide whether all of goods analyzed in a market are actually the same good. Is there such a thing as a market for "cars"? Some are high quality, some are low; different cars are used for different ends. In virtual economies, however, some markets do have perfectly homogeneous goods: every piece of linen cloth is exactly like any other. However, even here there are homogeneity issues. What about a more general market for virtual cloth? Yes, every linen cloth is the same, but there are also cotton cloth, silk cloth, and elfweave. Is it reasonable to lump all of these into the same market? The answer is once again not firm, but as a matter of judgment, one would place items together in the same market if they have the same sellers and the same buyers and the uses and production technologies are about the same. According to this insight, it might make more sense to lump together "all crafting resources for levels 60-70," rather than "all cloth crafting resources." Distance can also be a factor in homogeneity (see box 4.3).

The homogeneity assumption also covers the case of big goods. Typically we will be talking about the buying and selling of groups of small goods, like apples, and we will say, "When price falls, we buy more apples." What then about huge items, like virtual battleships? These may be a big one-time purchase for a single person, but the market as a whole moves many such things at a time. Even though battleships are big, there's still a supply of them and there is a demand for them. All of the logic in this chapter still applies, even for big items.

5. *Method of exchange*. It must be possible for users of a system to trade with one another. This is usually a given in the real world, but in markets mediated by digital communication systems, designers can write code that prevents people from finding, contacting, or exchanging anything with other people. Or they can place restrictions on when, where, and how such exchange may happen. The competitive market model

---

5. In advanced economics, allowances can be made for two or more markets where the markets are very closely related. The markets for high- and low-quality soybeans will be very closely related, so that, for example, if the price of high-quality soybeans were to rise, we could precisely predict a rise in the demand for low-quality soybeans.

Box 4.3

Market boundaries and arbitrage

A single market can encompass a large number of different marketplaces and over-the-counter trades for the same good. What determines the geographical boundaries of a market? Is the whole world part of the same market?

Figure 4.6 presents the market price of a Lizard Jerkin, a common piece of body armor in the virtual world of *Final Fantasy XI: Online*. The price is plotted over a period of six weeks for three different locations. In San d'Oria, the jerkin costs up to 3,500 Gil (the game's currency unit); in Windhurst, one can buy it for as little as 1,500 Gil, or less than half the price. Why is this? Why doesn't competition from Windhurst force prices down in San d'Oria and up in Windhurst? One possible explanation is that many buyers in San d'Oria simply don't know that the jerkin can be bought for much less in Windhurst (bounded rationality). Another possible explanation is that the journey to Windhurst is long and arduous. If you urgently need body armor in San d'Oria, it doesn't help you to know that it is available in Windhurst. "A jerkin in San d'Oria" and "a jerkin in Windhurst" are essentially two different goods. Thus, we say that San d'Oria and Windhurst are two different markets for jerkins.

Agents possessing the crucial information or transport capability that others lack can take advantage of a price difference between markets to earn profits. For example, someone who knows about the difference and is able to travel the distance with ease could buy discount jerkins in Windhurst and sell them with a big margin in San d'Oria. Buying from

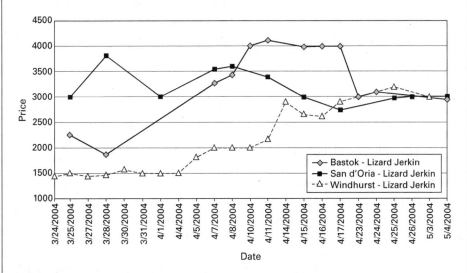

Figure 4.6

Price of Lizard Jerkin in three locations. Adapted from Nash and Schneyer (2004).

(Continued)

one market and selling to another to exploit a price difference is called *arbitrage*. The more arbitrage there is between two markets, the more their prices will converge toward the middle. If the arbitrageurs' activities cause the price difference to be erased entirely, the two markets are said to have integrated into a single market. This is what happened with Lizard Jerkins: increasing arbitrage caused the prices of all three markets to converge at 3,000 Gil. This new bigger market is more efficient: armorers in Windhurst get paid more for their products and consumers in San d'Oria enjoy cheaper armor.

Real arbitrageurs are not simply profiteers who contribute nothing to the economy. Arbitrage profits are the arbitrageurs' reward for making markets more efficient. But what is the arbitrageurs' purpose in a virtual economy, where designers could easily use their godlike powers to make the market more efficient (and thus less challenging) if they wanted to? The answer is that many economically minded players feel that seeking out and exploiting arbitrage opportunities is a lot of fun. In other words, arbitrage opportunities are a type of economic game content.

Arbitrage shows that the geographical boundaries of a market are set by the limits of effective communication and transport. Developments in communication and transport technologies make new trade and arbitrage opportunities feasible and thus drive market integration. In the real world, digital communication and global transport networks have become so advanced that for many goods, it is now possible to consider the entire world a single market.

assumes that users can freely trade with one another at a low personal cost.[6] Risk is an important element of cost; in some virtual environments, "trade" involves dropping things on the virtual ground and letting the other party pick them up. In that brief moment, though, anyone can pick up the good and make off with it. Search is another cost element: if it is hard to discover who is selling what and for what price, trades will not happen. Such things as search costs and risks of loss are part of the transaction costs that must be minimized if a perfectly competitive market is to emerge. Different kinds of exchange mechanisms are discussed in detail in chapter 7.

The five conditions of a competitive market are summarized in table 4.1.

What happens when things change?

The pressures that move prices toward a market-clearing anchor price were famously dubbed the "invisible hand" by Adam Smith, an eighteenth-century classical economist.

6. Transaction costs are often identified as the reason that economic agents sometimes form into larger associations. For example, if it is time-consuming and difficult for laborers to constantly renegotiate their pay with their employer, they may form a union and let the union representative do the negotiation for them all at once. Other types of transaction costs and institutions are discussed in chapter 9.

Table 4.1
Five conditions of a competitive market

1. Numbers	There are lots of buyers and sellers.
2. Specialization	People want and possess different things.
3. Free entry	The number of suppliers or consumers is not restricted.
4. Homogeneity	Goods being traded are mutually interchangeable.
5. Method of exchange	There is a cheap and easy way to conduct exchange.

Smith said that the economy did not arrive at its condition through the work of any one individual, but as the result of forces created when millions of individuals pursued their self-interest. The reality that the humble choices of millions of little people might produce anonymous, self-propelled, disembodied, and distributed social forces that determine much of our economic status is unsettling to some and frustrating to others, but it is an important realization for anyone trying to design an economy that will achieve specific outcomes. Besides, we have to thank Smith for providing a metaphor that is so ideally suited for making jokes and political one-liners.[7]

An increase in supply cost

The model of perfect competition can be used to predict how the invisible hand moves. Suppose that you decide to make it more expensive to produce apples. Suppose that apple harvesting is regulated by a timer bar, such that picking an apple takes 30 seconds. Now let's say that you decide to double that timer bar to 60 seconds. You have increased the time cost of producing apples. What is the impact on the apple market?

We will predict the outcome in three steps, beginning with a stable market, in figure 4.7A. The demand curve is unchanged from the previous graphs, but we now have two supply curves, S_1 and S_2. Focus on S_1; this is the "before" supply curve, that is, before any change. Where demand and S_1 meet, we have an equilibrium. The equilibrium price in the market is P_1 and the equilibrium quantity is Q_1.

Now we express the rise in the cost of producing apples as an upward shift in the supply curve. This is shown by the arrow labeled A. The shift has happened because making apples is more expensive for suppliers—it takes more time. Therefore, we must now pay suppliers more to bring any given quantity to the market. We cannot expect them to continue to make as many apples when it takes twice the time to make them. The suppliers' costs of making apples are higher; therefore, they will need to receive

7. Why was Adam Smith upset at his birthday party? The invisible hand was nowhere to be seen. How many economists does it take to change a lightbulb? None. They expect the invisible hand to do it.

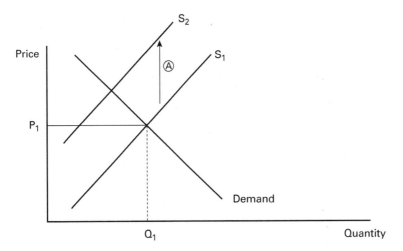

Figure 4.7A
Increase in apple production cost

more money to offer the same number of apples for sale. To reflect this fact, S_2 is higher than S_1.[8]

When supply shifts from S_1 to S_2, however, the market is thrown out of equilibrium, as shown in figure 4.7B.

At the current price of P_1, the quantity demanded remains at Q_1, as before. But the supply brought to the market is not dictated by the S_1 curve now. Instead, the S_2 curve tells us how many apples will be brought to market at a given price. And the S_2 curve says that at price P_1, only Q_2 apples will come to the market. With the higher production costs, many former sellers have decided to do something else. It takes more time now to make apples, and some suppliers have decided that the current price of apples doesn't make it worth doing any more. So they drop out, and the number of apples that get produced falls from Q_1 to Q_2.

This results in an apple shortage. The quantity demanded is still Q_1, but the quantity supplied now is only Q_2. At this point, the dynamics of price change kick in. As with any other shortage, the price of the good gets bid upward. This is shown in figure 4.7C.

In this shortage, people who want apples but can find none at all will attempt to strike deals with sellers at higher prices. Or some shrewd sellers will sniff the air and

8. In practice, the vertical distance between the two curves will be equal to the money value of the extra time suppliers must burn while making the apples. Such numbers can be estimated explicitly, but it requires fairly advanced econometrics. Greene (2011) provides an introduction. Increasingly, statistics packages such as R (open source) and Stata (Stat Corporation) attract communities of users, who prepare reasonably good surveys of the different tools of analysis and their application.

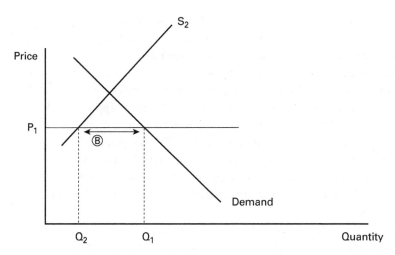

Figure 4.7B
Apple shortage

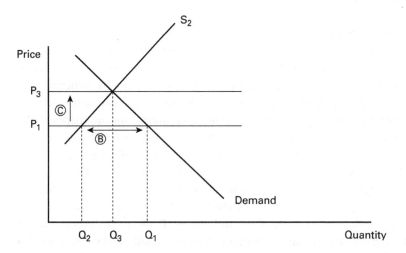

Figure 4.7C
Increase in apple price eliminates the shortage

realize, perhaps after a bit of experimenting, that they can sell their apples for quite a bit more than previously. As these decisions spread through the population, the observed market price of apples gradually rises. This is seen at C.

How long does the price rise? And how quickly? We can imagine that the price pressures are strongest at first, when the difference between buyer desires and seller stocks is greatest. Prices rise very quickly at first. But as the price approaches P_3, the new equilibrium price, things slow down. As the prices rise, the difference between quantity demanded and quantity supplied begins to fall. This happens for two reasons. First, as the price rises, some of the demanders are driven out; the quantity demanded falls. Second, as the price rises, some of the apple suppliers who had left come back. Quantity supplied rises again. The market mismatch is lessened from either end until, at P_3, it no longer exists.

The total effect of the design change to increase apple production time is visible in figure 4.7C. In the end, the price rises from P_1 to P_3, and the quantity falls from Q_1 to Q_3. Raising the cost of making apples reduces the number of apples sold and raises their price. It doesn't "destroy" the apple market; rather, it has a gradual, moderate, and measurable impact.

Estimating changes in practice

Above we showed how the apple market reacts to increased costs in abstract terms. Virtual economy managers can put this theory into practice and calculate actual numerical estimates for new equilibrium prices and quantities after a hypothetical cost adjustment. This can be highly useful in forecasting the effects of a planned patch.

The hardest part in putting the theory into practice is finding out the shapes of the current supply and demand curves. This can be achieved with A/B testing: hold the demand conditions for a good constant, change the supply conditions slightly, and then observe what happens to price and quantity. This traces out a part of the demand curve. Then hold supply conditions constant and vary the demand conditions slightly. Now the resulting changes trace out a part of the supply curve. Use the partial curves to extrapolate the approximate shapes of the full curves. To simplify things, you can assume that the "curves" are straight lines that can be expressed in the form Price = α × Quantity + β, where α is the slope of the line and β is the price intercept. Calculate the slopes and intercepts from your partial curves. Now that you know the shapes of the supply and demand curves, you can estimate the effects of cost and utility changes by changing the parameters and looking at where the new intersection point is. For example, to simulate an increase in production costs, increase the supply curve's β.

Markets in economic management

When all is said and done, what has the invisible hand accomplished? First, it translated your design choice into a new valuation of apples. You made apples harder to produce, and the market made the apples more expensive. This is good. The free market price of apples is showing to you (and anyone else who cares to look) what the *net social value* of an apple happens to be at the moment. It shows you what an apple is worth to people when you take into account all kinds of complicated things: the individual's desire and use for apples, the income they have to spend on apples, the time it takes producers to make apples, and the value of any other resources besides time (in this case, none) necessary to make those apples. It would be very hard to construct a generic "valuation engine" that could combine all of those bits of information into one number that expressed what an apple is worth. Even if you built such a thing, it would be very hard to get it to respond quickly and sensibly to changes. What if the value of a supplier's time changes? What if there's a change in halflings' dietary practice? What if someone figures out how to automate apple production? All of these changes would affect the scarcity and desirability of apples in this virtual world, and any valuation engine would be hard-pressed to keep up. Just gathering the input information would be hard. The advantage of the free market is that it gathers all this information for you (and all) and expresses it in a single number: "An apple, all things considered, is worth 8 coins to our users." This is incredibly important and useful information, and it is absolutely free. One caveat, though, is that this is a marginal figure: the value of the last apple produced. The total production includes apples that were more valuable to their consumers, thanks to diminishing marginal utility.

The second and equally important service provided by the invisible hand is that it moved resources to their most valued uses (on using the invisible hand to allocate user attention, see box 4.4). We saw that when a thing became more expensive to make, less of it was made. That's the right answer. If I am running an economy, and suddenly automobiles were to become ten times more expensive to make, I would have people switch to bikes and buses. But the market does this for me; I don't have to issue a law (or a patch). Similarly, when people desire more of a thing for some reason, the demand curve for it will shift outward. If you examine the previous figures, you will see that this will raise both the price of the good and its quantity. These are again the right answers. If I am the economy czar and my people express a new craving for apples, they should get more apples. Moreover, that new intensity of apple craving should be expressed in a higher price of apples—the stuff is more valuable to my people now. But no czar is needed to make these things happen. The free market does it on its own, moving resources into apple production and consumption. The invisible hand automatically translates the complex mix of individual desire, technology, and resources into action plans for the production, transfer, and consumption of valuable things.[9]

9. To dig deeper into the topics covered in this chapter so far, supply and demand analysis in a competitive market, consult any standard microeconomics textbook. We recommend Mankiw (2011, part 2) for its accessibility and Varian (2009, chapters 1–23) for its completeness.

Modeling fun

So far in this chapter, we have assumed that the act of producing things is not inherently enjoyable to the suppliers. This can be a reasonable assumption in the brick-and-mortar economy, but is it so in a virtual economy? At the end of chapter 2, we discussed the theory of play, which suggests that people derive some kind of satisfaction from artificial challenges. In chapter 3, we also discussed the social aspect of exchange: selling wares to other players can be mentally rewarding. In other words, virtual economic institutions like markets are not necessarily just means to ends; they can be enjoyable ends in themselves. If this is the case and our model fails to account for it, then its predictions will go wrong. In this section, we examine how the model of a competitive market can be amended to account for inherent fun in supply.

This easiest way to understand the fun of supply is as a modification of the supply curve. We described the supply curve as representing the amount of money you would have to pay someone to make a good and bring it to market. If the person likes making the good, you would not have to pay them at all. In fact, if they enjoy it so much, *they* might be willing to pay *you* for the privilege of doing the work!

To put these ideas into the model, consider the following formula:

Total compensation = Price received + joy of work

Now revisit what the supply curve is supposed to tell us: the price that exactly matches the cost of producing the item. In the case of virtual economies, that cost is usually the person's time: a person has to be paid that much to cover the cost of the time spent making the item. In a total compensation point of view, the amounts that a person is "paid" now include not just the price but the joy of work too. Thus, we have this equation:

Cost of producing the good = Total compensation

And therefore:

Cost of producing the good = Price received + joy of work

The usual supply curve shows all points where the cost of producing the good just equals the price received. We need a new curve showing the joy of work too.

Consider figure 4.7, total compensation. We have taken figure 4.5 and added a second curve to it: total compensation. Total compensation is equal to the vertical sum of the price the seller receives, plus their joy in doing the work. The supply curve is unchanged: it still shows how the price the seller receives is related to the quantity they bring to market. As before, this relationship slopes upward. As before, this results in an equilibrium price of P* and Q* that is subject to all the usual pressures of the invisible hand. But now we see that the seller receives additional compensation beyond the

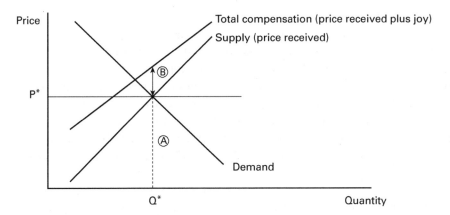

Figure 4.8
Total compensation

price. At Q*, they receive the price P* for their wares, shown by the height (A). However, they also receive joy that is certainly worth something, as shown by the height (A). Adding A to B reveals their total compensation for producing the goods.

Here's how the model can be used to understand the effect of people having fun at their work. Suppose you as the designer introduce a new fun element in the crafting of apples. Perhaps the interface makes a satisfying *pluck* sound with rustling leaves when an apple is harvested. If nothing else in the economy has changed, this effect will be represented in figure 4.7 by a downward shift in the supply curve. Why is this so? First, nothing has changed in the value of the seller's time and the economic costs of making apples, so the total compensation curve does not move. This curve still shows the total amount of benefit the seller must receive to bring apples to market, and that has not changed—they still need to be compensated just as much for their time. However, there is now more joy from producing apples, and therefore the composition of total compensation must have changed. If total compensation has not changed but there is more joy, then the price element must have fallen. In other words, since the seller is having more fun picking Apples, they do not need to receive as much coin as before to pick the same amount. Thus, the supply curve shifts down. All of the usual effects then follow. More apples will be produced. They will sell at a lower price. Because total compensation has not moved, height (A) gets smaller while height (B) gets bigger.

Imagine now an extreme case in which harvesting apples is so much fun that the supply curve shifts very far downward, so far in fact that the price at which supply meets demand is negative. In this case, the demanders get all the apples they want for free and there are still some left over. In other words, apples cease to be scarce and become economically worthless, like gravity. In practice, what happens in many games is that the suppliers sell the superfluous apples at negligible prices to NPC traders, who subsequently destroy them (this is discussed in the next chapter). If it is important to the suppliers that actual human players take the goods—for example, in order to get experience points—you might see a situation where suppliers are actually paying the demanders to accept more goods. Either way, the result no longer bears any resemblance to a market for actual apples, which might be disappointing from a narrative perspective and make it hard for players to feel immersed in the game. The lesson is that, strangely enough, creating a robust user-to-user market may require that users on the selling side experience little joy from production unless the goods are very hard to produce or the demand is massive.

This same model can also be used to assess situations where users get other types of nonmonetary rewards for production, such as experience points. The implications are the same.

Box 4.4
The economics of attention

Davenport and Beck argue that in today's affluent economies, the scarcest resource is increasingly human attention.[a] Nowhere is this more true than in virtual economies, where almost everything else can be duplicated at will except for attention. Below we present two basic economic models of capturing and allocating human attention.

Consider a jigsaw puzzle with only one piece—an extremely boring game that fails to capture anyone's attention at all. If we add some pieces to the puzzle, it becomes slightly less boring. Add a few pieces more, and the puzzle becomes quite interesting and starts to capture attention. But if we add too many pieces, so that the puzzle becomes too difficult, we start losing attention again. A puzzle with millions of pieces is too difficult to hold almost any attention at all. The key insights from this model are that (1) the amount of attention paid to a puzzle depends on the number of pieces and (2) the optimum number of pieces that earns the most attention is somewhere in the middle (point M in the figure here). This model can be used to analyze the optimum number of components in any game, content, or interface intended to capture attention. For example, it could be used to optimize the number of products presented in a virtual shop window.

Virtual economies with any kind of user-created content quickly run into the problem of how to help users find good content from among the chaff. For example, how can users find interesting locations in a user-created virtual world? How can buyers find relevant items in a marketplace featuring thousands of listings? If users have to spend lots of time searching or if their attention is diverted to irrelevant and low-quality content, then the user experience suffers. When users know beforehand what they are looking for, then simply providing powerful search tools is enough to solve the problem. In a typical MMO auction house, users can find exactly what they want by searching for items by name, level, and other common attributes. But this approach starts to fail if we introduce innovation into the economy. How could you search for a revolutionary new antilamp that sucks light out of the surrounding space if you never knew such a device existed?

Social media services commonly solve this problem through recommendations. The theory is that if someone else liked a product or piece of content, especially if that someone was your friend, then you might like it as well. Social media thus act as filtered funnels that allocate your attention to a small subset of all the possible content. But there are two fundamental problems with this approach. One is the bubble effect: interesting or important content that for one reason or another is not picked up by your social circles becomes invisible to you. Another problem is the Matthew effect: the rich get richer, and the poor get poorer. If contents are presented in the order of their popularity, then content that already has a lot of attention attracts even more attention, and content that so far has gotten little attention attracts even less attention. Popularity becomes a self-confirming hypothesis that may have little to do with the actual merits of the content.

Economists' standard solution to any allocation problem is to create a market. For example, a market for attention in a virtual environment could work as follows. Every time a user chooses a piece of content, reward its creator with points. Allow creators to spend the points to bump up their content's visibility in listings and search results. To break self-confirming feedback loops, allow creators to take risk and invest points up front into such promotion if they believe the content is good enough to recoup the investment through sales (i.e., the rewards for being chosen). And there you have it, a market for attention—also known as advertising! Advertising has a bad reputation because it by design diverts our attention, but it also has advantages, namely, reducing search costs and avoiding the bubble and Matthew effects. Implemented in new and creative ways, virtual advertising could significantly improve the allocation of user attention in virtual econo-

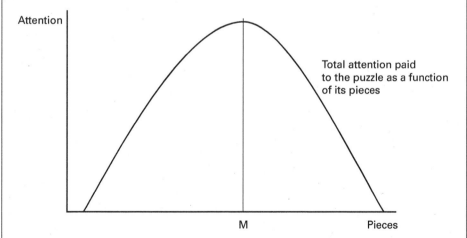

Figure 4.9
The puzzle model of capturing attention (first presented in Castronova 2002).

(Continued)

mies, and it does bring a certain amount of creativity and liveliness to an economy. If average users who are economically active could have the ability to create and display messages about their economic needs and offerings, the effect could be quite wholesome. At the very least, all of the users would know what is possible through the economics of the system. Just make sure to have some kind of advertising standards, filters, or reputation systems in place, though, because advertising that feeds false information into the market can lead to even worse allocations than having no information at all.[b]

a. Davenport and Beck (2001). Although the scarcity of attention has been analyzed by scholars much earlier (see Lanham 2007), management thinkers Thomas Davenport and John Beck are credited for popularizing the term attention economy and the new business challenges it implies.
b. To dig deeper into the economic analysis of attention and digital advertising, see Taylor (2013).

5   Regulating Markets

In the previous chapter, we introduced an ideal model of a competitive market, where anyone can join the market as a buyer or a seller and prices emerge freely from their interaction. However, most markets in virtual economies are not like this. Most are in one way or the other regulated by the publisher. For example, publishers often reserve the right to act as the sole supplier of premium virtual goods in their economy. No one else is allowed to compete with them. And in many ostensibly competitive markets, publishers actually enforce minimum or maximum prices, such as when nonplayer character (NPC) vendors in massively multiplayer online (MMO) games always offer a certain minimum price even for the most worthless items that players want to sell. In this chapter, we therefore focus on regulated, unfree markets: why and how to create them. This is a very important chapter because much of the art of designing a virtual economy consists of crafting different kinds of judiciously regulated markets that contribute toward the aims of the economy.[1]

Why regulate markets?

According to textbook economics, a perfectly competitive market is the best market because it leads to most efficient allocations. No real market is perfect, of course—often far from it. Thus, much of real-world market regulation, such as prohibitions on anti-competitive behavior, is aimed at pushing markets at least a little bit in the direction of the theoretical ideal. Virtual economists' aims are almost opposite. Most regulations are aimed at creating markets that are further away from the competitive ideal, not closer to it. Why is that? Recall from chapter 1 that efficiency is easy to achieve in virtual economies, but usually not their main concern. Instead, our chief objectives are

1. In standard microeconomic terms, this chapter deals with price controls, market structure, perfectly elastic demand, and perfectly elastic supply. Theoretical treatments of these topics can be found in standard microeconomic texts such as McConnell, Brue, and Flynn (2011), Mankiw (2011), and Varian (2009). This chapter focuses on their design and managerial applications.

providing content, attracting and retaining users, and earning revenues. It turns out that these objectives are often best pursued through unfree rather than free markets.

For example, consider revenue generation. If a game publisher has a multiplayer tank game and plans to monetize it by selling premium shells, the most straightforward way to do this is to create an unfree market where the publisher is a tank shell monopolist. The publisher could alternatively create a free, competitive market where anyone can craft tank shells and earn revenues by taxing this market. But this would be much more complicated and burden the players with a new game mechanic, one that might not contribute to the kind of action-oriented game experience that the designer had in mind (and it would actually still not be an entirely free market because taxes are a form of regulation too). Regulated markets are often the default option in virtual economy design: the simplest thing that gets the job done. Competitive markets are an advanced design element that many simple virtual economies don't feature at all. The only reason that we introduced competitive markets before regulated markets in this book is that in terms of economic theory, they are the baseline model on which our regulated markets are built.

Let's consider another example. This time the publisher has a subscription-based fantasy game. The designer is trying to create a virtual economy that provides a fun game experience to the players (i.e., the "providing content" and "attracting and retaining users" objectives). As discussed in the previous chapter, competitive markets can be great fun. Whether you're playing the role of an apple farmer or a dragon hunter, selling your wares to other players on a free market is satisfying. If one day some particular item is especially in demand, you can earn some extra gold by aiming your hunting trips or farming activities accordingly. But the flip side of the free market is that it also punishes for overproduction. If you've named your character Klim the Dragonslayer, bought all the premium dragon slayer equipment, and written a nice backstory about slaying dragons, the last thing you want to hear is that the price of dragon scales has plummeted due to an abundance of dragon slayers in the economy. Little will it relieve you to learn that there are more attractive opportunities available in the baking and healing industries. You wanted to be a dragon slayer, and now you're told to become a baker. It is precisely this kind of lack of control over one's own destiny that leads many to escape to online worlds in the first place. If you make players go through downsizing and restructuring inside your game, don't be surprised if they soon find another game to play. Because of game experience reasons such as this, designers often choose to enforce minimum and maximum prices on otherwise competitive virtual goods markets. The result may not be as immersive as a truly player-run economy, but it is easier to make it work as a game.

How not to regulate a market

The simplest way to regulate a market would seem to be to enact laws that require people to do what we want the market to do. For example, if we wanted to set minimum and maximum prices for a market, we would simply make a law that says so. Suppose the equilibrium price of bread is $5 a loaf and you want it to be only $2 a loaf. You could pass a price control law—nobody can sell bread for $5 because that is an outrageous price. All of the shops have to offer their bread for $2 a loaf. And they dutifully do so—in the front window. What's happening in the back alley? First, because the amount you can legally get for bread is now only $2 a loaf, a lot of suppliers have left the market. Bread is now scarcer than it was before. And the people who do make bread know they can't sell it for more—legally that is. But in the back alley, they can strike deals with black marketeers who buy the bread for the legal $2, plus a little extra for the baker. The black marketeers then turn around and sell the precious loaves for whatever the market will now bear, which certainly is more than $5 a loaf. The price control is actually counterproductive: less bread, higher price.

The same applies in a virtual economy. Even if you fixed the user interface so that it would accept no more than 2 coins as the asking price for a virtual loaf, bakers would simply ask for the remaining 3 coins as a gift, or as payment for some other, worthless item, or take the trade to an alternative marketplace. This is exactly what happened in dungeon-crawling game *Diablo III*, where transactions in the official real-money market were capped at $250. People took higher-value items to unsanctioned marketplaces and traded them there for whatever price the market would bear (we return to unsanctioned real-money trade in chapter 8). Even if you managed to close all the loopholes that make it possible to circumvent a price law, all you would achieve in the end is ensuring that the goods are mostly not offered on the market anymore, as few people find it in their advantage to sell them so much below the equilibrium price. So forget about the idea of using edicts to regulate markets. The most effective way to bend a virtual market to your will is through market structure.

Correct way to regulate: Market structure

"Market structure" is the answer to the question, Who are allowed to act as buyers and sellers on this market? Recall from chapter 1 that virtual economies contain different types of agents. Most have exactly two types of agents: users and the publisher, the latter often represented by computer-controlled NPC merchants. Although it is difficult for the publisher to impose on its users such specific rules as "you shall not ask for more than two coins for a loaf of virtual bread," it is relatively easy to enforce such rules as "you shall not sell virtual bread at all" or "NPCs too shall sell virtual bread." By varying which agent types are allowed to act as buyers and which agent types are allowed to act as sellers, we get nine different combinations of buyers and sellers. These combinations are the basic market structures.

The basic market structures are shown in table 5.1. There are six distinct market structures, plus a "no market" situation if we don't allow users to act as sellers or as buyers. Each of these structures results in a market with very different characteristics. A

Table 5.1
Basic market structures

| | | Buyer(s) | | |
		Publisher	*Users*	*Both*
	Publisher	(no market)	Monopoly	Monopoly
Seller(s)	*Users*	Monopsony	Unregulated	Price floor
	Both	Monopsony	Price ceiling	Price window

key point in virtual economy design is choosing the market structures that best support the economy's overall objectives. They are applicable in all kinds of virtual economies, from online communities to MMOs and mobile games. Below, we discuss what kind of aims each of the structures is suited for but first examine how designers can use market structures to support content and then consider their use in monetization.

Market structures for fun

The unregulated market, where players sell goods to other players, can be a fun market structure in games. It is used in MMO games like *EVE Online*. However, unless the quantities produced and consumed are very carefully managed, unregulated markets can find themselves in equilibria that break the game experience for many players. Prices of dragon scales may fall too low to sustain dragon slayers, for example. We will talk about managing production and consumption—known as *faucets and sinks* in virtual economy jargon—in chapters 11 and 12. For now, we will take base production and consumption as a given, and focus on how market structure and publisher involvement in the market can be used to control outcomes.

The *monopsony* structure, in which the publisher buys goods from users, addresses the problem of prices too low to sustain meaningful play. In this structure, the publisher, usually through NPC merchants, buys all the dragon scales from players at a fixed price. Other players are not involved as buyers. By guaranteeing a certain price no matter how much is produced, the publisher effectively eliminates the producers' risk and downside. However, this structure also eliminates the potential upside and general excitement of player-to-player trade.

The *price floor* structure represents a compromise between exciting but volatile free market prices and reliable but dull monopsony prices. In this structure, the publisher does not completely exclude user-buyers from the market, but acts as an additional buyer alongside them, usually in the form of NPC merchants. The NPCs will always offer a certain minimum price for any good, so that at times when other players are not willing to pay almost anything at all for dragon scales, the suppliers are nevertheless guaranteed a floor price. This floor price is in effect a subsidy, similar to agricultural subsidies in Western countries. Thanks to the subsidy, dragon hunters (and Western farmers) can enjoy the upsides of the market while not having to react to the downsides.

If the lack of demand (or excess production) on the market is chronic, then the price floor structure devolves into a near-monopsony. In such a situation, the price floor structure provides few if any benefits of user-to-user trade. Subsidies also raise the question of who pays for them. In a virtual economy, the money used to pay for subsidies can be created out of thin air. But this additional source of money flowing into the economy needs to be offset with a corresponding sink; otherwise it can cause inflation. Inflation is a subtle tax on everyone who owns money, so even virtual subsidies are not free.[2]

We have examined market structures from the perspective of players who want to sell goods. Next we examine market structures from the buyer's perspective. For players who want to buy goods, an unregulated player-to-player market is attractive for similar reasons as it is to the sellers. It can be fun to buy items from other players and occasionally haggle over prices. Free, fluctuating markets also make it possible to find lucky bargains. This also encourages players to log in often. On the negative side, large price fluctuations can result in unexpected ramifications for other parts of the buyers' game experience. For example, in *World of Warcraft*, some crafting materials occasionally become so expensive as to present problems for players who need them in their daily use of crafting skills. Chronically high materials prices can make crafting professions unplayable.

In the *monopoly* structure, the publisher (or NPCs) is the only seller and gets to dictate prices. It addresses the problems created by unregulated prices, but it also lacks the excitement of user-to-user trade. The *price ceiling* structure, where the publisher acts as a seller alongside user-sellers, is a compromise between an unregulated market and a monopoly. The publisher's offer price effectively creates a price ceiling on the market, as no buyer will need to pay more for the good than what the publisher is asking for it (see box 5.1). User-sellers can still carry on business provided that they can beat the publisher's prices. In this way, a lack of affordable materials will not become a bottleneck for crafters. But as the publisher creates the goods it sells out of thin air, care must be taken not to flood the economy with too many goods.

A market structure that simultaneously involves both a price floor and a price ceiling is called a *price window*. User-to-user trade will take place only at prices that fall within the window. Otherwise players trade with the publisher. The smaller the window, the more predictable the market is, but the less room there is for user-to-user exchanges. Choosing the right market structures and publisher prices to support the user experience involves striking a balance between too much regulation (boring) and too much freedom (undependable).

2. Monetary policy and balancing the inflows and outflows of money are discussed in chapter 12.

Box 5.1
Managing mineral prices in *EVE Online*

In *EVE Online*, the mineral titanium is a raw material that is used in the construction of all kinds of goods from spaceships to ammunition. It is obtained from asteroids that float in space. Players must fly their ships to asteroid belts, select an asteroid, and fire up their mining lasers. After a few moments, a certain amount of ore that can be refined into minerals is transferred into their hold. In time, the asteroid and the entire belt will be depleted. After a certain time (the *respawn time*), new asteroids appear, full of minerals. But before the respawn occurs, the only way to produce more minerals is to seek progressively more distant and dangerous asteroid belts. As a result, mineral production has an upward-sloping supply curve.

There used to be a price ceiling on the market for titanium. It was possible to acquire any quantity of the mineral at a fixed price of approximately 3.6 Interstellar Kredits (ISK) per unit. This could be done as follows. NPC suppliers would not sell titanium directly, but they sold unlimited quantities of certain spaceships and components at fixed prices. Skilled characters could recycle some of these goods back into titanium at a cost of 3.6 ISK per unit. So whenever supply and demand caused titanium's market price to exceed 3.6 ISK per unit, profit-seeking recyclers would start supplying the market with recycled titanium. This created an effective price ceiling for the mineral.

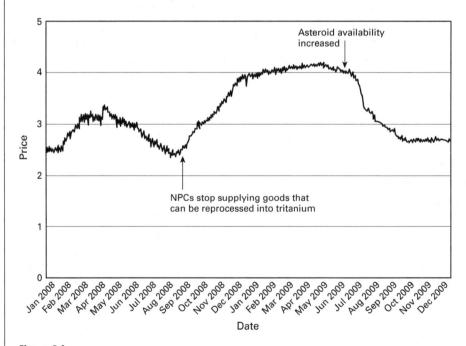

Figure 5.1
Price of titanium over time

(Continued)

In this case, the price ceiling was not an intentional design decision. The NPC suppliers that in effect created it were there only to provide certain conveniences and basic necessities in case the player-driven economy failed to provide them. The effect of the price ceiling was to cap the raw material costs of industrialists, but at the same time, it limited the profits and expansion of mining-oriented players. In 2008, in line with their aim to make *EVE*'s economy as player-driven as possible, the developers removed the NPC suppliers and thus eliminated the price ceiling.

The effect of the removal of the price ceiling can be seen in figure 5.1. Although the market wasn't clinging to the 3.6 ISK ceiling before the change because many factors caused it to fluctuate, it started on a steady upward course after the removal of the ceiling. An equilibrium price emerged at around 4.1 ISK. As the developers had expected, mining activity soared. But there were also further consequences. Asteroids became increasingly scarce, especially in safer areas. This had a negative impact on the game experience, especially for less experienced players. Industrialists' raw material costs also naturally increased.

On June 19, 2009, the developers made another change: the respawn rate for asteroids carrying tritanium ores was bumped up. According to our competitive market model, such a rightward shift in supply should decrease price and increase quantity. The market reacted just so. The price of tritanium fell 25 percent in two months and the quantity traded almost doubled. In terms of raw material costs and asteroid availability, the situation was now similar to how it had been before the price ceiling was removed. The difference was that the player mining industry was now much larger, standing in for the part that in the past had been supplied by NPCs.

The correct choice of market structure also depends in part on such factors as the target player demographic. Traditional MMO players are relatively dedicated gamers and can handle the occasional setback, especially if a corresponding upside is also possible. Thus, MMOs usually feature relatively unregulated user-to-user markets. In comparison, many mobile and social game developers cater to a much more mainstream audience that is more used to single-player casual games and noninteractive entertainment. Not surprisingly, then, the developers of so-called social games tend to go for the most asocial market structures, monopoly and monopsony, instead of structures that facilitate player-to-player engagement. Everything from strawberry bushes to restaurant chairs is sold at fixed prices from the publisher's catalogue. This allows designers to provide a game experience that is more consistent and predictable, if also less satisfying to some players.

The economics of NPC merchants

The basic idea in all the market structures where the publisher is involved as a buyer or seller is using computer-controlled agents to make sure that prices never reach below or above a certain limit. Let's call them *pricebots*. They typically appear as NPC merchants or simply as a "store" that lists items and prices. The distinguishing feature of a pricebot is that it is economically stupid. One version is the pricebot seller, which stupidly offers an unlimited number of a good for sale, at a single unchanging price, when any reasonable, rational economic agent would eventually run out of things to sell or would have to raise prices in order to procure more of the good. Similarly, a pricebot buyer will stupidly stand ready to buy an unlimited quantity of any garbage item that users bring it, again at an unchanging price. This behavior makes no sense at all; no real merchant or "store" would ever have enough money to endlessly buy worthless junk on demand. Any that tried would quickly go out of business, having no money and a warehouse full of, say, Dead Rat Head Soup. The only reason these bots can stay in business, of course, is that the designer provided them with an unlimited supply of credit. The designer let them mint any amount of coin needed to pay for all that garbage. You let them create any amount of goods, at zero cost, so that they can keep selling those goods at the same price. Anything the pricebots receive in exchange—the money or the Dead Rat Head Soup — the designer simply directs them to destroy.

Pricebots offer unlimited supply or demand to a market. Figure 5.2 shows how they can be used to affect market prices. The example here is of a buying pricebot. Left to itself, the market would achieve price P and quantity Q. However, you as designer introduce a merchant who stands ready to buy this good—call them apples—at the price PB, without limit. Immediately anyone who is selling apples to players at the price P leaves that business and takes their apples to the merchant, selling them for more and earning a tidy increase of PB − P coins on each one. People who want to buy apples find none on the market. People who sell apples are earning PB for each. How then will player-demanders get back into the market? Only by agreeing to pay as much

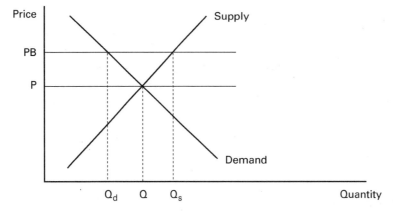

Figure 5.2
Price floor: The effect of a buying pricebot

as the buying pricebot does. An ordinary user who offers an apple maker anything less than PB will be refused. And thus, if they want apples, they have to pay what the competition pays: PB. It does not matter that the competition is a nonplayer character; all that matters is the bot's willingness to buy any amount of apples at price PB. This is the price floor market structure.

Besides increasing the going price to PB, the pricebot's purchases also have other effects on the market. At the new higher price, plenty of new human suppliers rush into the market. The total amount of apples made rises from Q to Q_s, a hefty increase. The pricebot has made apple selling more profitable, so more people are doing it. At the same time, though, the total amount of apples consumed by players has fallen. Of the Q_s apples produced, a significant amount ($Q_s - Q_d$) goes to the pricebot, who destroys them. Only Q_d is left for players, which is less than Q. Economists would say that the pricebot has crowded out some of the human players: it bought some apples that humans were going to get before.

Note that a buying pricebot operating at a price below the equilibrium will have no effect on the market. Sellers will sell for the highest price. If PB is below P, sellers will sell to other players, not to the bot. PB is a price floor: nothing can go below it, but it has no effect on what happens above it.

Now let's examine a selling pricebot. The bot sells an unlimited amount of a good at a fixed price to establish a price ceiling. If the price ceiling is higher than the market equilibrium, there is no effect; no buyers will purchase from a bot that's more expensive than what other users offer. Thus, the selling pricebot's price must be below the market equilibrium to have an effect. If it is, we would have similar effects. The market price would fall to the pricebot's price. Suppliers would be crowded out to some extent. They would have to compete with the pricebot seller and match its price. It's a lower price, so some of the human suppliers are driven out of the market. Demanders would get more of the good and pay a lower price for it.

Some virtual economies use buying and selling pricebots at the same time. This is the price window structure. A merchant may offer to buy an endless supply of apples for a low price and sell an endless supply of them for a very high price. As we have just noted, sellers at high prices and buyers at low prices can expect no business. Yet these prices put an effective bound on the markets, limits beyond which the market cannot go. If something breaks, for example, and suddenly the market is flooded with apples, their price will not fall to zero because there is a buying pricebot sitting there with a low price setting. It'll always buy at that price, no matter what. The selling pricebot with its high price puts a ceiling on the maximum price that the market will ever see; even if something goes wrong and suddenly the price of apples skyrockets, it can never be higher than the pricebot seller's price; he will always sell Apples for that price, no matter what. These two bots work in tandem to put a band around free market prices to force them inside a window.

(As an exercise, you might work through the effect of having a pricebot seller with a low price and a pricebot buyer with a high price. It is not pretty.)

Our discussion focused on the use of NPC merchants for creating price ceilings and price floors in order to regulate the market, but NPC merchants can also be used in more dynamic ways to put content and action into the economy. For example, new buyers and sellers could be programmed to enter markets periodically and create interesting fluctuations while at the same time guaranteeing that those who produce things are compensated at a rate they enjoy, while those who buy things find the prices reasonable.

Market structures for monetization

When a publisher uses virtual goods or currency sales as a way to turn its content into earnings, the question is not only what market structure provides a good user experience, but also what market structure yields the biggest revenues from a given set of content. From this perspective, an obvious choice is the monopoly structure, which is used in most social games. In this structure, the publisher sells currency or items designated as "cash items" to the users and will not permit the users to resell them to other users in order to prevent competition from second-hand sales. After all, virtual second-hand goods are identical to new ones. If second-hand sales were permitted, some of the users would buy used instead of new, and the publisher's sales would fall—right?

Amazon.com, the world's biggest bookstore, is so popular that many people don't even consider buying their books elsewhere. Just like successful virtual economy operators, Amazon has a considerable degree of monopoly power over its customers. But the market structure it has put in place for books on its site is not the monopoly structure; it's the price ceiling structure. For each title in its catalogue, Amazon lists not only the price of buying a new copy, but also offers from sellers of used books that carry the title. Buying a used one from a third-party bookseller is almost just as easy as buying a new one from Amazon. Why does Amazon do this? Sure, it earns a small commission on each used book sold through Amazon.com. But wouldn't it make more sense to assert a monopoly on its site?

The existence of a second-hand market, also known as a secondary market, certainly results in some consumers buying used instead of new (it "cannibalizes" primary market sales). But here's the trick: it will also result in some consumers buying new who would otherwise not have bought anything at all. This surprising effect is explained by the fact that the existence of a secondary market can increase the total lifetime value of a book to someone buying it from a store. After consuming the book's content, the reader now has the option of selling it to earn back some of their money. Consider the following inequalities. Without a secondary market, a rational consumer will purchase the book if the following condition is met:

price < value of the content

With a secondary market added, the condition becomes:

price < value of the content + resale price

In other words, the deal becomes attractive to a larger number of customers or at a higher price tag, or both. To make this model more realistic, we could also consider the residual value of keeping the book on your bookshelf (as a reference or to impress others), which is lost if the book is resold. In this case, adding a secondary market will make primary market prices more attractive only if

resale price > residual value of the book – cost of shelf space.

In the model, we assumed that the consumer knows the value of the book's content when deciding whether to purchase it. In reality, this is often not the case. Books are an example of experience goods (introduced in chapter 1): goods that are hard to assess for value before actually buying and consuming them. Buying an experience good is risky because you might find after reading the first few pages that the content fails to live up to your expectations. The existence of a secondary market reduces the risk of buying an experience good by allowing you as the buyer to recover at least part of the purchase price of the good in case it turns out to be bad. This is not much of an issue for virtual goods like swords and power-ups that have a predictable effect. But other virtual goods, such as complex game characters and whole games that have essentially been turned into virtual goods by means of digital rights/restrictions management (DRM), are to a great extent experience goods.

To summarize, the choice between a monopoly structure and a price ceiling structure (i.e., a monopoly with a secondary market) in markets intended for monetization depends on whether the introduction of a secondary market will increase primary market sales more than it cannibalizes them.

It is also possible to try to reduce the cannibalization effect. To understand how to achieve this, it is useful to view it as a price discrimination problem: you would like customers with a high willingness to pay to buy primary market goods and customers with a low willingness to pay to buy secondary market goods. Price discrimination techniques are discussed in chapter 4, but let's briefly examine a highly relevant example here. Teenage online hangout *Habbo*'s publisher Sulake makes money by selling virtual items to users. Users pay for the items using Habbo Credits, a currency that Sulake sells for national currency. But Sulake doesn't have a monopoly over the item sales: it allows users to resell virtual items to each other (using the same currency). However, *Habbo*'s users are keen on new content, which Sulake regularly publishes and promotes. Every time a new item is introduced, those who want it and are willing to pay a high price for it will buy it from Sulake. They can't buy it used, because it takes time for items to become available for sale used. Later, when used ones start to become available, those who weren't willing to pay Sulake's price can buy the item more cheaply. This is a type of intertemporal price discrimination. The longer the delay between the introduction of a new product on the primary market and the rise of the second-hand market, the less the latter will cannibalize the former.

Monetizing virtual currencies

In the *Habbo* example, the market for virtual items followed the price ceiling structure, but the market for Habbo Credits nevertheless followed a simple monopoly structure: the only agent selling Habbo Credits for euros and dollars was Sulake. This is probably the most typical way to monetize virtual currencies. However, it is also possible to use a price ceiling market structure for this purpose. In chapter 1, we introduced Q coin, the Chinese virtual currency that has begun to be accepted as payment for goods and services outside its host platform, Tencent QQ. Consumers who want to obtain Q coins can buy them from Tencent for a fixed price of 1 yuan per coin. Alternatively, they can purchase "used" coins from an unsanctioned third-party trader at the going market price. These used coins come from merchants who accept Q coins as payment.

So how does Tencent make money if the same used coins circulate between consumers and merchants? The answer is that on every turn of the cycle, some coins are spent on Tencent's official goods and value-added services. These goods and services are sinks: coins spent on them are retired from circulation. This reduces the total money supply and results in a slight increase in the secondary market price of the Q coin.[3] When the secondary market price starts to approach the primary market price, consumers might just as well buy new coins from Tencent instead of used ones. When they do, it provides revenue to Tencent and introduces new coins into circulation, which increases the money supply and eases the secondary market price. As a result, the secondary market price for Q coins tends to hover at around 0.9 yuan, never exceeding the price ceiling of 1 yuan.

What is the advantage of this rather complicated price ceiling arrangement compared to a simple monopoly? It is a very different strategy. Since account holders can use the market to convert virtual currency back into national currency, it becomes possible for third-party merchants and service providers to start accepting the virtual currency as payment. If they do, this increases the size of the currency area, attracts more consumers, and means that a greater amount of currency will be required to support the economy. For each new coin minted and sold to users, the publisher earns revenue. Economic growth thus translates into the publisher's earnings. These earnings continue as long as the economy keeps growing. After the growth stops, the publisher's revenues will come from coins minted to replace ones retired through sinks, as well as from any possible transaction fees. Monopolists benefit in the same way from

3. The relationship between money supply size and currency value is examined in detail in chapter 12 in the "Monetary Policy" section.

economic growth, but without third-party merchants, their economy is likely to grow much less. Simply opening up your currency is of course no guarantee that third parties actually start using it. Designing money that people will want to use is covered in detail in chapter 10.

Second Life's publisher, Linden Lab, uses a similar system to monetize its virtual currency, the Linden dollar (L$). Linden dollars are traded for US dollars (as well as for other national and virtual currencies) on several marketplaces, which together resemble an unregulated market. However, Linden Lab also participates as a seller on the market, selling newly minted Linden dollars to replace the money retired through sinks and to increase the total money supply in times of economic growth. The difference to Tencent is that Linden has not established a clearly defined ceiling price. It apparently seeks to maintain the exchange rate at around $1 = L$270, but is known to have sold Linden dollars at lower rates as well. This has earned the publisher accusations of undercutting the market from users trying to sell their Linden dollars. The long-term revenue potential of Linden's flexible ceiling model depends on exactly the same factors as that of Tencent's hard ceiling: economic growth and the net rate at which money is retired out of circulation. Tencent's model is better, however, because it is more predictable and transparent, and therefore instills confidence in the market.

One challenge with using the price ceiling structure for monetization is that the sources and sinks that determine the net rate at which money is retired out of circulation must be well balanced for each individual user. If they work well for most users but cause a few users to enjoy huge surpluses, then those rich users can sell the currency to every other user at rates that undercut the publisher, leaving it without revenues. In the monopoly strategy, this will not happen because users cannot sell their surpluses to others. Lost sales are thus limited to the few rich users. Many virtual economies avoid this potential problem altogether by providing no other sources for their hard currency (currency used for monetization) than purchases from the publisher. Sources and sinks are discussed in detail in chapter 11.

Perhaps the biggest disadvantage of the price ceiling strategy compared to the monopoly strategy is that it is much thornier from a regulatory compliance point of view. As a rule, governments dislike it if you attempt to supplant their legal tender. Using a virtual currency only within your own platform or in a closed loop involving only predefined merchants is unlikely to cause problems. Q coin got into trouble with the People's Bank of China, because it unintentionally became a general online currency. As the digital cryptocurrency Bitcoin is starting to emerge from under the radar, it is beginning to face similar troubles. We discuss Bitcoin in more detail in chapter 10.

Chaining multiple markets: Facebook credits

In January 2011, almost ten years after the Q coin was launched, Facebook released its own virtual currency, the Facebook Credit. Many people in the worlds of technology and finance believed that the Facebook Credit could disrupt entire global e-commerce. And not without reason: with 750 million active user accounts in 2011, Facebook was the biggest online membership service in the world, leaving Tencent QQ to second place. Like Q coins, Facebook Credits could be purchased from stores, earned from advertisers, and spent on virtual goods. Given the impact Q coin achieved in China, wouldn't Facebook Credit's global impact be massive?

To understand the true potential of Facebook Credits, you have to understand how the virtual economy around it was designed. The markets on which Facebook Credits and Q coins are exchanged are laid out differently. An entrepreneur sitting on a pile of Facebook Credits has but one potential buyer for them: Facebook. This monopsony allows Facebook to buy credits back for 30 percent less than what it sells them out for. It also makes Facebook Credits a closed loop economy, more akin to gift cards than a currency. This is a big relief to regulators, who can keep tabs on the size of the economy simply by following Facebook's finances. But it also means that the Facebook Credits economy could never start living a life of its own in the way that the competitive Q coin economy did.

Let's look at Facebook's economy in more detail. The way it works is that users buy credits from Facebook and then give them to application developers in exchange for virtual goods and services. Developers then redeem the credits back to US dollars with Facebook. What we have here is not one market, not even a combination of a primary and a secondary market, but three distinct markets for Facebook Credits, each with its own market structure. The agent that acts as the buyer in one market always acts as the seller in the next market, forming a chain of markets that starts and ends with the publisher itself. This market chain is presented in table 5.2.

Facebook's monetization model bears similarities to both *Habbo*'s simple monopoly and Tencent's price ceiling strategy. Like the price ceiling strategy, it supports third-party developers and merchants since it allows them to convert the virtual currency back to national currency. But unlike Tencent's strategy that treats both consumers and third-party developers as "users," Facebook makes a distinction between consumer accounts and developer accounts and gives them different market roles. Consumers are not allowed to sell credits to other consumers, even though they can sometimes "produce" them by obtaining them for free from Facebook or its partners as part of

Table 5.2
Facebook Credits market chain

	Seller(s)	Buyer(s)	Market structure
Market 1	Facebook	Users	Monopoly
Market 2	Users	Developers	Unregulated
Market 3	Developers	Facebook	Monopsony

promotions. Neither are developers allowed to sell the credits they earn back to consumers. This means that the consumers' only source of virtual currency is the publisher, just as in *Habbo*'s monopoly. In other words, if you are a consumer and want Facebook Credits, you have no choice but to pay Facebook's asking price for them. This is currently around $0.10 per credit, but varies a lot depending on the size of the bundle and on the payment method.

Similarly, the only agent to which third-party developers are able to sell the credits they earn from consumers is Facebook. Thanks to this lack of competition, Facebook is free to decide how much it will pay for the credits. It currently pays $0.07 per credit. Thus, the difference in the price paid by consumers and that earned by developers is around 30 percent; depending on payment method, it can be as much as 50 percent. Moreover, Facebook refuses to buy back credits that it distributes to users for free as part of promotions. Such credits are thus worthless to developers, even though they are required to accept them as payment.

Since all transactions in the Facebook economy ultimately have to go through Facebook's books, as opposed to merely through its technical infrastructure, as is the case with Q coin, there is a lot of friction in the economy. As a result, the Facebook Credit never took off in quite the same way as the Q coin did. Facebook has announced that it is going to phase out credits in favor of prices denominated in local national currencies by the time this book is out. This change by itself doesn't have an impact on our analysis unless it alters the structure of Facebook's markets. Whether Facebook credit balances are denominated in credits or dollars or euros does not change the fact that they are virtual money residing on Facebook's servers unless and until you are able to redeem them into bank money. We simply move from a Facebook Credit economy to a Facebook credit economy. Dropping the name of the unit of account in favor of plain old national currencies actually reflects the nature of the system better: it's not a new global money; it's a proprietary online payment system.

The market chain model is applicable to all kinds of situations where several different types of agents participate in the economy, and their roles and abilities need to be different. Facebook's economy was designed to facilitate third-party application developers, but in another economy, a distinct agent type could be advertisers, who buy virtual currency from the publisher and sell it to consumers in exchange for their attention.

Market or no market

In the previous sections, we discussed the use of different market structures for achieving various design aims. There is yet one more option that we did not discuss: not having a market at all. Because we were eager to cover markets, the defining institutions of economics, we jumped right in and have ignored this question thus far. But now that we've introduced both competitive and regulated markets, it is a good time to step back and ask, Are our design aims perhaps best served by not having any kind of market at all?

For material goods, markets emerge spontaneously as people exchange them from hand to hand. For virtual goods, this cannot be taken for granted. A virtual good cannot be transferred from one agent to another unless such a feature has been expressly enabled by the developer.[4] If there is no exchange mechanism, there is no market. Such an item is forever associated with the user who first acquired it, until and unless it is made to disappear from the system entirely. As with any other market-related design decision, the decision of whether to have a market is made separately for each item type. The guideline for making this decision is the same one that should inform all virtual economy design decisions: the design should contribute toward (1) providing content, (2) attracting and retaining users, and/or (3) monetization. Ultimately the right decision obviously depends on the context.

Let's take an example from the MMO world. In *World of Warcraft*, common items can be transferred freely between characters and traded in auction houses, but the rarest and most powerful items typically cannot be transferred between characters at all. Why enable a market for common items and disable it for rare ones? The rationale behind such design can be analyzed as follows.

First, there are several reasons that trading should be enabled. Player-to-player trade allows players to focus on those parts of the game content that they prefer the most and procure what else they need from others. For example, those who enjoy leatherworking can focus on leatherworking and use the earnings from the boots and bags they sell to purchase weapons and enchantments, which someone else enjoys producing. Crafters also find their occupation more fulfilling when other players purchase their wares. Moreover, player-to-player trade is a fun activity in itself: it can involve negotiation, arbitrage, attempts to corner the market, and so on. Enabling trading therefore works toward objective 1: providing content to users.

However, there are also reasons that player-to-player trade should not be enabled. When players exercise their comparative advantage in their area of specialization, producing only what they are good at and buying the rest from others, they are making the game easier for themselves. They are essentially skipping those puzzles that they find relatively difficult and focusing only on the easiest ones. As a result, they will consume the game's content faster than they would without trading. This can work against objectives 2 and 3, retaining and monetizing users. These objectives call for regulating the speed at which content is consumed in order to keep users hooked for as long as

4. Although in some cases, users have developed ways to work around this restriction and markets have pushed themselves into being even without the publisher's sanction. Such situations and how to deal with them are dealt with at the end of chapter 7 and in chapter 8.

possible. The faster the users burn through the game's content, the fewer subscription fees they will be paying and the less need they will feel to purchase boosts and other virtual goods from the publisher.

Another problem with enabling user-to-user trade is that items that can be transferred between players lose much of the signal value that they might otherwise have. An item that can be obtained only by overcoming an extremely difficult challenge signals that its bearer is a dedicated player. This not only enhances the player's social status but also helps others in gauging that person's level of experience. This can be very valuable information to anyone putting together an ad hoc group of players who don't know each other previously for the purposes of assaulting a difficult dungeon. But if there is a possibility that the item in question has been purchased rather than self-obtained, then the truthfulness of the signal is placed in question. This diminishes the value of the item and consequently also the players' motivation to go through hardships to obtain them, and thus works against objective 1: providing content.[5]

Considering these positives and negatives, should trading be enabled? In this case, the answer depends on the type of item in question. In the case of *World of Warcraft's* common items, the positives of player-to-player trade probably outweigh the negatives, because common items are in any case easy to produce and carry little signal value. In the case of rarer items that are more difficult to obtain and carry significant signal value, the negatives probably outweigh the positives. The quest to obtain a certain prestigious set of rare items is the main reason that many people keep playing the game. If these items could be easily purchased from a market, many players would reach their goals sooner and the goals would not feel as worthwhile in the first place. So the conclusion is a two-tier solution: *World of Warcraft's* designers have enabled trading for common items, but made it impossible to trade many of the rarer ones. To account for this apparent inconsistency in the game's physics, the designers have come up with a story device, "soulbinding," that provides an explanation for why some items cannot be transferred while others can.

Now to be precise, *World of Warcraft's* designers did not entirely eliminate the market even for the rarest items. Players can still sell them to NPC vendors for a minimal compensation. So there is a market; it's just that it's a monopsony, a market structure that involves no player-to-player trade. The negative consequences of player-to-player trade are eliminated, but players still have a way of selling off unwanted items. Are there any situations in which we truly want to eliminate the market completely? Yes, plenty. Things like levels, skill points, badges of achievement, high scores, likes, and upvotes are usually designed to be totally untradable and inalienable. In the sense that they are valuable and clearly something that users own, they are clearly virtual goods.

---

5. These same problems are also associated with unsanctioned real-money markets, where players buy and sell entire game accounts. This is discussed in chapter 8.

Yet because they cannot be transferred or traded, we often forget to think about them as goods. There are good reasons that these are usually not tradable, either to do with game design or with signal value. Still, their untradability is not absolute. In space MMO *Entropia Universe*, skill points that characters accumulate can be downloaded onto a chip and sold to other players on an open market. In Facebook and Twitter, there is an underground industry that trades likes and followers like cattle. We return to this in chapter 8. In the next chapter, we continue with the theme of limiting free competition, but from the perspective of a firm rather than of a regulator.

6 Market Power and Pricing

In this chapter, we go in detail into the concept of market power: what it is, how you obtain it, how you fight it, and what you can do with it. As is the case with many of the learnings in this book, the contents of this chapter can be applied on two levels. On one level, they can be applied in the internal design of a virtual economy. On another, they can be applied in the overall business of digital content publishing. The examples in this chapter are of publishers' wielding market power against each other, but the same models can also be used to understand how virtual entrepreneurs create and use market power inside platforms like *Second Life* and *IMVU*. Also, as is the case with many of the learnings in this book, the contents of this chapter can be applied in both design (how to benefit from monopoly power) and analysis (how the use of monopoly power is affecting the market). We start by discussing market power and its sources, and then move on to provide a detailed discussion of its main use: pricing goods in profitable ways.

What is market power?

In the previous chapter, we discussed the way publishers can act as monopolists in their own virtual economies in order to earn revenues. For example, *Habbo* is a teenage virtual world with a distinctive retro computer gaming visual style. In 2009, it generated $60 million in revenues for its publisher, Sulake. Most of the revenues came from quirky virtual items such as teleporters and ice cream machines that Sulake sells to *Habbo* users. Like most other publishers, Sulake does not allow anyone else to produce virtual items for *Habbo*. In effect, Sulake has a monopoly over new virtual item sales in *Habbo*.

The nice thing about being a monopolist is that you can dictate the prices of the goods you sell. Consumers then decide what quantities of goods, if any, they will purchase at the prices you ask. Alternatively, you can decide what quantity of goods to sell and let demand determine the price. This ability to dictate either prices or quantities is *monopoly power*. There is a microeconomic model of monopoly behavior that tells us that having this power is almost like a license to print money (in virtual economies, sometimes literally so). We'll skip the math and present just the general conclusions: a profit-maximizing monopolist will always produce a smaller quantity of goods at a higher price than what a perfectly competitive market would, and consequently earns a tidy monopoly profit above and beyond what suppliers in a perfectly competitive market could hope to earn.[1] The business implications are clear: monopoly power is great.

But does Sulake really wield monopoly power over its customers? Sure, it's the sole supplier of new virtual goods in *Habbo*. But *Habbo* is not the only teenage virtual world with virtual items. For example, *Gaia Online* is an anime-themed online hangout that targets a similar demographic with a similar virtual item–based revenue model. No doubt there is some kind of competition going on between these two platforms. If one of them tries to really screw its customers with massive price hikes, the customers might defect to the competitor. If so, the single-supplier monopoly model is probably not the most accurate description of the teenage virtual goods market. Still, a virtual item in *Gaia Online* is clearly not the same thing as a virtual item in *Habbo*, so the perfect competition model introduced in chapter 4 is not a very good fit either. Here we'll introduce a market power model of competition and see what it can teach us about competition between virtual economies.

Consider the following scenario.[2] An old man in a wooden cart at the end of a Tokyo clubbing street is selling steaming bowls of ramen noodle, a favorite after-hours snack among Tokyo clubgoers. Since there are no other ramen vendors in sight, he enjoys monopoly power over the market, setting his prices far above his marginal costs. One night, another ramen cart appears at the opposite end of the street. The old man's monopoly power is reduced: he can no longer ask quite as much for his bowls, lest customers walk over to the other cart.

However, the walk to the other end of the street is long, especially for a weary clubgoer at 5:00 a.m. This walk is a *switching cost:* a cost a customer has to pay in order to switch to the competing provider. Customers near the center of the street will find it easier to take the slightly longer walk than to pay the extra price. But for customers emerging from clubs right at the old man's end of the street, the cost is too high: they will put up with inflated prices rather than go through the trouble of walking to the other end of the street. Thanks to this switching cost, the old man is able to retain some of his price-setting power. It is no longer full monopoly power but what is known as *market power.*

1. The basic model of monopoly behavior, as well as models of competition in the presence of limited market power and differentiation, can be found in standard microeconomics textbooks, such as Mankiew (2011, chapters 15–17) and Varian (2009, chapters 24–29).
2. Based on a classic "linear city model" of competition by Harold Hotelling (1929), an influential statistician and economic theorist. Also based on a true story from Tokyo.

The situation in this night ramen market is now somewhat similar to what economists call monopolistic competition: it bears characteristics of both monopoly and competition.[3] In contrast to perfect competition, suppliers in monopolistic competition enjoy a degree of market power over their customers. Unlike in a pure monopoly, this power is nevertheless limited by a degree of competition. Monopolistic competition is probably the most commonly found situation in real-world markets. It is, unfortunately, also one of the most difficult to analyze.

How does the night ramen market relate to virtual economies? Imagine that the carts are platforms and the ramen bowls are virtual goods. The street represents a spectrum of different genres. The old man's cart is *Habbo*, and the competing cart is *Gaia Online*. Customers who love *Habbo*'s retro gaming style will not easily walk over to the anime end of the street: it's just too far from their tastes. Assuming these two platforms are the only ones on the market, this leaves both publishers with considerable price-setting power over their respective fans. But if one of the publishers attempts to price its virtual items too high, its fans may find it less painful to satisfy their desire for online sociability at the other site than to pay the extortionate fees. In other words, even though at first glance it may seem that publishers selling virtual goods on their platforms are enjoying a monopoly over their users, it becomes apparent when other platforms are taken into account that this power is never absolute. Like most businesses, virtual goods platforms have market power but not full monopoly power.

Still, even nonabsolute market power is great, because it allows businesses to set their prices higher than they would be able to in full competition. The more market power you have, the higher you can set your prices and the more profits you will earn. Table 6.1 shows examples of market power in action. The next question naturally is, Where can you get market power? If you already have some, where can you get more?

Building market power

In the scenario above, the suppliers' market power was based on *differentiation:* providing a good or service that differs from competing offerings, whether in terms of physical location or genre. Customers to whom a particular kind of specialized offering is very well suited will be reluctant to switch to a competing offering, even if it is cheaper, because it is less suited to them. Thus, the first method of building market power is differentiating your offering. On what dimensions you should differ from competition and in what directions depends on the preferences of the prospective customer base.

3. Since there are only two sellers, this market can also be described as an oligopoly. But textbooks such as Varian (2009) classify location models under monopolistic competition.

Table 6.1
Examples of market power

Market	Holder of market power	How the holder uses the power
New drugs	Drug patent holder	Price higher than marginal cost
Popular music	Music label	Price higher than marginal cost; fewer concerts
Computer operating systems	Software developer	Price higher than marginal cost; bundling of required software on equipment manufacturers; bugs
Mickey Mouse	Disney	Reduced quantity and high prices of mouse-themed apparel; high amusement park admission costs
Soccer	Fédération Internationale de Football Association (FIFA)	World Cup held only every four years
Lego	Lego	Small plastic blocks are quite expensive
Diamonds	De Beers	Reduced quantity and high prices of diamonds; artificial scarcity

However, differentation is often difficult to sustain. Consider what happens to the old ramen vendor. One evening before business starts in earnest, the competing ramen vendor moves their cart from the very end of the street one block toward the center of the street. As a result, some customers near the center of the street, who previously frequented the old man's cart, now defect to the competitor. To hold on to his market share, the old man responds in kind and moves his cart one block toward the center. Next evening the competitor makes another lunge for market share, and the old man responds. They repeat their actions several times until eventually both carts end up together at the center point of the street. This turns out to be the competitive equilibrium for this market: from here, neither cart can hope to increase its market share by moving. Both carts are now equally positioned to address the whole street, but the customers' switching cost that allowed the old man to exact monopoly profits is gone! Since the carts are right next to each other, any price reduction by one cart must immediately be matched by the other, lest all customers switch to the competing provider. The night ramen market has transitioned from market power–based competition into perfect competition.

In the same way, competition for market share erodes away differentiation in the digital publishing business. Games that reach for a bigger audience tend to do so by adapting to more mainstream tastes and conventions, much to the disappointment of fans at the edges of the audience, who prefer quirkier content. *Habbo* and *Gaia Online* have so far avoided this path, instead holding relatively fast to their original designs. This can be a smart strategy when the center is already contested. But even if a publisher sticks with an original design that appeals to a certain audience, it often happens that when it reaches enough success, similar competing titles appear to exploit the opportunity. The original title becomes the center point of a new line of similar offerings, and its uniqueness is eaten away. This is to some extent what happened to *Habbo*, a teenage virtual world that was launched back in 2000. Teen virtual worlds sprang up left and right, some very successful, and *Habbo* started to have a hard time standing out.

World of Warcraft has been subject to both types of competitive erosion. First, it was positioned from the start as a rather generic fantasy in order to attract a large mainstream audience. Second, the original elements it had were soon imitated by numerous new entrants. Games like *Tower of AION* offer striking similarity from game mechanics all the way down to user interface design. Yet despite this lack of differentiation, *World of Warcraft* remains a great business. Almost ten years after it was launched, it is still able to fetch a monthly subscription fee of around $10 to $15 from millions of people. How is this possible? In the following sections, we examine what other sources of monopoly power there are besides differentiation.

Switching costs

Differentiation builds market power by increasing customer switching costs. Other factors as well contribute to customers' cost of switching to a competitor. Common factors across industries are the cost of searching for alternatives and learning about their quality, the cost of learning how to use a new service, and durable investments in complementary assets such as guidebooks and special hardware. Consumers' switching decisions are also influenced by cognitive biases, such as a tendency to stick with a previous choice even when an objective observer might conclude that it is no longer the best one (known as the fanboy effect). In many industries, suppliers also create switching costs through fixed-term contracts, low-frequency subscription billing, and upfront payments, such as when buying a bunch of virtual currency to be used later.

Below, we highlight two types of switching costs, social networks and virtual assets, that are especially characteristic of online games and communities, and consider what steps publishers can take to maximize these switching costs to enhance their market power. We then move on discuss how to fight against these strategies.[4]

4. For an introduction to the theory and managerial implications of switching costs and positive network externalities in the information goods business, see Shapiro and Varian (1999, chapters 5–8). The version developed here addresses today's social web and virtual goods platforms.

Social networks

Many online services, including online games and communities, exhibit *network externalities:* the value of the service to a user depends on the number of other users currently using it. The more members a social networking site has, the more useful it is to individual users, since they can connect with more people. If they were to switch to a smaller social networking service, they would experience a drop in value. In general, the more users a network has, the bigger the cost of switching away from it. For this reason, the social networking market tends to *tip*: once one service has achieved a critical mass of users, it starts to grow rapidly and forces all similar services out of business. In other words, positive network externalities give rise to natural monopolies.

But online games and communities can also involve *negative* network externalities. A massively multiplayer online (MMO) server with too many players is slow to respond. A chat channel with too many people is difficult to follow. In these cases, every additional user past a certain threshold decreases the value of the network to the users. Such networks have a limited optimum size. Publishers can circumvent this limit by running several separate instances of their platform in parallel, as is common in MMO games, but this curbs the positive externalities. To mitigate this, many MMOs allow players to migrate between servers to join their friends. *EVE Online* is a rare exception in that its advanced "single shard" server infrastructure allows every player to always participate in the same fictional universe—although not without occasional problems with server response times.

A further point to note about the special nature of network externalities in games and online communities is that it is often not so much the absolute number of other users that matters to the individual user but the number of friends or acquaintances who are participating. Users pay a high social cost for switching away from a game or community where they have an existing network of friends and relationships, regardless of whether the absolute number of users in that community is very high. The absolute number of users is more important in an infrastructural communication network such as the telephone or the Internet.

To increase social switching costs, developers can use promotions to encourage users to bring their friends and family members into the platform. They can also encourage the forging of new relationships and institutions inside the platform by providing communication tools, friend lists, team play features, and sophisticated support for guilds and clans.[5] In many MMOs, guilds and clans end up setting up forums and event calendars on third-party servers because the publisher of the MMO fails to provide them with suitable social tools. This makes it extremely easy for the guild as a whole to switch to a competing game whenever its members wish (more on this below).

5. We return to the role of institutions like guilds and virtual corporations in improving user retention in chapter 9.

One thing that is often forgotten about social networks is that antagonistic relationships are relationships too. Hard-core gamers may rather give up friends and allies than lose the dear enemy whose defeat is the whole purpose of their virtual struggle.

Virtual assets

Switching to a competing platform entails losing all of one's virtual items, points, badges, achievements, titles, and other persistent assets accumulated on the old platform. This can be a major switching cost that keeps users loyal—and another argument for implementing a simple virtual economy in almost any platform. However, the loss is a switching cost only if the lost articles are somehow valuable to the user. Pointless points, meaningless awards, and an epic weapon of yesteryear that is no match to today's monsters will not stop a user from switching.

To create virtual asset switching costs, designers need to make it possible for users to accumulate some kind of persistent assets on the platform. Then they need to ensure that the assets are desirable and remain so over time (virtual goods design was discussed in chapter 3). One simple asset that is not to be overlooked is the age of the user's account. People can be immensely proud of owning an old account because it proves that they are a veteran member. All you need to do is to make the age visible somehow, so that it can be flaunted. The ICQ numbers introduced at the beginning of this book are a good example of this. Another notable example are user identifier numbers in Slashdot, a technology news site and online community. As with ICQ, rare numbers are sometimes traded on eBay. The site's publisher itself once auctioned off a three-digit number for charity.

The numbers trade also exposes a notable danger in basing market power on virtual asset switching costs alone. If a market emerges where users are able to liquidate their assets into more portable assets such as money, then the assets will cease to act as a switching cost. This applies to real-money markets as well as simple barter. On discussion forums catering to teenage virtual world fans, we have seen numerous offers to trade *Habbo* accounts to accounts in *RuneScape* (a fantasy game appealing to the same demographic) and vice versa. We offer some strategies for dealing with unwanted markets in chapter 8.

Mobile and social games publisher Digital Chocolate once launched a line of premium virtual characters called NanoStars that could be used simultaneously in a range of different games. When a new NanoStars-compatible game was launched, all of the users' old characters immediately became usable in the new game. The idea was that this would increase users' loyalty to the Digital Chocolate brand across different genres. For a user, investing in portable virtual goods like NanoStars is less risky than investing in virtual goods that are locked into a single game. On the flip side, such a network can accumulate a lot of virtual goods in the long run, which can become a problem for game balance and monetization. We discuss how to deal with virtual goods accumulation in chapters 11 and 12.

Fighting against market power

What if you are launching a new title and all your potential customers are already locked into incumbent titles using the techniques discussed above? What can a new entrant do to diminish the incumbents' market power? Since market power is based on customer switching costs, the new entrant must try to find ways to either reduce the switching costs or compensate the customers for incurring them.

Compensating customers' switching costs
In subscription-based games, the most obvious way to compensate customers for making the switch is to offer them an initial discount—first month free, for example. Compared to staying with the incumbent, the customer saves one month's subscription's worth of money by switching—enough for some people to compensate for the friends and assets they will be leaving behind. In free-to-play titles, where revenues are generated through virtual goods sales, the analogous move is to give new users some free items or virtual currency when they join up.

But the problem with using virtual goods as compensation is that their value is often based on their scarcity. If you give every new user a rare, unique, and powerful item as an initial sweetener, the item will soon become common trash and cease to serve its purpose as attractive compensation. An initial endowment of currency will likewise come to be seen as nothing but the minimum necessary to buy what every newbie has. Virtual goods retain their allure better if they are awarded only selectively as part of limited campaigns.

When you compensate users for making the switch, you are effectively turning their costs into your costs. This initial investment into acquiring the customers is worth it if their total lifetime value exceeds the acquisition cost. But beware of churn: people who just sign up for the free gift and switch to the next platform as soon as it's used up.

Reducing customer switching costs
When Lufthansa opened new routes in northern Europe, the business travelers in the region already had platinum memberships with the incumbent airlines. Switching to the new entrant would have meant a downgrade for them in terms of status and lounge access. Lufthansa could have compensated for this with lower ticket prices, but this would have been costly for the airline. Instead, it started a campaign where new customers could instantly jump to the membership level that corresponds with their membership level in the incumbent's program. In other words, Lufthansa allowed new

customers to import their virtual assets from the previous platform, thus eliminating a major switching cost.

This strategy can work in online games and communities as well. Many online services allow users to import their contacts from another platform. Importing virtual items and character levels is trickier because their attributes and functions differ among platforms. Allowing users to start from the top may also reduce their appetite for additional purchases and subscription months.[6] A potentially better way to implement imports might be to provide users with nonfunctional badges that record their achievements in the previous platform without conferring any tangible advantages in the new platform. Making imports one time only discourages users from going back to the old platform.

To reduce customers' social cost of switching away from the platform where all their friends are, it is useful to try to get people to switch in groups. For example, a new MMO publisher in a competitive genre could focus its marketing efforts on getting whole guilds to switch. An executive at an MMO publisher in China told us that Chinese MMO publishers sometimes pay hard cash to guilds or guild leaders to get them to switch to a new title. Once the game has a comfortable following of guildsters, positive network externalities kick in and it becomes easier to attract additional players.

Using market power to price virtual goods

Now that we have examined ways in which suppliers can build market power even in a competitive market environment, we spend the rest of this chapter examining how that power can be put to profitable use in pricing. The main pricing theories that we cover are optimum pricing through price elasticity, price discrimination, and bundling. There is a large variety of practical tricks and strategies in pricing that we are not able to fully cover here, but usually they can ultimately be traced back to the theories we present next or to the behavioral theories discussed in chapter 2. Before we go to the actual theories, we start with some practical advice on how to set initial prices by looking at what competitors are doing.

Setting initial prices using benchmarking

Before we can use any clever strategies to optimize our virtual goods pricing, we need some kind of initial starting prices that represent the best guess of what the optimal prices might be. Coming up with such guesses can be tricky. If you have never sold

---

6. Airlines do not have this problem because their levels are perishable: if Lufthansa's new platinum members don't buy lots of flights during the year, they will soon find themselves automatically downgraded. Perishable virtual goods and similar strategies for maintaining a balanced virtual economy are explored in chapter 11.

anything similar before, you have no idea what prices the market will bear. A physical producer can derive a reasonable guess of a good price by adding a markup on the marginal production cost, but virtual goods vendors don't have simple guidelines like this. For virtual goods vendors, the best approach is therefore to benchmark against competitors, which can be done in two ways: benchmarking revenues and benchmarking price tags.

Benchmarking revenues means using revenue per user figures from competing virtual goods platforms as guidance in setting your prices. For example, if the average revenue per user (ARPU) in other similar games is $2 per month and you have designed a game in which players need to buy approximately 10 coins per month, then your guess at a realistic initial price is $.20 per coin. The theory here is that consumers would be willing to pay a similar price for a similar game regardless of what number of coins or other tokens it entails. The problem with this approach is that average figures can be highly misleading. In most free-to-play games, the majority of revenues come from a small percentage of players who spend much more than the average figure, while most players spend nothing at all. To avoid setting your prices too low, you thus have to optimize them for the spenders rather than for nonexistent "average" consumers, but such data can be hard to come by.

Benchmarking price tags is simple: look at what competing games are charging for different types of virtual goods, and price your own goods and currencies in a similar way. For example, if a competitor is charging the virtual currency equivalent of $1 for a purely decorative virtual hat, then price your hat at 10 coins and your coin at $0.10, or any other combination that results in the total real-money price of $1. The theory here is that people are willing to pay a similar price for a similar benefit. In this approach, you don't need to worry about the difference between top spenders and nonspenders. You are also not locked into the assumption that your game needs to produce a similar ARPU as competing games, which may or may not be a good assumption. Figure 6.1 shows what kinds of prices publishers typically charge for virtual goods in mobile games.

Price elasticity of demand

Now let's assume that we have a game publisher that sells virtual coins to its players and sets the initial price for the coins by benchmarking against other similar games. Next, we want to find out how the coin price should be adjusted to maximize revenues. What happens to revenues if we increase the price per coin? Two things: (1) the *price effect:* an increase in the price per unit increases the revenue generated from each unit sold, increasing total revenues; and (2) the *quantity effect:* an increase in the unit price tends to result in fewer units sold, decreasing total revenues.

The price and quantity effects are illustrated in figure 6.2. Initially total revenues are equal to $P_1 \times Q_1$, as represented by areas A and B. Increasing the price from P_1 to P_2

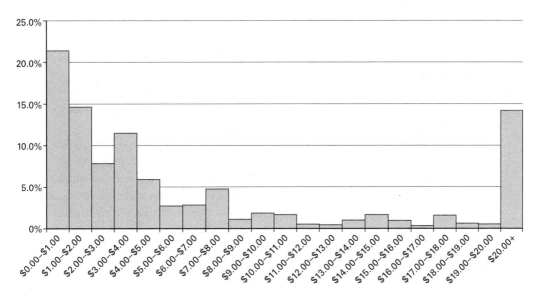

Figure 6.1
Distribution of virtual goods prices in leading mobile games. Adapted from Lehdonvirta and Joas (2012b). The sample consists of 2,096 premium virtual goods in twenty-six leading mobile games. Prices were converted from virtual currencies into US dollars using an average exchange rate of the virtual currency packages in each game.

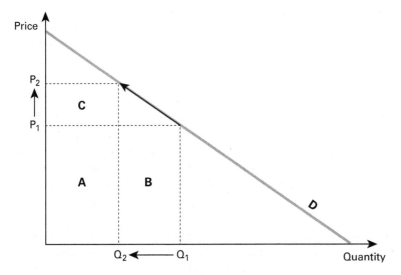

Figure 6.2
How total revenue changes when price is increased.

results in the quantity sold falling from Q_1 to Q_2. The new total revenues are therefore equal to $P_2 \times Q_2$, as represented by areas A and C. Area B was lost to the quantity effect, and area C was gained thanks to the price effect. In this case, comparing the sizes of areas B and C suggests that the price increase was not worth it: the quantity effect was stronger than the price effect, so that the total revenues are actually lower after the price hike than before it. In this situation, the right thing to have done to improve revenues would have been to reduce the price, not increase it.

To determine which of the effects dominates, that is, whether we should increase or decrease the price to improve revenues, we can use a simple economic tool, *price elasticity of demand* (PED). Price elasticity of demand is a number that answers the question, "If price increases by 1 percent, by how many percent will the quantity demanded decrease in response?"[7] In other words, it measures how sensitive the demand is to changes in price. Goods that consumers are highly dependent on tend to have a PED below 1. For example, one study found that the PED for gasoline in the United States is 0.26.[8] A 10 percent increase in the price of gasoline would result in a meager 2.6 percent reduction in gasoline consumption. Gasoline demand is thus not very sensitive to price changes; people prefer to save money somewhere else than reduce gasoline consumption. Someone with a monopoly over gasoline production could increase revenues by increasing its price.

PED is not fixed. If we increase the price of a good, PED tends to increase with it. At relatively low price levels, PED is often small: a 1 percent increase in the price of a $1 good is not a big deal for the consumer, so the quantity bought is relatively unaffected. But at higher price levels, a 1 percent price increase starts to translate to a lot of money. As a result, consumers begin to respond to price hikes with relatively larger reductions in the quantities bought, increasing the PED. When PED reaches 1, it means that the next price hike would be met with a one-to-one reduction in the quantity demanded. It would not have any net effect on revenue: the price effect and the quantity effect would balance each other out.

Luxury goods often have PED values over 1. For example, one study found that the PED for high-end Chevrolet automobiles at their current prices is around 4. A 10 percent price increase would lead to a massive 40 percent drop in the number of cars sold. Total revenues could be increased by reducing the price. As the price is reduced, PED also tends to drop. Important PED values and their implications for pricing are summarized in table 6.2.

7. Economics textbooks usually present PED in a slightly different way: if price increases by 1 percent, by how many percent will the quantity demanded increase in response? Because quantity demanded typically falls rather than increases, as the price increases, this definition results in PED being a negative number. Negative numbers are inconvenient to discuss in text, so everyone usually just drops the minus sign.

8. Espey (1996).

Table 6.2
Critical PED values and implications for pricing

PED	If price increases	How to increase revenues
> 1	Demand falls dramatically	Decrease price
= 1	Demand falls in proportion	Optimum price; don't change
< 1	Demand falls slightly	Increase price

We can therefore conclude that the price that yields the greatest possible revenues is one where PED equals exactly 1. Why, then, is gasoline sold at such a low price that its PED is a lowly 0.26? Because competition keeps gas prices in check. Why, then, does General Motors price its high-end Chevrolets so high that their PED is a whopping 4? Because car manufacturing involves significant marginal costs. General Motors earns a bigger profit by selling a smaller number of expensive cars than by selling a large number of cars at a price at which it can barely recoup the cost. Virtual coin vendors don't have to worry about these factors. Our game publisher should adjust the price of its virtual coins until PED hits exactly 1.

So how do you determine PED? By looking at how people have reacted to price changes in past sales data, asking customers or beta testers what their likely reactions to different price levels would be, or conducting pricing experiments. Past sales data may not be available, and even if they are, it can be hard to distinguish the influence of price changes from other factors like marketing campaigns, patches, and seasonal variation. Asking people is often easiest, but the problem with asking is that what people say in surveys and do in practice can be different. Pricing experiments (i.e., A/B testing), where you try out a proposed new price with a small sample of users, can yield the most reliable data.

Finally, an important additional factor to keep in mind with PED is that there is a difference between users' immediate responses to price changes and their behavior in the longer term. Gasoline's short-run PED was found to be 0.26, but in the long run (defined as longer than one year), the same study found gasoline's PED to be almost twice as high, at 0.58.[9] This is because after some time, people start adjusting their habits to the new price. Revenue increases from price changes can therefore be transitory. Instead of permanently lowering the price of a virtual currency, consider driving sales through campaigns where prices are reduced for limited periods. This prevents users from becoming habituated to the lower price.[10]

9. Espey (1996).
10. To dig deeper into the theory of price elasticity, see Mankiw (2011, chapter 5). Recently the game publisher Valve conducted experiments explicitly designed to measure the PED of their products and found them to be very, very high, http://www.techspot.com/news/45989-valve-cofounder-explains-steams-ongoing-price-experiments.html.

Price discrimination

In the previous section, we assumed that we have to charge the same price from every consumer. What if we could charge different prices for the same product from different consumers? We could set the price for each consumer so that it corresponds with individual willingness to pay. This would give much better revenues than a single compromise price that is too low for some consumers and so high for others that it scares them off. Charging different prices from different consumers is known as *price discrimination*.

The ethicality of price discrimination is debatable. On one hand, it seems unfair to charge some people more than others for the same product. On the other hand, being able to charge some people less than others means that the product reaches and perhaps benefits a larger number of people than it otherwise would. This is the justification offered by textbook publishers when they sell the same textbook at radically different prices in the United States and India. In any case, consumers on the wrong side of price discrimination understandably tend to get upset about it, a factor that even the most unscrupulous supplier needs to consider. Lost consumer trust through short-term optimization can have a serious impact on the long-term bottom line.

In theory, it is possible to implement perfect price discrimination in a virtual economy. Just use A/B testing as described in the previous section to determine the price elasticity of demand and the optimal price for each individual user instead of the overall demand curve. Charge users that optimal price. In practice, it is not quite as easy, because a few data points per user are not enough to reveal much about their preferences. But with more data and more sophisticated techniques, something approaching perfect price discrimination is quite possible; it is already being done to some extent by some social game companies, and to a greater extent by the brick-and-mortar retail industry. To avoid consumer backlash, retailers use personalized discount coupons instead of meddling with price tags.

Less perfect price discrimination can be implemented through much simpler means. These can be divided into two categories: group discrimination and consumer self-selection. Group discrimination involves dividing the consumers into groups based on some convenient variable that is likely to be correlated with their willingness to pay. Typically this means the user's country of residence. It is easy to identify from their point of entry into the system or their IP address. To maximize sales, users from poor countries should be charged less, and users from rich countries more. For example, Sulake charges its US customers 20 cents for one *Habbo* coin, while Ecuadorian customers pay only 17 cents per coin (although Sulake tells us that this reflects cost differences rather than intentional price discrimination).

Consumer self-selection can be implemented alongside group discrimination or instead of it. The basic idea is to provide several differently priced versions of the product and get each consumer to select the one that best corresponds with their willingness to pay. Typically this means providing a no-frills version for the thrifty consumer, a middle-class version for the slightly more affluent consumer, and a luxury version for the rich consumer. There does not necessarily have to be any functional difference between the versions; it is more important to construct the appropriate images through marketing and presentation and let social processes do the rest. As discussed in chapter 3, price itself can be a signal that sets one good apart from another. In an online game, this might mean offering the basic game for free and then providing a range of differently priced hats for progressively more affluent consumers to splurge on (see box 6.1). It can be highly effective to "help" consumer self-selection by using data to identify top spenders and ensure that they always see the most expensive options first. This is a good alternative to perfect price discrimination in that it makes use of data but mitigates the user acceptance and ethical questions by giving users the final choice.

Another approach to consumer self-selection is to make use of the fact that affluent consumers often have a lower marginal utility for money and poor consumers a lower marginal utility for time. In lay terms, affluent consumers have more money than time and poor consumers more time than money. To discriminate, offer the same product using two different methods, one of which requires the consumer to spend a lot of time but little money and the other of which requires little time but a lot of money. In traditional retail, this was achieved by distributing discount coupons in newspapers. Those who valued their time little enough to look for and cut out the coupons would pay less for the products. In free-to-play games, the same virtual goods can often be obtained either for free through "grinding," that is, time-consuming repetitive play, or for a fee through instantaneous purchase. What is sometimes missing is the middle ground. *World of Tanks*, an action MMO, allows players to obtain new tanks through three alternative routes: purchasing a premium tank (instantaneous; costs around $50

Box 6.1
Going after whales with harpoons

People who spend a lot of money on a game are known as "whales." A typical definition is that a whale is a gamer whose lifetime value exceeds $500. Like high rollers in the casino business, whales represent a small minority of customers, but an extremely economically important group to publishers who succeed in catering for them. For example, in a mobile game with in-app purchases, whales can represent less than 10 percent of paying customers but account for more than 50 percent of revenues.

In many games, spending and thus revenues, are in effect capped by the fact that players run out of worthwhile things to buy. Even a whale cannot spend $500 if there are only $50 worth of products available. One simple way to deal with this issue is to create "harpoons": high-priced super-items aimed specifically at whales. Table 6.3 shows the most expensive items available for purchase in a sample of leading mobile games.

(Continued)

The most expensive harpoon in this list is the Legendary Monster, priced at over $200 each. Besides in-app purchase, the monster can also be acquired by a combination of persistent effort and amazing luck. Its buyer can thus plausibly claim to have acquired it by investing effort instead of money. The most expensive whale harpoon we have seen anywhere is Shark Skin Sword, a weapon in the Facebook game *Ninja Saga* that kills everything with one hit. It is priced at approximately $850.

However, as with real whaling, the morality of these practices is sometimes suspect, especially when the targets are calves. Make sure your users are competent and know what they are buying, or whales may come back to haunt you.

Table 6.3

Title	Item name	Durability	Price
Tiny Monsters	Legendary Monsters	Durable	$211.86
Deer Hunter Reloaded	Multiple Items (3)	Durable	$139.89
iMob2	Disrespect: Im Rich	Consumable	$113.64
Race Or Die	Burn: Hate Stain	Consumable	$113.64
DragonVale	Leap Year Dragon	Durable	$88.00
Crime City	Onslaught Shotgun	Durable	$74.00
Monopoly Hotels	Film Reel Room	Durable	$71.01
Kingdom Age	Roc	Durable	$64.00
Modern War	Tactical Nuke	Durable	$63.60
Battle Nations	Compound	Durable	$55.56
Tiny Village	Multiple Items (14)	Durable	$36.62
Kingdoms of Camelot	Magical Restoration	Consumable	$34.62
Pet Hotel	Mountain	Durable	$27.92
Tap Paradise Cove	Santa Maria	Durable	$23.92
The Sims Freeplay	Pirate Statue	Durable	$16.67
Temple Run	Multiple Items (4)	Durable	$14.29
Original Gangstaz	Link Breaker	Durable	$13.16
Global War	Link Breaker	Durable	$13.16
Snoopy's Street Fair	Woodstock	Consumable	$12.50

Note: Adapted from Lehdonvirta and Joas (2012). Prices were converted from virtual currencies into US dollars using an average exchange rate of the virtual currency packages in each game.

Table 6.4
Valuations

	Apples	Pears
Adam	$2	$4
Steve	$4	$2

for a high-end model), a combination of grinding and paying for gold (takes perhaps 10 hours and $10 for a comparable model), or pure grinding (takes tens of hours but is free).[11]

Bundling

So far we have focused on pricing a single good and its substitutes. If there are multiple different goods for sale at the same time, we have another strategy for improving revenues without resorting to price discrimination: bundling. The theory behind it is as follows. Assume that there are two goods, apples and pears, and two consumers, Adam and Steve. The two consumers have different preferences so they value the goods quite differently. Their valuations are presented in table 6.4.

The apple and pear supplier knows these valuations thanks to analyzing point-of-sale data. And even if it didn't, it could guess that there are most likely some consumers who value apples more than pears and vice versa. Given these valuations, how can the supplier maximize its revenues without resorting to price discrimination? If it prices apples and pears at $4 each, it will sell one of each, earn $8 and miss two potential $2 sales. If it prices the goods at $2 each, it will sell two of each, earn $8, and know that it charged two times $2 less than what the consumers were willing to pay. There is a total of $12 of consumer value on the table. How can the supplier get all of it instead of just $8? The answer is bundling. Create a new bundle product, "apple and pear," and give it a price that equals consumers' highest and lowest valuations for two products, which is $6. Both Adam and Steve will find this bundle acceptable, but for different reasons: one sees it as containing a $2 apple and $4 pear, while the other sees it as containing a $4 apple and $2 pear. Both buy it, and total sales equal $12—the full consumer value.

In practice, things are of course more complicated because there are more products and more consumers and the valuations are not as well known. But the basic idea is the same: find two products that many consumers are likely to want but hold very different valuations for them. Set their individual prices at the highest valuation and offer a bundle priced at the sum of the highest and the lowest valuation that you want to support.

11. To dig deeper into the theory of price discrimination, see Varian (2009, chapter 25).

Policy implications

In this chapter, we showed how publishers with significant market power can act almost like monopolists inside their own virtual goods platforms. Economic theory suggests that compared to a perfectly competitive market, a monopoly produces a smaller number of goods at a higher price, which results in a loss of social welfare. Based on this economic argument, society prefers competitive markets and often regulates against monopolies. What policy implications should we draw from this to virtual economies? Should publisher Sulake's monopoly over virtual goods sales in *Habbo* be broken? Would the society be better off if anyone could generate virtual items inside the virtual hangout and compete the prices of those items down to marginal cost, which in virtual environments is zero? Meticulous application of textbook economics would suggest that this is the case, but game designers' intuition strongly suggests otherwise. Game designers are right, because as we discussed in chapter 3, the value of virtual goods is based on their scarcity and their relationship to each other and the virtual context in which they are used. They are part of an overall service provided by the publisher, and thus it is the publisher's job to regulate their supply in a way that maximizes the overall value of the service rather than simply minimizing prices (for an example of virtual market power regulation inside a game, see box 6.2).

In other words, real-world regulators should typically keep their hands off markets inside virtual economies. The market between virtual economies is a different matter. This market in which publishers compete against each other is a fairly typical consumer market with differentiated offerings and some positive network externalities, with the addition of virtual goods that can create strong additional switching costs.

Box 6.2
Market power inside a virtual economy: From oligopoly to free market

Market power works the same way inside virtual economies as it does outside and can give rise to interesting dynamics. For years, so-called Tech II spaceships in *EVE Online* could be manufactured only by those in possession of appropriate blueprints, an extremely scarce resource. This meant that the market for Tech II ships was *oligopolistic:* it had only a small number of suppliers, who at times competed against each other and at times colluded to create cartels to charge higher prices from consumers. Limited market power was thus an engine of much user-created content in the game.

In 2006, the developers determined that the prices of Tech II ships were too high and the quantities produced too low to yield the optimal game experience overall. How did they increase the supply? One possibility would have been to decrease production costs by, for example, reducing the number of components required. But since the market was oligopolistic rather than perfectly competitive, meaning that the suppliers could potentially collude with each other, this change might have ended up only increasing the suppliers' margins. Prices and quantities might have been unaffected.

(Continued)

Instead, the developers decided to let more suppliers enter the market, transitioning it from a near-oligopoly into a more competitive market. They did this by making it possible for characters with suitable skills to "invent" more Tech II blueprints, the resource that was limiting entry to the market. Invention was difficult and expensive, so the immediate effect on the market was small, as figure 6.3 shows. But it added up over the years: After one year, the quantity of Tech II ships produced, as measured in ship tonnage, had doubled. In two years, it had quadrupled. Prices stabilized at around 30 percent of what they had been before the change.

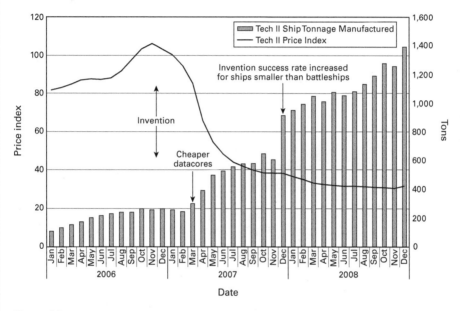

Figure 6.3
Tech II spaceship manufacturing output and price index over time

Normal regulatory oversight that aims to maintain fair competition is as appropriate as in any other market. One area that might require attention is ensuring that consumers are adequately informed about their rights in the virtual goods that they accumulate. Using cloud services for storing books, games, and currencies is a relatively new trend, and it may not be obvious to consumers that in contrast to their physical counterparts, these services often place heavy restrictions on the transferability of their contents. Another issue is ensuring that pricing remains clear and understandable despite the emergence of dynamic pricing schemes of the kind we have described. Consumers need to be able to make informed decisions about their choice of platform for competition to work.

7   Methods of Exchange

In this chapter, we return to the internal workings of a virtual economy to address a practical design question: What kind of mechanisms should we provide to users for carrying out trade? Storefronts? Auction houses? Or something much simpler? Recall that in chapter 4, we said that a market can consist of any arrangement through which buyers and sellers meet for the purposes of exchange. In chapter 5, we talked about who those buyers and sellers are on different kinds of markets. We left open the more practical question of how the exchange actually takes place. In this chapter, we review the main types of exchange mechanisms found in an economy, whether national or virtual, and then consider how to choose which exchange mechanisms to implement in a virtual economy. Finally, we round off our four-chapter series on markets by examining the limits of market design: how the threat of unsanctioned markets places limits on what kind of market design decisions we can feasibly hope to implement.

Common exchange mechanisms

Personal trade

The simplest imaginable exchange mechanism is a physical meeting of two individuals who strike a deal over an object one of them has in their possession.[1] Payment is carried out, and the item changes hands on the spot. This was the only exchange mechanism available in the earliest MMO games. In *Ultima Online* and *EverQuest*, people would walk around the game world shouting what they wanted to buy or sell until they bumped

---

1. Exchange mechanisms are presented in this chapter roughly in the order they appeared in virtual economies. To some extent, the order also reflects the development of commerce in general economic history, but it should be noted that early human societies relied on nonmarket allocation mechanisms, such as reciprocity and economic rights and obligations structured according to kinship networks (Polanyi 2001). Extensive trade was a later development, and a society structured by markets is an entirely modern invention. We discuss nonmarket allocation mechanisms in chapter 9.

into someone willing to negotiate. If they managed to agree on a price, one of the players would click on the other's avatar, opening a trade window. The buyer would place money in their side of the trade window, and the seller would place the item in their side. Once both players clicked Confirm, the deal was executed. A number of such deals, occurring over a span of time and space, constituted the market. Personal trade can be facilitated by a currency or it can be pure barter, where goods are exchanged for other goods (we return to barter versus currency in chapter 10).

Escrow

When *Habbo* was first launched, it did not feature a trade window. The only way to transfer an item from one avatar to another was to drop it on the ground and have another avatar pick it up. Personal exchanges were conducted by having the seller drop the item being sold at the same time as the buyer dropped the payment. But this made it easy to commit fraud: one of the parties could simply fail to drop their part and grab whatever the other party had dropped. As a result, trading was something that could take place only between people who trusted each other—and trust was scarce in a pseudonymous open online environment. One way in which traders could get around this problem was to use a third party that both users trusted as an intermediary. The intermediary would take the item from the seller and the payment from the buyer and, once in possession of both, drop them to their new owners. Such an intermediary is known as an *escrow*. Escrows are widely used in many markets, such as the market for second-hand Internet domain names, a type of virtual good. By bridging gaps in trust, escrows enable exchanges that would otherwise not be possible and thus improve the efficiency of a market.

In a subsequent update, *Habbo* implemented the same kind of a trade window that *Ultima Online* and *EverQuest* already had. This kind of a trade window can be seen as an automatic escrow, a software replacement for a human intermediary. Several of the exchange mechanisms described below are commonly implemented with a built-in escrow system.

The fair

The problem with personal trade is that the resulting market is inefficient. Chance meetings between suitable trading partners are rare. Buyers miss bargains, sellers miss buyers, and everyone spends a lot of time walking around and shouting. Very quickly, certain institutions begin to emerge from such disorder. Buyers and sellers start to look for each other in the same crossroads. Certain days begin to be favored as trading days over others. Before long, an improved version of the basic exchange mechanism has emerged: the *fair*, a periodic or ongoing meeting of buyers and sellers at a fixed location. Such gatherings and sites are also commonly known as markets, but because *market* also refers to the more general economic concept, we use the alternative term *fair* to talk about them. Fairs emerged in both ancient human societies and early MMOs. They made it much easier for everyone to find suitable trading partners and thus increased the efficiency of trade.[2] (See box 7.1.)

Silent fair

In *Ultima Online*, an open area in the city of Britain, in front of the First Bank of Britain, quickly emerged as the principal fairground. In *EverQuest*, an area known as the East Commons usually obtained this role. Both games had so much economic activity that the fair was an all-day, every-day event. The old trade window was still used to carry out the exchanges, but finding trading partners was now easier. As the fairs grew, a problem started to emerge, however: with so many people hawking their wares in the same area, the public chat window was starting to be overloaded with messages, to the point of becoming almost useless. *EverQuest*'s designers addressed this problem by introducing a new exchange mechanism: a trade interface where players attending the fair could silently list the items they wanted to buy or sell, along with requested prices. Other players could then use a search interface to examine these offers. When they found an offer they wanted to take, the system would provide them with directions to the location where the person making the offer was standing. The deal was then completed face to face, so to speak. This enabled a "silent fair": although there was still a lot of shouting and hawking going on, it did not impede on people's ability to find what they wanted, as they could use the search interface for that.

Bazaar and retail store

Even with fairs that gather buyers and sellers in the same location, finding suitable trading partners can still be somewhat time-consuming and troublesome. As a seller, you have to be in your stall for long periods of time to catch the best customers. You also have to be prepared to hawk and advertise your wares, which can be intimidating for those unused to it. What if you could outsource the job to a professional? Indeed, the next step in the evolution of exchange is the involvement of professional merchants who buy goods from producers and sell them on to buyers. Thanks to merchants, every day can be a market day. Consumers and producers can trade whenever they want to, and the market becomes even more efficient. We refer to marketplaces staffed by dedicated merchants as *bazaars*, in contrast to fairs, in which producers act as sellers themselves. Thanks to the dedicated merchants, bazaars tend to be more permanent affairs than fairs. The Grand Bazaar of Istanbul has been going on since the fifteenth century and today consists of over 4,000 merchants in little stalls and shops.

2. To dig deeper into the theory and practice of fairs and related institutions, see Dijkman's (2011) history of medieval commodity markets.

Box 7.1

Emergence of fairs in *EverQuest*

In 2001, the makers of the game *EverQuest* experienced an interesting problem: its markets were empty, and its empty spaces were markets. *EverQuest* was a "gear game," one in which a character's items had a big impact on its competitiveness. Gear could also be traded with other players, but in the game's first years (it was launched in 1999), *EverQuest* had no interface for doing so other than personal trade windows. There was no auction house where players could go to post items for sale. Nor was there any way for players to browse the items of other players to see what might be for sale. Rather, all negotiation happened through the chat system. Players with items to sell would write long chat messages that listed the items and the prices. Other players who saw these messages would then scroll through them, looking for things they might want. If they found something, they would send a message to the seller, asking for the character's location. Then they would move their own character into close proximity to the seller's character (which could take minutes or even hours, depending on how far apart the characters were), click on the selling character, and open a "trade window." In the trade window, the seller would place the item he wanted to sell, and the buyer would place his money. Each party would have to click "Agree," and then the trade would take place.

This cumbersome way of doing business provoked a very interesting economic dynamic. First, since chat channels were limited by region, certain regions became the "market regions." If you entered a market region, your chat box would suddenly light up with lengthy messages listing items and prices. All of the vendors concentrated in one spot. Why? Because the concentration of vendors made the region the top place for buyers to go. And the top location for buyers is of course the only place a vendor wants to be. The location of this fair was thus a self-confirming choice on the part of buyers and sellers. It was a classic coordination equilibrium: Because buyers were there, sellers were there, and because sellers were there, buyers were there.

Proof that *EverQuest*'s markets were a coordination equilibrium could be found in the nature of the precise locations that became the fairgrounds. One of the interesting aspects of coordination outcomes is that there can be many possibilities that would work just as well, but only one of them ends up chosen. In the case of *EverQuest*, there were many possible fairgrounds, but on any given server (the game was divided into dozens of servers that replicated the same basic world), only one spot served as the fairground. On a few servers, the fairground was in a forest. On most others, it was in a tunnel. Interestingly, on none of the servers was the fairground in the North Freeport Market, a location the designers had specifically created for that purpose. The North Freeport Market was not accessible to about 25 percent of users (the evil characters) and thus lost out to places such as the East Commons Tunnel. The tunnel was made by the designers to allow evil characters to bypass Freeport, a city that hated them. Naturally, the fair appeared there and not in town, because markets don't care if their users are good or evil or something in between, as long as they do business. Markets only care about maximizing the amount and efficiency of trade. Thus, the market in *EverQuest* was empty, and the empty space, a tunnel, was the market.

Independent *retail stores* are basically merchants who are so successful that they can attract buyers to their own location instead of having to vie for them among other merchants inside a bazaar. Retail stores and bazaars can also operate in reverse, buying goods from individuals instead of selling them. As discussed in chapter 5, NPC vendors in MMO games have an important role in buying items as well as selling them.

However, playing the role of a full-time salesperson is not what most players have in mind when they enter a game. Few player-merchants ever emerged in *Ultima Online* or *EverQuest*. Most people would prefer to be producers (hunters, crafters, explorers and so on) and leave shopkeeping to someone else. The developers of *Ultima Online* addressed this by creating an artificial salesperson: a robot that players could purchase and place outside their homes. Once activated, it would sell items from its inventory to passersby at prices fixed by the master. But the effect of this feature went further than making life easier for player-merchants: it largely eliminated the need for any dedicated merchant players at all, as it allowed almost anyone to sell items twenty-four hours a day. Players acting as salespersons or even true retail store owners remain uncommon in virtual economies to this day.

Auction

Rare and unique items are difficult to sell through retail stores and other mechanisms that require the seller to set an asking price, because it is hard for the seller to estimate a good asking price for an item that is rarely traded. The seller can hazard a guess, but it will most likely be either too high, in which case the item fails to sell, or too low, in which case the seller leaves money on the table. For rare and thinly traded goods, an *auction* is a better choice of exchange mechanism. Economic theory suggests that a suitably designed auction will not only succeed in selling the item but also do so for almost the maximum price the buyers are willing to pay. Auctions are thus great price discovery tools for thinly traded items.

Auctions exist in numerous different varieties. Wholesalers of flowers and produce traditionally use a dutch auction, where the seller announces progressively lower asking prices until one of the buyers accepts the price. The simultaneous ascending auction, introduced in the beginning of this book as a game governments use to allocate radio frequencies, is a sophisticated auction combined with cleverly designed virtual goods.

In early MMOs, players often organized auctions where the seller or their agent would stand on a virtual podium and announce the items to be sold, one at a time. After each item was announced, prospective buyers would shout out their bids, and the highest bid would win. Lots of drama, tension, and even fights would develop as the bidders sought to intimidate each other into giving up while trying hard not to get carried away and end up paying too much themselves. In a bazaar with many sellers and few buyers, a reverse-auction situation can sometimes develop, where sellers publicly compete in who can offer the lowest price for a commodity to a buyer.[3]

Auction house

Today old-fashioned auctions involving shouting and hand-waving have to a large extent been replaced by digital equivalents in both national and virtual economies. In fantasy MMO games, *World of Warcraft*'s highly automated *auction house* has set the standard for efficient trade. A seller simply goes to the auction house, drags the item to sell to the selling interface, sets the starting bid, and chooses a duration between twelve and forty-eight hours. Buyers use a sophisticated search interface to find their desired items. When a buyer places a bid, the money is automatically moved from their wallet into escrow. When the auction runs out of time, the person making the highest bid is declared the winner and receives the item through the in-game mail service. The seller receives the price less a transaction tax by mail. All other bidders have their bids returned to them from escrow by mail. Traders like the auction house because it is very efficient compared to any of the other exchange mechanisms discussed so far.

Buyout house

In a typical auction house, sellers also have the option of setting buyout prices for their goods. Any buyer willing to pay the buyout price can buy the item immediately, without having to wait for the auction to end. This saves time and working capital for both parties, making the market more efficient. The buyout price is used especially in auctions involving frequently traded commodities, because for such goods, the seller already has a good idea, based on previous trades, of what buyers are willing to pay. Since the seller is able to set the buyout price very close to the price that an auction would produce, actual auctions are rendered largely unnecessary. As a result, for cheap and frequently traded items, the auction house tends to devolve into a *buyout house,* where people just use buyouts and forgo time-consuming auctions. Buyout houses can also be created by design. *Habbo*'s centralized Marketplace is a buyout house where sellers post sell offers (i.e., buyout prices) and buyers see only the cheapest available price for the item they are seeking. When an item is sold, the next best offer pops to the top of the stack, displayed to prospective buyers. There is no reason to wade through pages of similar listings to find the cheapest offer.

The buyout house is not well suited for every kind of item, however. For rare and thinly traded items, it is very difficult for a seller to accurately estimate buyers' willingness to pay. If an item has only one sell offer listed, it is also very hard for an inexperienced buyer to know whether the price is fair, or possibly an attempt at gouging. For these reasons, people prefer trading rare items in an auction. If a rare item is sold in a

---

3. For an introduction to auction theory and modern national auctions, see Klemperer (2004).

buyout even when auctions are available, this probably indicates that the seller under-estimated the value of the item and set the buyout price too low, or that the seller was in a great hurry to liquidate the item, as when selling stolen property.

Bourse

Stock markets, the pinnacle of financial capitalism, are like buyout houses where both buyers and sellers can enter offers into a central registry. A trader in the market wishing to buy a given stock has two options. The first is to take the best sell offer currently in the registry and pay the seller's asking price, as in the buyout house example. But if that price seems too high, the stock market gives the aspiring buyer a second option: enter a new buy offer into the registry with a lower price, and wait. Someone looking to sell the stock might come along and take up that offer, assuming no better buy offers are available. Buy offers are known as bids and sell offers as asks. The difference between the highest bid and the lowest ask is known as the spread. A narrow spread suggests that the market is efficient. This system of trading that stock markets use is called an *exchange* or a *bourse*. Since *exchange* is also a more general term, we use the term *bourse* to avoid confusion. The bourse system is commonly used to trade not only securities but also gold, oil, foreign currencies, and the digital currency Bitcoin (figure 7.1). Like the buyout house, the bourse is suited for frequently traded commodities rather than unique, rarely traded items.[4]

In the virtual economy of *EVE Online*, the bourse is the most commonly used exchange mechanism. Everything, from minerals to missiles and from spaceship hulls to trade goods, is traded using a bourse system. When a player places a sell offer, the item in question is moved from their hangar into escrow and released only when the item is purchased or when the offer is canceled or expires. When a player places a buy

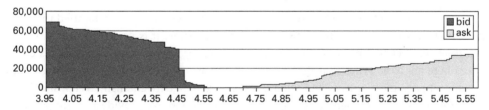

Figure 7.1
Buy offers and sell offers for bitcoins in the Mt. Gox bourse. The vertical axis indicates US dollar values. The horizontal axis indicates the number of bitcoins available for sale and purchase at each dollar value. The chart is cumulative, so that bitcoins available for purchase at a given price also include those available at previous prices. The snapshot was taken on October 6, 2011.

4. For a detailed description of the structures and functioning of modern bourses, see Harris (2003).

Table 7.1

Ten exchange mechanisms that implement markets

Personal trade	Two persons meet, negotiate, and trade.
Escrow	Two persons execute a trade by using a trusted third party as an intermediary.
Fair	Many individuals meet at a fixed location to negotiate and trade.
Silent fair	Many individuals meet at a fixed location to negotiate and trade; buy and sell offers are listed in a central registry to facilitate finding a buyer or seller.
Bazaar	Professional merchants buy and sell goods at a fixed location; prices are negotiable.
Retail store	A professional merchant offers goods for sale at fixed prices at a fixed location.
Auction	A seller announces an item for sale; buyers announce their bids.
Auction house	Sellers list goods for sale in a central registry; buyers bid for them through the registry; the highest bid wins.
Buyout house	Sellers list sell offers in a registry at fixed prices; buyers make deals through the registry.
Bourse	Sellers list sell offers; buyers list buy offers; deals are conducted through the registry.

offer, the amount of money being offered is similarly moved into escrow. Thanks to this, deals can always be completed immediately when another player takes up on an offer.

We have now covered a variety of exchange mechanisms used in virtual as well as national economies. These mechanisms are summarized in table 7.1.

Choosing an exchange mechanism

In the previous section, we identified ten exchange mechanisms that are used to carry out trade in markets. This list is by no means exhaustive. It is possible to imagine an infinite number of variations in how exchange is carried out. The mechanisms covered here are basic types that developers can use as inspiration when designing their own exchange mechanisms. But what is a good exchange mechanism? What should a designer look out for when designing one? In this section, we provide a few important guidelines on how to choose exchange mechanisms for a virtual economy.

Exchange mechanisms and market efficiency

We mentioned several times how the more advanced exchange mechanisms improved the efficiency of the market. The more efficient a market is, the easier it is for everyone to get what they want. If the market for, say, wheat was hopelessly inefficient, so that wheat was extremely troublesome to obtain, there would not be many bakers in the economy. Efficiency is thus an important factor to consider when choosing an exchange mechanism. Markets for basic necessities should be efficient so as not to jeopardize other aspects of play or participation. Markets for naturally scarce things, like advertising space, should be as efficient as possible to ensure that resources are put to their most valuable uses.

That said, efficiency is not always the objective in virtual economy design. Recall from chapter 1 that one of the aims of virtual economy design is to regulate the speed at which content is consumed. A frustratingly inefficient market will block players' progress too much. But an overly efficient market might allow players to cruise through items and levels too quickly and thus reduce the publisher's earnings. This means that sometimes a designer might want to intentionally slow users down with an inefficient exchange mechanism. In *EVE Online*, the main exchange mechanism for trading almost everything is a highly efficient bourse. However, *EVE*'s designers have intentionally crippled the bourse somewhat by limiting its geographical scope: only goods located in the same region as the player's avatar are displayed in the trading interface. This makes it necessary to travel and ask around to get a fuller picture of what different goods cost around the universe at any given time.

World of Warcraft's auction houses are also designed to be less efficient to use than they would have to be. First, the trading interface cannot be called up just anywhere: the avatar needs to move to the actual Auction House building located in a major city. Second, because of the way the logistics of the auctions are designed, high-volume trading requires lots of running about between the auction house, a mailbox, and a bank—and needless to say, these three are situated apart. Blizzard offers a mobile smart phone client that allows players to bypass all these limitations and access the auctions from anywhere, but this feature comes with an additional monthly subscription fee. This tiered system is perfectly in tune with the objectives of virtual economy design: users who consume content slowly pay less; users who rush through the game faster must pay more per time unit.

Exchange mechanisms and engagement

Another factor to consider in exchange mechanism design is *engagement*. By *engagement*, we refer here to anything that the exchange mechanism requires the participants to engage in doing in order to trade successfully. This could be negotiating, haggling, hawking, touting, searching around, establishing trust, and so on. Recall that one of the objectives of virtual economy design is providing attractive content to users. The kind of engagement we are describing here is a subset of content.

In conventional economic analysis, actions like negotiating and searching represent transaction costs. Advanced exchange mechanisms achieve efficiency precisely by eliminating actions such as these. Buying or selling something through a streamlined digital bourse involves no social interaction at all. Having a comprehensive search

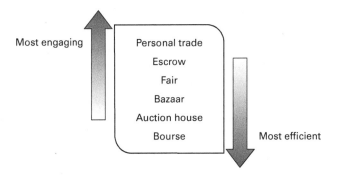

Figure 7.2
Exchange mechanisms listed in the order of efficiency and engagement

index makes finding goods and bargains so easy as to present no challenge. But from a game design perspective, inefficiencies like negotiation and search might be desirable. Eliminating them might eliminate what was interesting about the market in the first place. There is thus a trade-off between efficiency and engagement.

In summary, a market rich in engagement provides users with lots of things to do, while an efficient market that avoids all engagement provides little. Still, the kind of content engendered by inefficiency is not always the most attractive kind. Searching around and negotiating is fun only to a certain extent, after which the deal needs to succeed so that participants can move on to other types of content.

Figure 7.2 lists some of the basic exchange mechanisms roughly in order of increasing efficiency and decreasing engagement.

Exchange mechanisms and information
In chapter 2, we introduced the idea of bounded rationality: that people's decisions are limited by the information available to them. If you don't know how much an item is worth, you might end up paying too much for it or selling it too cheaply. This creates arbitrage opportunities for experienced participants but can lead to new users being ripped off.

Exchange mechanisms differ in how much information the user needs to already have to make good trades with them. At one end of the spectrum, auctions have an in-built mechanism of revealing information about people's willingness to pay for a given item, so even if you have no idea how much an item is worth, you are likely to get something close to the current market price if you sell it in an auction house. At the other end of the spectrum is personal trade: all you know is what the other person is telling you, and they might be lying.

Habbo originally supported only personal trade and fair-type "trading rooms" that emerged spontaneously. Very quickly, users started to maintain third-party market information sites that collated and published information about the current market prices of different items in trading rooms, thus helping to add information to the market. However, not all the information provided by these user-managed sites was necessarily impartial. Later, *Habbo*'s developers created a buyout house—not to replace personal trade and trading rooms but to complement them with an additional exchange mechanism that would also act as a centralized source of price information. *Habbo*'s buyout house allows users to see the price history of any item traded in the house, helping people make informed trading decisions even when they execute the trade using a different exchange mechanism.

In general, rare and thinly traded goods are most efficiently exchanged in auctions because they facilitate price discovery for items with little or no price history. This also applies to unique items and items with variations in quality. Frequently traded commodities can be more efficiently exchanged by simple retail stores. Bazaars, buyout houses, and bourses fall somewhere in between; they allow more opportunities for price discovery and bazaars also for observing differences in quality among suppliers. In other words, the choice of exchange mechanism also depends on the characteristics of the good being traded and how that influences information needs.

Information can also be affected by the form of presentation. A price can be hidden or loudly reported. Dense tables reward analytical folks but leave average users in the dark. In most cases, data about economic activity and choices should be easy for users to access and sort.[5]

Exchange mechanisms and market structure

Some of the exchange mechanisms we have described are commonly found in user-to-user markets but not in publisher-to-user markets. The auction house is one example. Other mechanisms, such as retail stores, are more common in publisher-to-user markets than in user-to-user trade. This suggests that the question of which agents participate in the market as buyers and sellers, also known as market structure, influences exchange mechanism design. More precisely, the number of agents participating as buyers and sellers influences which exchange mechanisms can be used.

For example, it is simply not possible to have an auction on a monopsony-structured market because by definition, such a market has only one buyer, while an auction by definition involves several buyers. For this reason, players in fantasy MMOs sell their items back to the publisher using retail stores—nonplayer character (NPC)

---

5. Interfaces are always too crowded, of course, and so user interface designers are never happy to hear that users really need to be provided with even more information. This isn't just a virtual problem; there's a reason that merchants at bazaars are shouting all the time, and our web browsers are packed with ads. Attention is a scarce commodity. The economics of attention, and some solutions to it, were discussed in chapter 4, box 4.4.

vendors—rather than some kind of fair or auction. Similarly, reverse auctions are not possible on monopoly markets. On a market with only one seller, fairs and bazaars are reduced to retail stores.

This applies when all NPCs behave similarly, so that they are essentially manifestations of a single agent, the publisher. NPCs can of course also be equipped with distinct artificial intelligences (AI) and wallets, and made to operate on the market as independent agents (see box 7.2 for an example). This would allow players to auction off their items to multiple NPCs competing against each other, for example. In other words, it would allow more engaging exchange mechanisms to be implemented even in publisher-to-user markets. The downside is that designing such AIs and ensuring

Box 7.2
NPC traders in *EVE Online*

EVE Online's economy features many NPC-run corporations, with names such as Allotek Industries and Further Foodstuffs. These corporations specialize in buying and selling trade goods that player-run corporations have no real use for, such as livestock and consumer electronics. Their purpose is to create a basic set of trading opportunities for beginner player merchants who can buy cheap NPC goods from one corporation and sell them to another in a different star system. The NPCs carry out exchange by posting buy offers and sell offers in *EVE*'s regional bourses in the same way as player traders do. This makes the experience of trading with them somewhat similar to player-to-player trade.

Despite trading on bourses, the NPC traders' AIs are very simple. Each good has a default buy price and a default sell price with a small margin in between for players to make a profit. When an AI has its buy offer fulfilled, it adjusts the price downward and posts another offer. Responding to a sell offer will likewise cause that AI's sell offer price to increase, until eventually the trade route becomes unprofitable. This way, the profits that can be made from trading with NPCs are in practice capped, even though in principle the NPC corporations have infinite stocks and wallets. After a day or two, the AIs adjust their offer prices back toward the defaults, making the trade route profitable again. As the goods in question are such that players themselves can neither produce nor consume them, the AI does not have to worry about any player-driven market prices in its pricing decisions.

EVE's NPC corporations are not truly independent agents, as they do not attempt any strategic behavior, such as undercutting competition. This limits the engagement value of trading with them. In recent patches, *EVE*'s developers have eliminated much of the NPC trade as they have added new types of player production into the economy. Most trade goods are now produced and consumed by player characters as part of new industrial processes carried out on planetary surfaces. Perhaps the best use for simple AI traders is in bootstrapping merchant play in a virtual economy that does not yet have sufficient player-driven demand for it.

that they work together reasonably (not flooding the market with cash as they try to beat each other in an auction, for example) is more challenging.

Multiple exchange mechanisms in one market

Different exchange mechanisms have complementary features. Personal trade facilitates building social relationships that can be useful later, while buyout houses and bourses are good for buying things in quantity. There is no reason that multiple exchange mechanisms could not coexist in a given market. Player-to-player markets in MMOs typically support at least personal trade and fairs (which arise spontaneously from the former) in addition to an advanced mechanism, such as an auction house or a bourse.

Limits of market design: Unsanctioned markets

Based on what we discussed in this chapter and in chapter 5, the task of designing a market for a given good in a virtual economy can be summarized as a set of three decisions: (1) whether to have a market for this good in the first place, (2) which market structure to impose on the market, and (3) which exchange mechanisms to make available for the market. The optimal choice in each case was described in terms of what would be most beneficial to the publisher that runs the economy. However, sometimes the interests of the publisher are in conflict with the interests of individual users. When this conflict is strong enough, users will attempt to find ways to circumvent the publisher's design and put in place unsanctioned markets with characteristics better attuned to their own interests. Designers should always keep this possibility in mind because it in effect imposes limits on how far they can go to shape markets. We finish this chapter, and the four-chapter series on markets, with three stories on how users took market design matters to their own hands.

Circumventing exchange mechanisms: Habbo trading forums

Until recently, teenage online hangout *Habbo* featured only very basic exchange mechanisms: personal one-on-one trade windows and trade rooms where people congregate to trade ("fairs" in our categorization). This lack of sophisticated support systems and user interfaces for market transactions was well in tune with the hangout's focus on low entry barriers, open-ended design, and social interaction. But for users who tended to trade a lot, like big builders and collectors, it meant that trading could be a time-consuming and laborious activity. Some users consequently decided to add a new exchange mechanism to *Habbo*: they opened a *Habbo* trading forum on an external site. On the forum, users could post sell offers and buy offers, browse offers, negotiate deals, and even organize auctions—all without having to navigate *Habbo*'s crowded rooms and corridors. Only actual delivery and payment had to be conducted inside *Habbo*. Today, such forums are a common player-created complement to many online games and hangouts. This allows users to circumvent more laborious exchange mechanisms, even if designers originally imposed those mechanisms on users for a reason.

Circumventing market structure: Q coin trading

In chapter 1, we told the story of the Q coin: the virtual currency that almost became the Chinese economy's de facto online currency. That was most likely not what the publisher Tencent had intended. Q coin was designed as a currency that users would buy from Tencent and spend on Tencent's virtual goods and services. In other words, the publisher intended to have a monopoly over Q coin. But they left a small crack in the design: a gifting feature through which users could send Q coins to their friends. That crack widened into a huge market as online retailers started to accept Q coins as payment for goods and services and sell the coins back to users in online auctions. Because Tencent was no longer the only party selling Q coins to users, the market structure transformed from a monopoly structure into a price ceiling structure. Tencent's selling price became the ceiling price that users would take when no cheaper options were available. This was not necessarily a bad deal for the publisher, though. The size of the market grew enormously, and thanks to some currency being constantly retired from circulation, there was always demand for replacement currency from Tencent.

After the People's Bank of China got nervous about Q coin's reach and Tencent significantly limited the amount of currency that could be transferred between user accounts, users came up with another circumvention method: instead of transferring currency between accounts, they started to transfer whole accounts that contained standardized amounts of currency. Transferring an account is, after all, a simple matter of letting the other person know the password. Thus accounts became a kind of superunit of the Q coin money, similar to high-denomination bills that complement coins used in smaller transactions. The designers' intent was again circumvented.

Circumventing the absence of a market: Dragon kill points

What if no transfers, trades, or giftings are possible at all? Can players find ways to circumvent the entire absence of a market? As mentioned earlier, most high-level items in *World of Warcraft* are designed so that they cannot be traded between players. Once a player picks up an item, that item is forever their. Thus there is no way for players to buy high-level items; they must simply keep playing until they obtain the items that they want. However, guild players have come up with a method that makes it possible to partly circumvent this embargo. So-called DKP systems (from "dragon kill points") are accounting systems created by player guilds to ensure that over time, items obtained from multiparticipant missions or "raids" are distributed fairly among the guild's members. Members receive points for participating in raids and spend those points to "buy" from other participants the right to pick up a specific item that drops during a raid. In this way, effort is rewarded and items are allocated to those who value them the most. However, some guilds also permit accumulated DKP points to be transferred between players. This opens up the possibility of using money to buy points and, by extension, the items that those points allow claim to. A relatively inexperienced player could thus spend their way to high-level gear in a short span of time, something that *World of Warcraft*'s design was supposed to make impossible. In practice, though, such markets are limited and have not been a serious issue in the game.[6]

6. For a detailed study of one DKP system, see Castronova and Fairfield (2007).

8 Externalities and Secondary Market Trade

In this chapter, our theoretical focus moves away from markets and into the concept of externalities: costs and benefits caused by an action to a third party. In terms of practical subject matter, we nevertheless continue with markets, as the topic of the chapter is applying the theory of externalities to analyze unsanctioned secondary market trade of virtual goods.

The term *secondary market trade* refers to users' trading virtual goods between themselves for real money. The first virtual goods secondary markets consisted of MMO players trading game items and characters on Internet auction sites like eBay. Since then, similar real-money markets have emerged for very different kinds of virtual goods, from virtual poker chips to Facebook likes and Twitter followers.

Secondary market trade is controversial: many gamers equate it with cheating, and most publishers forbid it in their user agreements. But some players argue that it is their natural right to dispose of their game assets as they see fit. Who is right? This kind of moral argument is difficult to settle. A school of thought known as law and economics posits that such questions should be addressed through economic analysis. According to this school, the favored outcome is the one that leads to the greatest net social benefit, regardless of what moral arguments can be mustered in its support.

To analyze the net social impact of secondary market trading, we introduce the concept of externalities: costs or benefits caused by a transaction on a third party. To provide designers with tools to combat secondary market trading and its harmful side effects, we describe strategies that economists have outlined for dealing with externalities and examine the applicability of these strategies to virtual goods trade.

Introduction to secondary market trade

Virtual goods earned through gameplay

In a typical online game, players earn some kind of virtual assets through gameplay: character attributes, items, coins, and so on. Since the earliest online games with assets that persist over game sessions, players have occasionally traded these goods for real money. In more recent games, this has become fairly commonplace: three surveys conducted between 2005 and 2009 suggested that around one in four or five MMO players traded game goods for real money.[1] A player wanting to sell their virtual goods typically lists them on a third-party auction site that specializes in virtual goods trade. Prospective buyers then bid on the goods. Payment is carried out through PayPal or similar means. The buyer and the seller then log into the game, and the seller hands over the goods. If the product traded was an entire account, the seller simply e-mails or messages the account details to the buyer.

At first this phenomenon was simply called real-money trade (RMT). But since virtual goods are now sold for real money by game publishers as well, we need a more precise term to refer specifically to player-to-player real-money trade. A term that has been used alongside RMT for a long time is secondary market trade, a term borrowed from finance. In finance, a primary market is where the original issuer of a security sells the security to investors. When investors subsequently sell the security to other investors, those transactions are called the secondary market. In the case of virtual goods, the primary market is where the publisher sells its virtual goods to players or players earn them through gameplay. Subsequent trades of those goods between players for real money constitute the secondary market.

The secondary market for virtual goods in online games is now huge (table 8.1). Since there is real money to be made in virtual goods trade, many kinds of professionals have entered the market. Julian Dibbell wrote a book about his experiences as a professional virtual goods dealer.[2] He and his fellow dealers bought underappreciated MMO accounts at auctions, refurbished them, and sold them for a profit. A company called IGE attained a name as a virtual currency exchange office, buying and selling virtual

Table 8.1

Estimated sizes of secondary markets for virtual goods in online games, 2009

North America, Europe, Japan	Korea	China	Other	Global total
$ 2.4 billion	$620 million	$1,510 million	$320 million	$4.9 billion

Note: Adapted from Lehdonvirta and Ernkvist (2011). The original source has an error in the calculation that gives a much lower number for North America, Europe, and Japan (p. 15, table 7). The number presented here corrects the error.

1. Yee (2005) reported 22 percent, CNNIC (2009) reported 24.9 percent, and KOCCA (2010) reported 24.2 percent. Developers we talked to said that these percentages seemed too high, but admitted that they had no way of estimating the true incidence. In any case, the incidence of secondary market trading varies significantly between game titles and categories, so aggregate numbers like these should be taken only as suggestive.
2. Dibbell (2006). Julian Dibbell is an American technology journalist who has written influential articles about life in online games and communities.

currencies for dollars and euros. So-called gold farms—workshops full of computers staffed by professional players harvesting virtual goods for a living—began to supply IGE and similar resellers with virtual currency. According to a report coauthored by one of us and published by the World Bank, something like 100,000 full-time game laborers may have been employed in gold farming in 2009.[3] What's more, gold farming is in fact only part of a whole third-party gaming services industry (box 8.1).

Many MMO players and publishers see secondary market trading and the use of third-party gaming services as cheating. They also claim that it hurts the game experience and provides an incentive for cybercriminals. We will analyze these claims in the next section. First, let's look at what other kinds of virtual goods are being commonly traded on secondary markets.

Premium virtual goods

Secondary market trading is not limited to goods earned through gameplay. In many games and online hangouts, virtual goods are primarily obtained through purchases from the publisher, but they are also actively traded on secondary markets. Cards used in trading card games such as Magic: The Gathering (MTG) are a classic example. Players purchase these cards from the publisher at fixed prices without knowing exactly what cards they will get. They then swap and trade cards between each other and between professional intermediaries to obtain the sets that they want. Over ten years after a digital online version of MTG was launched, there continues to be a vibrant second-hand market for virtual cards, which change hands for anything from a few cents to hundreds of dollars apiece. In contrast to MMOs, in trading card games, secondary markets are an integral part of the social aspect of the hobby. Since all cards are originally purchased rather than earned through gameplay, trading cannot be seen as cheating. This applies generally to all premium virtual goods: buying them used is no more cheating than buying them new.

Yet secondary markets for premium virtual goods can cause other kinds of headaches to publishers. *Zynga Poker* is an online Texas hold 'em game where users can buy poker chips but not redeem them back to real money because the game is not intended to be a real gambling game.[4] However, a secondary market has emerged where winning players can sell their accumulated chips to other players. Many players prefer to buy used chips rather than new chips from *Zynga* as the latter are more expensive. This is a serious concern for the publisher not mainly because of the revenue impact, but because if regulators start regarding the game as real gambling, it might inadvertently find itself subject to gambling regulation. In many jurisdictions, online gambling is

3. Lehdonvirta and Ernkvist (2011).
4. As of January 2012, *Zynga* was reported to be interested in entering real-money gambling as regulations in the United States are being relaxed.

Box 8.1
The third-party gaming services industry

The companies that develop and publish online games are called the online game industry. They are shadowed by a whole ecosystem of shady groups and companies that have discovered business opportunities within the contents of their games. The term *gold farming*, which describes one aspect of this ecosystem, fails to capture the full range of services and functions involved. A World Bank report coauthored by Lehdonvirta refers to this ecosystem as the "third-party gaming services industry."[a] According to the report, this shadow industry consists of the following kinds of specialized groups and companies.

Gaming studios

If game studios are companies that develop games, gaming studios are companies that play games. Also known as "gold farms" or "virtual sweatshops," these are small offices and warehouses in which young men in countries with low incomes but high affinity for online games, such as China and Vietnam, play games for a living. Their main products are virtual currency, game characters, and "powerleveling," that is, player-for-hire services. The biggest operational cost for gaming studios is labor, but game account subscriptions and CD keys can also be a major money sink.

Bot farms

Bot farms produce the same outputs as gaming studios with approximately one-tenth of the labor cost. They achieve this by using software that largely automates the task of playing the game, turning the player's character into a robot. But the use of botting software is strictly forbidden by most game publishers. As a result, bot farm operators may invest significant resources on research and development to create bots that beat the publishers' countermeasures.

Hacker groups

The most unscrupulous way of harvesting virtual goods for sale is to steal them from other players. Hacker groups use the same kinds of phishing attacks to gain access to game accounts as they use against online banks. Hacker groups also supply unscrupulous bot farms and gaming studios with "black accounts": stolen game accounts that have been stripped of possessions but can still be used for gold farming before they are shut down. Thanks to their economic value, virtual goods are among the most-sought-after commodities in today's global hacking scene, and entire families of malware are dedicated to stealing them.[b]

(Continued)

Wholesalers

Wholesalers buy virtual currency from smaller gaming studios, bot farms, and hacker groups and sell them on to retailers.

Retailers

Retailers are companies that specialize in marketing and selling the products of the third-party industry to the end customers, the gamers. Retailers maintain websites, buy advertising space in search engines, develop customer databases, operate call centers with staff who understand the customers' languages, and handle billing. Virtual goods retailers that target Western gamers were originally Western companies staffed with Western sales managers. Only production was outsourced to low-income countries. But by the mid-2000s, Chinese virtual goods entrepreneurs developed sufficient marketing and language skills to be able to expand to the whole value chain, from production to marketing. Since then, the industry has been dominated by Chinese entrepreneurs.

The third-party gaming services industry may already have seen its heyday. It grew rapidly in the mid-2000s, as MMO games grew in popularity, led by the hit title *World of Warcraft*. But today things are different. The MMO market is saturated. Publishers have become savvier with their revenue models, selling virtual goods to players directly and limiting player-to-player trading opportunities. Growth in gaming takes place on new platforms such as smart phones and tablets, but third-party service providers have largely failed to break into these media. It seems as if gold farming, a phenomenon that earned the interest of so many journalists and scholars, and the ire of so many players, is returning to the shadows. Our industry informants confirm that Chinese gaming studios are being shuttered, in some cases possibly moved to countries with lower labor costs.

The global virtual economy will continue to produce strange new industries that thrive for a while until the structures change again. Yesterday's gold farmers are today's paid Twitter followers. Sooner or later a similarly extraordinary industry is bound to emerge from mobile computing ecosystems.

a. Lehdonvirta and Ernkvist (2011).
b. Krebs (2009).

outright prohibited. Zynga has used lawsuits to go after secondary market intermediaries, but to little apparent effect.

Japanese publishers of highly popular virtual card battle games have experienced similar troubles. Players have been trading rare cards on Yahoo! Auction Japan for tens of thousands of yen (hundreds of dollars) per card, which in itself is not necessarily a problem. But the trading phenomenon helped draw media attention to the publishers' revenue models, which made heavy use of gambling and slot machine–style mechanics (buying cards at random to complete sets to win prizes). In May 2012, the Japanese Consumer Affairs Agency concluded that such models were against the law, forcing the publishers to make costly adjustments.[5]

Facebook likes and other social media votes

Game assets are not the only virtual goods being traded for real money. Facebook likes, Twitter followers, YouTube subscribers, Reddit upvotes, and many other kinds of "votes" that measure popularity on social media platforms are also being bought and sold for US dollars. Just like game items, social media votes are artificially scarce markers that afford status and advantage to those who accumulate them. Someone with a large number of votes or endorsements shows up at the top of lists and search results, and any message that person publishes is afforded more attention and credibility. As a result, social media votes are very valuable to advertisers, politicians, and anyone else wishing to influence people. Given this demand and the limited supply, it is no wonder that a market has emerged.

The designers of social media platforms intended that votes be "earned" by posting interesting content or by being popular for one reason or another. But they also made it possible to indirectly purchase votes by buying advertising space that drives likes and follows. In the last few years, third-party vendors have entered this market and started to sell votes directly. Dozens of online stores openly offer Facebook likes, Twitter followers, and other votes for sale. Prices range from a couple of cents to over a dollar per vote. The vendors obtain these votes from either real users, who are paid to like and follow specific brands, or arrays of fake user accounts controlled by unscrupulous entrepreneurs—just like gold farmers versus bot farms in the third-party gaming services industry. If the analogy holds, we may yet see cyberattacks designed to "steal" social media votes—a worm or trojan that uses your account to like its paymaster's Facebook page, for example.

Real users who "produce" social media votes on demand are recruited through so-called paid-to-click sites and paid crowdsourcing platforms. They typically earn no more than a few cents per click. Our observations suggest that they often come from

5. Yomiuri Shimbun (2012).

Net-savvy low-income countries, where such earnings can represent meaningful supplementary income. Some Filipino click workers we interviewed as part of an ongoing research project into virtual work reported earning their entire income from crowdsourcing and paid-to-click sites. The bulk of their earnings fortunately came from useful microtasks rather than fake social media votes.

Theory of externalities

Above we learned about the secondary market trading of various kinds of virtual goods. Next we want to understand its effects on a virtual economy and its publisher. For that purpose, we go back into microeconomic theory for a set of concepts that is useful in analyzing the net social impact of an action.

In theory, free trade is a boon to society because it allocates resources to their most productive uses. But markets that exhibit externalities are an exception. Externalities, also known as a spillover effects, are costs or benefits caused by a transaction on a third party. Since they affect a third party and not someone who has a voice in the transaction, they are not reflected in the transaction price. This distorts resource allocation. Externalities can be caused by production, consumption, or the act of exchange itself.

The classic example of a negative externality is pollution generated by a factory. The owner of the factory has to pay for the land, labor, and raw materials used in the production of goods but not for the polluted air. That cost is mostly borne by everyone else, in the form of illnesses, lower agricultural output, and so on. Someone who buys the factory's product obtains all of the product's benefits but pays only a part of its true costs. As a result, a larger quantity of the product is produced and sold at a lower price than what would be socially optimal (figure 8.1).

Positive externalities can arise, for example, when someone paints their house. Neighbors benefit from the new paint aesthetically and can even benefit financially as property values increase slightly in response to the increased attractiveness of the neighborhood. However, these benefits are not reflected in the cost of the paint, which the homeowner alone must pay. Homeowners will thus paint their houses less often than would be optimal for the entire neighborhood.

In the presence of externalities, the free market price of a transaction does not fully reflect its overall costs and benefits to society. As a result, private and public interest diverge: the optimum level of production for market participants is too much or too little for the society at large. In the presence of negative externalities, markets produce too much of a good. In the presence of positive externalities, they produce too little. Both are a type of what economists call *market failure:* a situation where individuals' pursuit of self-interest leads to an inefficient outcome from a societal point of view.

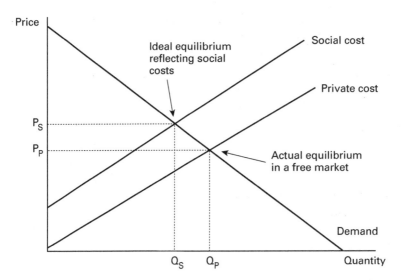

Figure 8.1
A negative externality causes private cost and social cost to diverge

In other words, negative externalities are problematic not because they represent costs—all economic activity involves some kind of costs—but because they represent costs that are not included in the free market price of the activity.[6]

Negative externalities in criminology

Some criminologists suggest that many crimes can be examined partly as negative externalities resulting from perfectly legal transactions.[7] For example, assault is highly correlated with alcohol consumption in historical, comparative, and individual analyses. Although alcohol consumption is no excuse for assault, in economic terms, it can be seen as a negative externality of alcohol consumption. Bars and liquor stores benefit from alcohol consumption, but in a free economy they pay only a small part of its true social costs. In this sense, they are comparable to the polluting factory, except that the pollution they produce as a side effect of their business is not a chemical but crime. Indeed, alcohol purveyors have been subject to prohibition and taxation, two of the main approaches for dealing with negative externalities. We cover these approaches later. First, we analyze secondary market trade from the perspective of externalities.

6. To dig deeper into the theory of externalities, consult a standard microeconomics textbook. We recommend Mankiw (2011, chapter 10) for accessibility and Varian (2009, chapter 34) for depth.
7. Farrell and Roman (2006).

Negative externalities in secondary market trade

In general, economists believe that trade is a social good—that is, the more people are allowed to trade, the better off the society will be. This applies to games as well. A secondary market trade can be shown to produce many kinds of benefits to players who participate in it. It makes it possible for players to buy used gear that suits their play style or fashion sense, fast-forward parts of the game that they find boring, and keep up with friends who are able to play more. It can allow the most dedicated players to finance their gaming hobby through gameplay. And when a player wants to move to another game or another hobby altogether, secondary markets allow them to liquidate their gaming investments and carry them to the next venue. Similarly, in social media platforms, the trade of likes and followers for real money allows users to earn money and advertisers to boost their credibility.

As a general statement, we can say that the trade of virtual goods on a free market benefits both the buyers and the sellers who participate in it. Otherwise they would not be doing it. Individual trades may end in disappointment because of asymmetric information or outright fraud, but on average, market participants walk out satisfied. When we look only at the buyer and the seller, secondary market trade thus seems to have an unambiguously positive social impact. But what kind of effects does it have on other people? In other words, what kind of externalities does it involve?

Diminished information value of possessions

As discussed in chapter 3, virtual goods are not only means toward ends; they are also markers that signal something about their owners to others. In the context of an online game, a high-level character signals that the player has spent considerable time playing the game and can be assumed to be familiar with the common tactics and conversational conventions of the game. An extremely hard-to-get object signals even stronger commitment and perhaps even above-average skill. Possessions can also reveal where in the game world players have adventured and what play styles they prefer. All such information has practical value in situations such as choosing members to a group or a guild. It can, moreover, accrue respect or status to the player among their peers, which for many MMO players is the main underlying motivation for participating in the game in the first place.

Secondary market trade allows players to obtain high-level characters and goods without necessarily expending any effort to get them. It therefore undermines the information content of those goods. The more players buy goods from the secondary market, the less likely it is that a signal given by a good is honest, that is, indicates that the possessor really performed the deeds associated with the item. This makes it costlier (in terms of time and effort) for players to find suitable partners to form groups with. It also reduces the social status value of the items. Dedicated players find that the trophies they have obtained through patient gameplay are devalued by what they see as plain cheating. In this way, every secondary market transaction inflicts a small negative externality on other players, especially those with significant in-game possessions. This obviously applies only in games where goods are obtained through gameplay. If the goods were obtained by purchase from the publisher, then they had little information value to start out with (see box 8.2).

Note that this problem is not limited to real-money secondary market trading. Any market, including perfectly sanctioned in-game player-to-player markets that use virtual currency, can reduce the information value of possessions by obscuring their origin. We discussed this issue in chapter 5. But unlike real-money markets, in-game markets don't allow complete newcomers to suddenly obtain large amounts of virtual wealth, so the effect is more limited. In this sense, real-money markets are more dangerous to signal value than virtual currency markets.

The same information value analysis also applies to the trade of social media votes. Acquiring a large number of Facebook likes or Twitter followers is hard. A lot of people have to be at least slightly interested in you. As a result, we tend to treat the fact that some brand or artist has managed to obtain a large number of votes as a signal of quality. It's not a perfect signal for sure, but at least some kind of an indicator. This information value is really the only value that social media votes have, both for someone possessing the votes and someone observing them. If likes and followers can be purchased for real money, then the honesty of such signals is placed in question. The more prevalent this trading is, the less meaning users can ascribe to a like. In the extreme case, social media cease to act as a useful social filter at all and turn into just another medium where money equals visibility. Every social media vote sold for real money inflicts a small negative externality on everyone else using the system in the form of diminished information about participants' true interests.

Crime pollution

Secondary markets provide an economic incentive for various antisocial behaviors, and especially for committing fraud and breaking into accounts to steal virtual goods from users. Thanks to secondary markets, virtual goods are highly sought-after commodities among cybercriminals. Fraud involving virtual goods is also very common. In a typical swindle, the villain offers an item for sale, collects the payment, but then fails to deliver or delivers an item of lesser value. The fraudster may also offer to buy a good and collect it but fail to pay. These behaviors obviously have a big negative impact on users' well-being. They also cause direct costs to publishers: at one point in *EverQuest II*, over 40 percent of customer service time was spent on disputes over virtual item sales.[8]

8. Robischon (2006).

Box 8.2

Time aristocracy versus money aristocracy

Throughout history, dress and personal objects have had a strong relationship with social status. In many cultures, it was possible to discern a person's position from their dress. Nobles could be recognized from silk and swords, and purple, a rare dye, was a sure sign of royalty. The basis of this relationship was a scarcity of goods and an economic system that distributed wealth according to rank. But as societies became more affluent and trade connections improved, wider ranks of society began to gain access to goods that once were limited to the privileged. Moral panic ensued: How could society continue to function if the servant became indistinguishable from the master? The higher classes would stand to lose if class distinctions were to be evened out in this way.

In many cultures, the elite responded by creating sumptuary laws: mandatory rules that determine what each social class is permitted or required to wear and consume. For example, in the increasingly affluent Renaissance England, Tudor monarchs saw it necessary to prescribe by law everything from the permissible colors, cuts, and materials of the clothes that different levels of nobility and bourgeoisie could wear, all the way down to the maximum permissible lengths of their swords and daggers. The explicit purpose of this legislation was to ensure that appearance closely reflected social position.

The controversy over real-money trade in online games can be framed as a struggle between "time aristocracy," such as students and those who are retired, and "money aristocracy," such as working adults. Online games have traditionally granted the best items, and consequently the best social positions, to those with lots of time at their disposal. This is the time aristocracy, a term coined by Joshua Fairfield. Real-money trade threatens this regime because it allows those with little time but lots of money at their disposal to reach the same ranks. These are the usurpers, the money aristocracy. Consequently, the time aristocracy lobbies for "sumptuary laws," or prohibitions on all kinds of real-money trade. Their success has been varied. Many games remain in the hands of the time aristocracy, but many newer games are increasingly ruled by the money aristocracy.

In the future, the gap between time and money gamers might be reduced by digital microwork and paid crowdsourcing platforms such as Amazon Mechanical Turk, which allow online time to be flexibly converted into money.

The crime pollution analysis introduced earlier suggests that these antisocial behaviors should be counted as a negative externality of secondary market trade. Some might argue that this is unfair, as every market by its very existence creates a financial incentive to steal. We hardly blame car buyers for auto theft, even though their demand is what motivates professional thieves. But secondary market trade also incentivizes a range of other antisocial behaviors: spam advertising in in-game chat channels, disruptive gold farming activities in game economies, and even cyberattacks directed at game servers to dupe them into yielding valuable assets. It seems reasonable to take these into account when assessing the net social impact of secondary market trade.

The idea that secondary market traders somehow "unbalance" the game economy comes up often in discussions among MMO players. Whether a player plays the game themself or pays someone else to do it should in theory have no impact on the game's virtual economy. In practice, problems can arise because professional gold farmers' play styles differ from normal players' behavior. Characters controlled by professional farmers can sit in one place for days or weeks, monopolizing limited resources far more tenaciously than any normal player would. Farmers are also less likely to communicate with other players, possibly disrupting the social fabric of the game. In these respects, a sociable player for hire working alone may be quite indistinguishable from a normal player, while automated bot farmers are likely to impair other players' game experience the most. Games with highly player-driven economies, such as *EVE Online*, are more vulnerable to the negative effects of farming than games where players' economic behavior has less impact on others, such as *World of Warcraft*.

Publishers' diminished ability to monetize their content

Often one of the key objectives of a virtual economy is to monetize content: to withhold the best virtual items or experiences until the user unlocks them through microtransactions, or to spoon content to the user at a carefully designed pace to keep subscription or advertising revenues flowing. Secondary market trade can undermine such designs. If an online gamer rapidly buys their way up to a high-level character, they in effect consume the game's content faster than originally designed. Sometimes this can be good for the publisher, as it allows the publisher to hold on to subscribers who prefer faster access to content. But it can also mean that players burn through the game's content quickly and then rapidly move on to the next game. According to one analysis, this kind of "premature aging" through secondary market trade contributed to the rapid decline of the highly anticipated MMO *Lineage 2* in Korea.[9] To add insult to injury, the publisher does not even get compensated for the content speedup: the revenue from providing this service goes largely to third-party gaming services providers.

9. Huhh (2005).

Today's content publishers are savvier with their revenue models, preferring virtual goods sales and downloadable content to flat subscription fees. In this model, if players want to consume content faster, they can do so by paying to the publisher, not to a third party. But here too, secondary markets can subvert revenues by competing with the primary market. All kinds of virtual goods, from *Zynga Poker* chips to Steam game accounts containing dozens of PC games, are being traded "used" on online marketplaces at prices below the primary market price of a "new" good. However, the interplay between primary and secondary markets is complex. Under some circumstances, the existence of a secondary market can boost primary market sales instead of merely cannibalizing them. This is why Magic: The Gathering is a trading card game rather than just a collectible card game.[10]

Dealing with negative externalities

We saw that secondary market trading can cause various kinds of negative externalities to other people. Economists and policymakers have come up with several potential approaches to dealing with negative externalities. The simplest policy is to prohibit the activity that causes the externalities. A more sophisticated approach is to impose on the activity a tax that is equal but opposite to the value of the negative externalities. The most sophisticated approach that economists have come up with is defining property rights in such a way that a market emerges for the externalities, and they in effect become internalized. In virtual economies, we have the further option of changing the rules of physics in such a way as to eliminate or minimize negative externalities. These approaches are listed in table 8.2. We next describe each approach in more detail and assess its viability.

Prohibition
The most straightforward way to deal with negative externalities is simply to prohibit the activity that causes them. Assuming that the net social impact of the activity is negative, eliminating the activity will increase net well-being. This is the path most game publishers choose: they prohibit secondary market trading in their terms of service and threaten to freeze accounts that are found to infringe on the prohibition.

Prohibition is a simple policy to understand, but there are three problems associated with it. The first is that prohibiting an activity eliminates both its positive and negative effects. You might want to eliminate fraud while making it possible for users to buy their favorite items, for example. The second problem is that enforcing prohibition is in practice often exceedingly difficult. Despite strict legal prohibitions and freezings of

10. See the "Market Structures for Monetization" section in chapter 5 for a theoretical discussion of the effects of secondary market trade on primary market sales.

Table 8.2
Possible responses to the negative external effects of individual behavior

Response	Benefits	Costs
Prohibition: Declare a rule and ban people who break it	Removes violators completely	Errors in judgment lead to public relations problems. Optimal amount of behavior may not be zero.
Impose a tax ("Pigouvian") on the undesired behavior	Soft enforcement, achieves social optimum	Hard to know what the right tax is. Hard to tax the right people.
Coasean bargaining: Create property rights to the externality and let people trade it	Negative consequences become priced by the market	Hard for all the affected to come together to negotiate efficiently.
Resilient design: Anticipate the problem and design around it	Minimizes consequences before the environment is live	Requires good foresight of potential behavior once system goes live

tens, if not hundreds, of thousands of accounts, Blizzard has never been able to stop secondary market trading around *World of Warcraft*. Unsanctioned markets for virtual gold and player-for-hire services have never been more than a web search away. Legitimate users may also be banned by accident.

The third, and perhaps the most serious, problem with prohibition is that it can actually aggravate some of the negative effects of the activity by pushing it underground. The high incidence of fraud in MMO-related secondary market trade is at least partly attributable to the fact that publishers have made it very difficult for secondary market participants to use secure mainstream ecommerce tools such as eBay and PayPal. As a result, much of the trading takes place on the shadier alleys of the web, where fraudsters ply their trade with impunity.

In summary, while prohibition is a simple and straightforward policy, it is not always the most effective one for improving net social impact.

Pigouvian tax

A more progressive approach to dealing with negative externalities is to tax the root activity instead of prohibiting it outright. Recall that the main problem with negative externalities is not that they represent costs, but that they represent costs that are not included in the free market price of the good, leading to more of the activity than would be socially optimal. The idea with Pigouvian taxes is that we increase the price of the activity to the socially optimal level through taxation. For example, many jurisdictions impose an extra tax on alcohol to reduce its consumption to levels that cause less harm in relation to the benefits. The money raised through the tax can also be allocated toward repairing some of the damage done. By avoiding outright prohibition, taxing can also reduce criminal activities that flourish when the activity is forced underground.

Over the years, several game publishers have experimented with taxation as an alternative to prohibition in dealing with secondary market trade. How does it work? Let's look at two examples: *EverQuest 2* and *Diablo III*. In 2005, Sony Online Entertainment opened Station Exchange, a sanctioned real-money marketplace for items, coins, and characters belonging to its flagship MMO, *EverQuest 2*. Players accessed Station Exchange through a website. In form and function, it was not very different from eBay and the many unsanctioned virtual goods auction sites. Sellers would list virtual goods, currencies, and characters for sale and buyers would bid on them. From every successful transaction, Sony collected a rather substantial tax of 10 percent of the final closing price. Sellers were also charged a $1 listing fee for listing items and coins and a $10 fee for listing characters, mostly to disincentivize nonsensical listings.[11]

In one year, the marketplace facilitated almost 40,000 successful auctions with a total value of $1.87 million. Sony's income from the system was $274,083, chiefly from transaction taxes. Compared to overall revenues from the subscription-based game, this income was not huge, probably equaling less than 10 percent of the subscription revenues from players who could access the market. It is impossible to say whether the income was enough to compensate for the game's possible premature aging and other loss of revenue caused by secondary market trading, but it was obviously more than what Sony was earning under its earlier ineffectual prohibition policy.

A big difference between Station Exchange and unsanctioned trading sites was that the former was directly connected to Sony's game servers and billing systems. This meant that money and goods could be assigned to their new owners automatically and instantaneously, making most types of fraud impossible. Indeed, one year after the launch of the service, the company reported that overall customer service time spent had dropped by 30 percent, a result at least partly attributable to reduced disputes over virtual goods trade. Station Exchange thus seemed to mitigate crime pollution externalities quite effectively. Station Exchange was never enabled on all of *EverQuest 2*'s servers, but it was extended to some of Sony's other online titles. The marketplace operated until 2011, when *EverQuest II* transitioned from a subscription model to a free-to-play model.[12]

In 2012, Blizzard opened a similar real-money auction house in its highly anticipated dungeon-crawling game *Diablo III*. The tax structure is slightly more complex.

11. The source for these and subsequent figures on Station Exchange is Robischon (2006).
12. In other words, Sony began to sell virtual goods directly to players and probably did not want to have to compete with the secondary market, preferring the monopoly model instead. See the "Market Structures for Monetization" section in chapter 5 for a discussion of the effects of secondary market trade on primary market sales.

Blizzard collects a fixed transaction fee of $1 from all item trades. But if the seller wants to cash out earnings, an additional 15 percent fee is deducted. Otherwise the earnings remain on the players' game account and are usable in future purchases within *Diablo III* or Blizzard's other titles. By taxing purchases lightly and cash-outs heavily, Blizzard perhaps attempts to guide players toward depositing money into their game accounts and leaving it there to be spent on Blizzard's other products. Another notable feature of the auction house is that bids are capped at a maximum of $250. We can speculate that this decision springs from concerns with consumer protection and financial regulation. But as discussed in chapter 5, a price law that attempts to force a market below the equilibrium price is a losing proposition.

Many players were unhappy with these terms. The market equilibrium price of many *Diablo III* items proved to be far higher than $250, making it an unappealing prospect to sell them over Blizzard's system. Moreover, the cash-out tax was perceived as high. Not surprisingly, many players chose to continue using unsanctioned third-party marketplaces. Despite the risks, heavy traders found these virtual "tax havens" more attractive than the official auction house. Sony's Station Exchange was never able to completely replace unsanctioned marketplaces. With these parameters, Blizzard's auction house will not be able to do so either.

This story illustrates that imposing Pigouvian taxes on a market can be far from easy. Even if everyone agreed that in the end it would be better for all if everyone paid taxes, each individual considered in isolation has an incentive to shirk and freeload on others rather than pay. Tax collection therefore needs to be an enforced rather than a voluntary system. But publishers, like governments, are able to enforce tax laws effectively only on their own territories. That is why publishers must create marketplaces on their own territory to compete with the unsanctioned ones. The challenge is to get users to use these official marketplaces instead of the unofficial tax havens. Publishers, like governments, can try to make their local marketplaces more attractive than the tax havens by relaxing the tax rate. But this makes sense only to the extent that it doesn't compromise the original aim of the taxes: reducing negative externalities. Thus, publishers, like governments, must also use legal prohibitions and threats of account seizure against traders on unsanctioned marketplaces. However, from the previous discussion on prohibition, we know that there are limits to how effective these methods are.[13]

Coasean bargaining

Besides enforcement, another problem with the Pigouvian tax approach is that it is very hard for a policymaker to accurately estimate the economic value of some negative externality. Without this information, setting the tax rate at the socially optimal

---

13. For more on the theory of Pigouvian taxes, see Mankiw (2011, chapter 10) or Varian (2009, chapter 34).

level is impossible. Markets are usually much better at estimating the economic value of things. Is there any way we could use markets to value externalities? Yes, if we are able to define property rights in them. This is the idea behind so-called Coasean bargaining.

Consider the following example. Two college students share a dorm room. Student A likes to listen to Irish folk music using his loudspeakers. Student B hates Irish folk but can't escape hearing it if A plays it. In other words, A's music consumption creates a negative externality for B. How do we reconcile the situation? Let's create a property right in the room's aural environment and assign it to A. The owner of the right gets to decide what music, if any, is played. Now if B suffers from the folk music more than A benefits from it, then B can simply buy the property right away from A. If A benefits from the folk music more than B suffers from it, then he can keep playing. Here's the neat part: it doesn't matter to whom the property right is initially assigned; the end result of the bargaining is always the same socially optimal arrangement. If we initially assigned the aural rights to B and A benefited from them more, then A could simply buy them from B.

The example, and Coasean bargaining in general, rests on the assumption that the concerned parties are able to negotiate over the rights without being hindered by transaction costs. In the case of two students in a dorm room, this may not be too unrealistic. But what would a negotiation over the negative externalities caused by a secondary market transaction look like? On one side, you would have the trader, and on the other side, the publisher and all the rest of the player base—not a realistic proposition, let alone one with zero transaction costs. Coasean bargaining is not a viable approach to dealing with large-scale secondary market trade, but it is a useful model to keep in mind for possible application in situations involving conflicting interests between small numbers of parties.[14]

Resilient design

We have exhausted the main tools against negative externalities that textbook economists and policymakers possess, but virtual economists have one more ace up their sleeve. We call it *resilient design*: economic design that is planned from the ground up in such a way as not to break when subjected to the eventual emergence of secondary markets and other unorthodox user behavior. Consider the following example. The designers of *EverQuest* never expected secondary markets, so they didn't practice resilient design. They put a small number of unique monsters into the world that yield superior rewards. Professional gold farmers quickly set up perimeters around these monsters and monopolized them day and night. As a result, normal players could not

---

14. For more on the theory of Coasean bargaining, see Mankiw (2011, chapter 10) or Varian (2009, chapter 34).

enjoy this important part of the game, and their experience suffered. Contrast this with *World of Warcraft*, which was designed many years later, when secondary markets were already well established. In *World of Warcraft*, unique monsters are nonrivalrous: they exist in a separate parallel reality for each player and group, making it possible for everyone to experience the same content without stepping on others' toes.

Of course, taken to the extreme, *World of Warcraft*'s approach simply means building single-player games. So-called social games tend to have very resilient and predictable economies, but the flip side is that there is little economic interaction among players. Together with negative externalities, they also lose the positive externalities of a multiparticipant economy: novelty and innovation. Designers who aim to use the virtual economy as a wellspring of emergent content need to be bolder. CCP Games allows console FPS gamers in *Dust 514* and PC MMO gamers in *EVE Online* to interact in the same virtual economy, but through a strictly defined protocol. Good resilient design can be seen as the art of making only the necessary compromises that enable the economy to function reasonably regardless of what the users get up to.

9 Institutions and Nonmarket Allocation

Much of economics is concerned with the functioning of markets, but markets are not the only way by which resources are allocated. Companies and organizations distribute goods and services internally according to their own hierarchies. Parents provide food to their children without demanding anything in exchange. Governments levy taxes to provide public goods and social welfare. Criminals steal wealth from others to consume it themselves. These are examples of nonmarket institutions and allocation mechanisms, which we focus on in this chapter. In ancient economies, nonmarket allocation was the norm and markets the exception. In today's national economies, markets are emphasized, but nonmarket allocation mechanisms nevertheless remain crucial. For virtual economy designers, the institutions and mechanisms described in this chapter are building blocks for economic design, and they can also be used as analytical tools for understanding and anticipating emergent user behaviors.

What are institutions?

In chapter 3, we introduced the concept of equilibrium, a target outcome toward which a social system tends to drift. The first and most famous equilibrium in economic theory is the equilibrium price in a competitive market. This was a price that no one predicted or ordered, but that emerged by itself from the interactions of millions of people. Despite being completely unauthored, the equilibrium price is a compelling force: you won't be able to buy a good for less than its equilibrium price, and you won't be able to sell it for more. Not even the government, with all of its laws and powers, can do much to change it.

In this chapter, we use the concept of equilibrium more generally. There are many social situations that have target outcomes that emerge and persist the way equilibrium prices do. Take, for example, driving. In the United States and Finland, people drive on the right side of the road. In the United Kingdom and Japan, they drive on the left. Which side is used doesn't matter as long as everyone uses the same side. Yet none of this was initially commanded by anyone; the laws we have today merely codify a practice that began ages ago, when people rode on horses and in wagons. These patterns emerged by themselves from the interactions of millions of people and still have compelling force today. (If you don't agree, try driving on the wrong side of the road.)

Social scientists have a general term for social equilibria of all stripes: *institutions*. An institution, in this technical sense, is a persistent social pattern that is emergent and self-enforcing. Prices and right-driving are institutions. So is the norm of holding the door open for others. Fashion is an institution. At a higher level, the European Union and the Constitution of the United States are both institutions: they persist because they induce supporting social interactions among millions of people.

In this chapter we use the notion of institutions as social equilibria to talk about numerous ways other than markets whereby economic goods and services can be produced and transferred, in national as well as virtual economies. For example, in families, breadwinners distribute the fruits of their labor to the rest of the family. In modern corporations, goods and resources flow from one person and business unit to another according to predefined hierarchies and plans. In MMO guilds, members share loot between each other and provide equipment to new players.

Institutions versus markets

Many institutions form relatively stable structures of resource allocation that persist over time. These can be contrasted with competitive market-based allocation, which in its ideal form takes place between ever-changing anonymous market participants, who neither give nor expect any loyalty from each other. Examples of how the same goods can be allocated via both markets and institutions are given in table 9.1. If competitive markets are the most efficient way to allocate resources, then why do other institutions exist? Are they some kind of irrational historical vestiges that will soon be extinct?

Resource sharing in families is perfectly rational when we include facts of biology into the analysis. From an evolutionary standpoint, an individual's chief concern is not

Table 9.1
Examples of market allocation versus institutional allocation

Good	Market allocation	Institutional allocation
Food	Grocery store; farmer's market	Family distribution at mealtime; school cafeteria
Child care	Nursery school; baby sitters	Parental care
Entertainment	Ticketed concerts and sporting events	Free play
Parking	Private parking garages charging a fee	Parking permits issued by a university for no charge
Health care	Over-the-counter cold remedies	Organ transplant lists
Scenic beauty	Private tourism attractions	Nature preserves

the most efficient fulfillment of their own wants, but the propagation of their genes. A question that has vexed economists considerably more is the existence of the institutions known as companies. For example, why does the CEO of CCP Games always use the same person—his lead maintenance programmer—to fix bugs in *EVE Online* instead of requesting competitive bids from the market? Many functions that were once central to companies are today outsourced to the market: accounting, security, facility management, customer support, secretarial services, and so on. Is it only a matter of time until absolutely everything is outsourced, so that every task is carried out by an ad hoc network of one-person companies? Will the rigid hierarchies known as companies eventually disappear?

It turns out that in many cases, it is actually more efficient to always use the same person for a task rather than to buy the service from a market. Even though you might be able to find a better price or a better-quality service from the market, using the market incurs *transaction costs:* costs like the trouble of finding, hiring, training, monitoring, trusting, and paying a suitable supplier. For common and well-defined tasks, such as operating a company cafeteria or providing security for a building, it is relatively easy and cheap to find suitable suppliers from the market, so those tasks are more readily outsourced. But for extremely specialized tasks like fixing bugs in a specific MMO, locating and training a suitable person is very expensive. Once you do find and train one, the most efficient course of action is to use the same person over and over again. Thus, we have the institution of employment in a company. In general, economists think that institutions represent social equilibria, or outcomes where different economic and social forces balance each other out so as to produce a stable solution.

Just because institutions represent social equilibria, however, does not mean that they are always fair or desirable. A mafia extortion business can be a highly stable arrangement because of the victims' fear of severe punishment. Institutions can also be dynamic equilibria, continuously cycling between a set of outcomes. An example is a two-party political system that seesaws between two similar governments while having forces in place to prevent a third alternative from emerging.

Groups and corporations

Institutions naturally also exist in virtual economies. Perhaps the most typical virtual institutions are various kinds of groups and corporations. Most MMOs have guilds or clans that organize group activities, distribute loot to raid participants, grant material support to new members, and provide "career paths" to dedicated players. More open-ended platforms like *Second Life*, *Habbo*, and *EVE Online* have spawned a huge variety of institutions, ranging from banks and stock exchanges to charities and tourism offices.

Economists see group formation as another form of equilibrium behavior. One model is simple reciprocity, "You scratch my back, and I'll scratch yours," which has been shown to be an equilibrium behavior in economic analysis. People who help one another in groups are often helping themselves. Group members who enforce group norms through stigma or other forms of punishment are solidifying the group and making all of its members more successful. Large numbers of economists have studied when such arrangements might actually work out and when they would be eroded by selfish or pathological people. Their basic conclusion is that there's an economic rationale for playing as a team.

Teams and groups are of course a core part of almost any multiuser digital experience. There seem to be three natural group-size equilibria: small teams, clubs, and networks. Small team groups are 5 to 8 members formed and disbanded within a few hours. Clubs are longer-lived institutions of perhaps 50 to 150 people. Networks are larger, more or less permanent webs of connection that extend to several thousand people. We suspect that these sizes exist because they balance competing forces. On the one hand, every group faces an inertial dissipating force—people always have the option of going their own way. On the other, the rewards of grouping are attractive. These group-size equilibria are places where the attractive power of group rewards just matches the incentive to go solo.

Group equilibria also give rise to internal reputation economies. The concept of social or political capital is a social scientist's way of accounting for the ability of some people to acquire goods or attention on the basis of past behavior. Doing certain things that improve one's standing in a group also creates a kind of virtual currency in the group's collective mind, and that currency can be paid out when needed. People who run out of such capital are booted from the group; those who have the most become leaders.[1]

Why groups and corporations?

From a publisher's perspective, institutions like groups and corporations can have many benefits in a virtual economy. They can help new users feel part of the community through being socialized into its norms. They can increase user engagement and retention as participants seek to fulfill their obligations and avoid disappointing their peers. They can provide participants with meaningful things to do, whether it is participating in a group or opposing it (see box 9.1). And in many cases, they help mend gaps in the system's original design or implementation. For example, in *Habbo* and *Second Life*, users created tourism offices and guided tours to overcome the chaotic new user experience that these open-ended online hangouts were offering. In early MMOs such as *Asheron's Call*, *Ultima Online*, and *Lineage 2*, users created commodity currencies to continue trading when the official currency hyperinflated due to bugs.[2]

1. See the discussion on Dragon Kill Points at the end of chapter 7 for an example of a system where aspects of participants' social capital are formalized into a digital point system.
2. Virtual commodity money is discussed in detail in chapter 10.

Box 9.1

Centralized economic coordination in a player alliance

> Ascendant Frontier Alliance was a virtual *EVE Online* organization that in its heyday con-
> sisted of over a thousand members. Under its visionary headman, Cyvok, the leaders of
> the alliance undertook to build the first ever Titan-class starship of the *EVE* universe: a
> gigantic mother ship with a doomsday weapon more powerful than anything seen in the
> game so far. The project had to be conducted in absolute secrecy lest enemies of the alli-
> ance find out and attempt to sabotage it.
>
> For eight months, the miners of the alliance mined minerals, industrial facilities pro-
> duced materials, and freighters hauled components to the hidden main construction site.
> Numerous cover projects were started, among them a second construction site for a smaller
> capital ship. Enemies of the alliance came close to discovering the location of the main
> construction site only two weeks before the Titan became operational. When the launch
> of the megaship was announced, the whole EVE community was taken by surprise. The
> alliance had used its institutional power to coordinate a massive amount of economic
> activity outside the usual galactic markets.

Designing groups and corporations

Given that institutions are behavioral equilibria that emerge among agents, they cannot be directly created by designers. However, designers can take several approaches
to promote the emergence of institutions. The most straightforward approach is to
provide players with the formal tools and trappings that the designer believes will be
needed by a particular kind of institution. For example, *EVE Online*'s designers thought
that the game world should have corporations, so they provided players with a corporation user interface that allows players to start a new corporation, add members to the
roster, and maintain a corporate currency account that qualified officers can access.
Such features are great for institutions that fit the mold envisioned by the designer.
However, they can be useless or even obstructive to institutions that follow a different
pattern. *EVE*'s corporation management user interface used to contain a feature for
distributing shares to corporation members, but it was almost never used because it did
not serve any useful purpose for the kinds of organizations that *EVE*'s players were in
practice creating. In later updates, *EVE*'s designers brought the features better in line
with the player-run organizations' actual needs. Meanwhile, *EVE*'s player community
also created a wealth of third-party tools, using *EVE*'s in-game browser and data API,
that support their own institutional forms.

Another approach to institution design that is complementary to providing tools and
trappings is to think carefully about what kinds of incentives would lead to the desired
social equilibrium. For example, if you want players to band together to form corporations or groups, then one good way to incentivize that is to promote skill specialization while ensuring that the challenges that the players face require the application of

several skills in combination. In fantasy MMOs, a clichéd convention is to have players specialize in dishing out damage, absorbing damage, or healing damage. In *EVE*, players specialize in activities such as mining, production, or security. A successful group requires a variety of skills, which promotes banding. The more complex an institution is, the harder it is to set up in this way.

Finally, the most open-ended approach to institution design is simply to create conditions that are favorable for institutions to emerge without necessarily giving too much thought to what kinds of institutions they should be. If the service has a suitably sizable and active user base, users will start coming up with their own institutions. The conditions are simple. First, users need to have relative freedom of action. If they are railroaded into a particular style of use, then it is naturally hard for them to innovate new institutions. Second, users need to have some kind of conflicting or complementary interests that compel them to seek coordination with others. Often such interests emerge from the content of the service or from users' personal preferences quite spontaneously. Third, to hold institutions together, there has to be some mechanism for creating trust among users or, failing that, for exacting punishment on transgressors.

Trust and justice

Institutions often require *trust* to emerge. Trust refers to the assumption by people that the promises they receive will be fulfilled. Coordinating institutions like right-driving or holding a fair every first Sunday of the month don't require much trust to emerge, because there is nothing to be gained and much to be lost by deviating from the norm. But in other institutions, members stand to gain at others' expense by not holding up their end of the bargain. This is typically the case in institutions that unfold over time. For example, having secured a monthly salary, a maintenance programmer might choose to go fishing instead of showing up at work. Or an entrepreneur might take investors' money and run with it instead of using it to grow a business. Other examples are shown in table 9.2. The mere possibility of such things happening can prevent these beneficial institutions from forming in the first place. Trust is therefore considered a foundational input to almost any kind of economy. You just can't have much in the way of markets and growth without trust.

Trust is created by meta-institutions like *morals* and *reputation*. Morals are standards of behavior that are considered acceptable in a culture. They consist of axioms like, "You should keep your promises." They are held to be self-evident, but often they also make great economic sense. Deviations from moral behavior are discouraged by social punishments, which can range from eye rolling to complete exclusion from the community. Another related meta-institution is reputation, which is a kind of track record of past behavior that can be used to predict a person's future behavior. Someone with a

Table 9.2
Examples of trust in economic affairs

Situation	Agent who must trust	Agent who must be trusted
Repair a car	Car owner	Mechanic
Loan money to a new business	Bank	Entrepreneur
Accountants in a practice	All	All
Telecommuting	Manager	Worker
Internet access contract	User	Service provider
Education	Student	Professor
Health care	Patient	Doctor

good track record can be trusted to keep promises in the future as well, while someone with a bad reputation should probably be avoided. These meta-institutions help the development of more complex institutions like employment and trade with credit and curtail antisocial institutions like extortion rackets.

In addition to informal meta-institutions, societies have also developed formal institutions for enforcing moral behavior and holding people up to their promises. These are known as the *justice system*. Criminal justice upholds certain moral institutions like the prohibition against murder and the institution of private property. Civil justice settles disputes between people and ensures promises are held. Both types of justice are ultimately enforced by state coercion, violent if necessary. Promises backed by a justice system can thus be stronger than promises backed by reputation only. An entrepreneur who runs off with the investors' money can be tracked down and have their assets seized. But formal justice tends to cost a lot of time, effort, and money to obtain. Justice is thus not a replacement but a complement to informal trust, necessary for enabling larger business deals but mostly unneeded in daily life. We would not want to live in a society where the only thing that prevents others from cheating, robbing, and murdering us is the fear of law enforcement.[3]

Trust and justice in virtual economies

Trust is a scarce commodity in many virtual economies.[4] It exists between friends and teammates but is hard to find between strangers. The loss of one's reputation is not a serious punishment in most virtual economies because alternative identities can be created quite easily. Perpetrators of fraud can launder their gains by transferring them

3. To dig deeper into the economic analysis of law and justice, see Mercuro and Medema (2006).
4. For a more detailed account of trust and its antecedents in virtual environments, see Schroeder (2011, chapter 5). Ralph Schroeder is a social scientist who pioneered the study of virtual reality and avatar-mediated social interaction.

privately to another account and then continue their enriched virtual lives under that name. This lack of effectiveness of informal trust mechanisms is partly offset by formal justice frameworks put in place by the developers. Usually these consist of two parts. The first part is a terms of service and code of conduct that acts as a sort of high-level criminal law and prohibits such actions as harassment (known as "griefing" in games). This law is mostly enforced by the publisher's support staff. Enforcement by humans is very expensive, so publishers try to minimize this type of law.

The second and bigger part of the virtual justice system is a set of rules enforced by the platform's code. For example, it is usually physically impossible for a character to steal a virtual item from another character or to fail to pay for an item won in an auction. These rules are automatically enforced by the programming. However, a significant limitation of such automated justice systems is that they can enforce only contracts and institutions programmed in by the designers. They are not able to settle difficult disputes or enforce new and innovative contractual arrangements in the way human judges do. This limits the emergence and longevity of new user-created institutions such as virtual companies, securities, co-ops, charities, and any other arrangements where misappropriation is possible (see box 9.2).

There are exceptions: in *Second Life*, participants were able to set up an entire virtual stock exchange called SLCapex, complete with a regulatory commission and self-licensed stockbrokers.[5] Despite its almost complete lack of legal protections against fraud or insider trading, entrepreneurs using SLCapex succeeded in raising the equivalent of approximately $145,000 from investors. This was possible because of exceptionally strong trust developed within *Second Life*'s relatively mature community. However, it turned out that at least some of this trust was misplaced. The market value of the investments grew to $900,000 before eventually plummeting, while at least some entrepreneurs shirked their duties. SLCapex continues to exist and operate to this day, however.

Real law in a virtual economy

Some entrepreneurs operating in *Second Life* have overcome the paucity of trust and enforceable contracts in the economy by simply invoking national law: signing real, binding contracts that pertain to virtual dollars instead of national ones. On several occasions, national criminal justice systems have also been invoked to deal with the theft of virtual goods by out-of-game means. In several cases, these bids have been successful, and courts have agreed to protect virtual property interests. But the introduction of national law into virtual economies raises a multitude of difficult questions. What kinds of virtual property interests should be protected? Can users' property rights

5. Bloomfield and Cho (2011). Robert Bloomfield is a professor of management and accounting and probably the leading academic expert on *Second Life*'s economy.

Box 9.2

The EVE Intergalactic Bank

Press release March 30, 2006

After months of development, the EIB has officially opened its doors for business.

What is the EIB you ask? The EIB (Eve Intergalactic Bank) is the first true bank service in the EVE galaxy. Striving to offer our clients the best financial services possible, we endeavor to become the largest financial institute the galaxy has ever seen.

Offering bank accounts, insurance, and loans, the EIB has filled a void of financial instability many inhabitants of EVE face on a daily basis.

Here is a rundown of what services we can offer:

Bank accounts, with a minimum interest rate of 3.5% per month
Various Insurance deals for all our clients
Loans
Escrow services
Financial Planning
Advice on shares purchasing and other investment opportunities

If you would like more information, visit our website at www.theeib.com, email our support department or contact Cally in game.

Cally
Chief Executive Officer
Eve Intergalactic Bank

EVE Online's virtual economy features an ever-changing variety of player-created institutions, from companies and stock exchanges to casinos and banks. One of the earliest and biggest was the EVE Intergalactic Bank. Its interest-bearing savings accounts offered a very attractive alternative to the zero-interest accounts of the game's built-in financial system. Deposits poured in, and the start-up quickly ballooned into a huge financial institution.

After six months of operations, disaster struck: the bank's CEO, Cally, announced that he had grown tired of his job and had decided to embezzle the institution's assets. He claimed to have stolen approximately 790 billion ISK, a colossal sum within the context of the game's economy. It would have been enough to build three Titan-class spaceships, of which not a single one had been built at that time. Various estimates placed the real-world exchange value of the credits at between $100,000 and $170,000. Players who had trusted EIB with their savings were devastated, but there was nothing they could do—no authority they could turn to.

The scandal provoked *EVE*'s publisher, CCP Games, to hold an online press conference. In the conference, the company stated that as long as events that would be termed fraud or embezzlement in a real-world context happened within the context of the game and did not break the terms of service, the publisher would not intervene. CCP did, however, say that it would closely monitor the funds in question to ensure that they would not be converted into real money on secondary markets, which would be a terms-of-service violation.

(Continued)

Since EIB, several scams of similar and even greater magnitude have rocked EVE's economy. Many of the perpetrators claim that they initially had honest intentions, but eventually gave in to either the temptation or simply the boredom of running an institution with accounts to keep and paperwork to deal with. Many more virtual businesses probably fizzle out quietly simply because the manager stops logging in. No commitment package or golden handshake is enough if you grow weary of the whole world in which your business takes place.

Since charters and securities in *EVE* cannot be legally enforced and rely instead on trust, the institutional landscape is fragile and constantly changing, as players come and go. In any national economy, this would be disastrous for economic development, but in a virtual economy, such dynamism can also have the benefit of keeping things interesting.

interfere with publishers' rights to manage their virtual economies? What if theft or fraud is part of the game?

These and other questions have been debated for years in scholarly circles and also increasingly in courtrooms. Greg Lastowka provides the most thorough and insightful review of the cases and issues at stake.[6] Legal analysis is outside the scope of this book, but we briefly offer our view of the current practical situation with regard to virtual economies and national justice. National justice systems shy away from intervening in the internal workings of a game or service that does not actively seek to blur the boundaries between the virtual and the national economy. National courts will not hear cases of in-game theft or disputes relating to the disappearance of gold coins from a guild vault unless such cases also involve some significant out-of-game component such as hacking or coercion. But if a virtual economy integrates directly with the national economy—for example, by allowing participants to exchange virtual currency back to real money, like *Second Life*—then national justice starts to play a bigger part. Regulatory compliance becomes an issue: the economy can no longer be managed as if it was just a game. *Second Life* prohibited gambling within its virtual economy following an FBI investigation. The U.S. Internal Revenue Service found that virtual greeters working in *Second Life* were real employees and subject to federal income tax withholding. But for contracts and disputes between normal users and user-created institutions that involve little out-of-game financial value, national courts

6. Lastowka (2010). On the intersection of law and virtual economies, see also Duranske (2008), Lastowka and Hunter (2004), Balkin (2004), Fairfield (2005), and Lehdonvirta and Virtanen (2010). Legal scholars were among the first to seriously study virtual economies and their real-world effects. Many legal analysts approach the subject from a law-and-economics perspective, and many economic insights can be gained from the legal literature.

are in practice not very feasible providers of justice because the transaction costs are simply too high.

User-generated justice

Given that neither automated justice systems nor human courts can feasibly provide comprehensive justice in a virtual economy, how about the users themselves? Could they create the institutions of justice in the same way they have created other institutions?

Examples of player-created justice systems emerging in virtual economies are extremely rare. The reason may rather ironically be in their lack of violence. While online games feature plenty of violent imagery, it is usually physically impossible for players to engage each other in any truly coercive or violent way that would have significant consequences. This means that even if users could come up with their own legal norms, they would have no means of enforcing them effectively. A partial exception to this is *EVE Online*, where players can cause irrecoverable damage to others' virtual ships and equipment. Some strong alliances have used the threat of such violence as a means to protect third parties against attack and theft on the alliance's territory, creating what amounts to rudimentary criminal justice. But at the same time, even the most powerful alliance in *EVE Online* would find it very difficult to enforce a simple commercial contract because *EVE*'s automated banking and warehouse systems will not honor player-created judicial orders to seize accounts or property. To our knowledge, no effective player-created justice systems encompassing both criminal and civil law exist, probably because of the difficulties of enforcing them.

There is, of course, a very good reason that game developers are extremely wary of giving players wide powers to hurt and coerce each other: the first thing that arises from such powers is not a justice system but violence and coercion. A fair justice system might emerge from the chaos at some point, but by that time, it is doubtful if there would be any justice-loving players left in the game.

A knowledgeable reader might object that at least small-scale player-run justice systems have operated successfully; the most famous is probably in *LambdaMOO*, a text-based virtual environment where users create legal norms through a democratic process.[7] But *LambdaMOO*'s system is not purely user run: norms created by the users are ultimately enforced by the administrators of the service, not by the users themselves, who lack such capabilities. Because of human resource costs, this approach is most likely not viable in commercial scale virtual economies.

One potential approach to user-created justice that to our knowledge has not been attempted is a competing regimes model: create a number of parallel domains, each with its own player overlord or assembly that has a monopoly on violence. Domains

7. Mnookin (1996).

that use this monopoly to protect citizens and enforce contracts will attract creativity and commerce, while domains that use it for nefarious purposes will find their lands deserted.

Redistribution

Justice systems are usually part of a larger institution called government that not only enables advanced markets to function by providing a justice framework but is also tasked with regulating the markets in order to prevent market failures and other undesirable outcomes.[8] In many societies, government is also tasked with filling the social welfare gaps and moderating the income inequalities that markets tend to generate. This creates a significant form of nonmarket allocation called government redistribution. Government redistribution essentially involves taking wealth from the rich and giving it to the poor. The taking part is typically accomplished through progressive taxation. The giving part is accomplished not only by dishing out money and subsidies, but also by providing free services. A typical redistribution scheme consists of tax-funded social security, health care, pension benefits, education, infrastructure, and other government services. In Finland, a fairly typical Nordic welfare state, the public sector spent and redistributed a whopping 55 percent of the country's gross domestic product in 2010.

Why redistribute?

The macroeconomic objectives of government redistribution are achieving greater social welfare and income equality, which are associated with a large number of societal benefits, including increased generalized trust, which boosts commerce.[9] Extreme redistribution in the absence of other motivators than money, however, can act as a significant dampener on individual productivity and innovation. In contrast to charity (see the next section), it is usually not voluntary for an individual to give. For this reason, hardcore libertarians see redistribution as a form of institutionalized theft (see the section on crime in this chapter).

Well before the age of welfare states, redistribution was extensively practiced in traditional kinship communities.[10] In such communities, the leader would take some or all of a year's harvest and distribute it among the members of the community according to some system of social status or role in the community. Similar practices are today found in some MMO guilds that tax their members. This kind of communal redistribution can be used to promote collaboration instead of competition between members and to share risk.

8. For an example of market failure, see chapter 8 on externalities.
9. Wilkinson and Pickett (2009).
10. Polanyi (2001).

In virtual game economies, equity and redistribution are not societal concerns in the same way as they are in a material economy, but they can be related to the game design concept of balance. Players of a game have a sense of equity that may be triggered in different ways. Economists have written of "horizontal equity" as the desire to make sure that people in similar circumstances receive similar economic rewards. "Vertical equity" is the standard that those who deserve greater rewards actually receive greater rewards. In a game design context, this looks much like the designer's objective of offering equal rewards to players showing the same level of skill and effort and higher rewards to players who have better skill and show more effort.

Besides equity considerations, it is also important to ensure that every player always has at least the minimum set of resources necessary to participate in the game, so as not to be inadvertently locked out of it. For example, players who lose all of their ships in *EVE Online* are gifted a new starter ship. From the perspective of preventing player churn, it may in some circumstances make sense to be even more generous and implement social security payments that are somehow relative to the player's wealth or income level prior to their economic demise.

Designing redistribution

So some type of equity and minimum social security are necessary even in a virtual economy, but do we need redistribution to achieve them? Can we not simply create goods out of thin air to distribute to the needy without having to take anything away from anyone? Yes, but creating goods out of thin air has its complications. If the virtual goods in question are positional goods, then the act of creating more of the goods will diminish the value of the existing stock of goods.[11] So in practice, we end up implicitly taxing the existing owners of the goods in the same way as printing more money is a tax on money owners, whose wealth is diminished by the resulting inflation. And in any case, new virtual goods flowing into the economy will upset the macroeconomic balance unless they are offset by corresponding reductions elsewhere.[12] Thus, every time we open the faucets to give more goods to one segment of the player population, we need to take goods away from some other segment to maintain balance. In effect, we practice redistribution.

How to implement redistribution correctly? One of the findings of inequality research is that it is very hard to achieve one form of equity without being accused of violating the other. Users will have their own ideas about what makes cases "similar" and about how much more reward a "better" player should receive than a "worse" one. Typically those notions will be biased in favor of the person speaking. There is no evidence, for example, in public opinion polling that the opinions of people are consistent when it comes to equality.

11. For an introduction to positional goods, see the final section of chapter 3.
12. See chapter 11 on macroeconomic design.

Thus, it is best that those who design redistribution schemes make the scheme explicit, obvious, and justifiable to the users. A fee on auction house use redistributes wealth if rich users trade more than poor users do. Yet it would seem justifiable to most users that those who put a heavier load on a system pay more. Ability to play also bears some significance: those with many virtual resources have an easier time paying any given fee. Seemingly capricious and unpredictable schemes are far more likely to be met with outrage. Hiding such a scheme only risks a major political problem on the day it is (inevitably) discovered. The lesson of "treat the same the same and the different differently" is easier to understand than implement.

We will return to this topic again in chapter 12, in the "Inequality" section, where we will discuss practical measures and methods of managing distribution on the macroeconomic level.

Charity and gift giving

Another significant form of nonmarket allocation is charity and gift giving. Gift giving happens in the context of a large variety of customs or institutions that demand it: birthday presents, Christmas presents, corporate gifts, anniversary presents, a bottle of wine when you're visiting someone's house, a box of chocolates to coworkers, and so on. Gift giving fuels a huge amount of economic activity: many producers of flowers, chocolate, design pottery, and neckties exist almost entirely thanks to gift giving. People also frequently give self-made items and self-produced foodstuffs as gifts to each other instead of selling them through a market. Individuals and corporations donate significant sums of money to causes that they support. Charity and gift giving are by definition nonmarket activities because they involve giving away something of value without receiving a payment in exchange.

Why do people give?
Recurrent gift giving between the same people, such as birthday presents, can be understood and analyzed as behavior that relates to the performance of social roles and relationships.[13] Other types of giving, such as donating money to a school, have characteristics that resemble market transactions: the people involved are not necessarily close to each other, there is an element of value assessment involved (Does this recipient need help?), and the transaction is a one-off event. Indeed, there is a popular theoretical angle that frames giving as a sort of trade in disguise. According to *social exchange theory*, even though gift givers receive no material compensation for what they give, they gain gratitude, respect, and social capital that offsets the value they relinquish, making the transaction socioeconomically worthwhile for them. This

13. See chapter 3.

gratitude may later be translated into actual material benefits if recipients reciprocate the gift. An object given as a gift, such as a decorative vase that sits in the recipient's living room, acts as a constant reminder of the debt that was incurred by receiving it. Help always benefits the giver, and sometimes the recipient too.

People also help each other in cases where the likelihood that the help will ever be reciprocated in any way is extremely small—for example, when giving money to a beggar on the street. This is called *altruism*. Altruism can be understood as motivated by indirect reciprocity: the expectation that someone else will one day help the helper and thus pay back the original help. Altruism is a self-reinforcing institution: the more people help others, the more likely they feel they themselves might one day be helped too.

Conjectures in evolutionary psychology provide another way of explaining altruism that doesn't rely on any kind of reciprocity. People are predisposed to help other genetically connected beings because it helps their genes to survive even if it does not benefit them in person. Empirical studies support this idea to some extent, as they suggest that people are more likely to be altruistic toward persons similar to themselves than to those who are dissimilar, ethnically or otherwise. In any case, we are in no way slaves to our genes: we can donate our time to improving Wikipedia if we so choose or even choose to help a different species. Altruism without any expectation of return, direct or indirect, is called pure altruism. Table 9.3 shows examples of how the same behaviors can often be interpreted as either pure altruism or as exchange.

Interestingly, paying someone for a contribution that they have thus far given purely altruistically can cause a crowding out of the altruistic motivation, which can lead them to contribute less, not more. You have to pay a lot of money to get something that a person wants to give for free. Thus, things like blood donations can be more effectively supplied by charity than by markets.[14]

Table 9.3
Is it a gift?

Behavior	As pure altruism	As an exchange
Loan tool to a neighbor	Just trying to help him out	May get loans in return
Take care of child	Paternal love	Child will take care of parent in old age
Community service	Helping the community	Nicer community is nicer to live in
Political office	Public servant	Power
Take care of an ill person	Helping the sick	Others may be more likely to help me if I am sick

14. To dig deeper into the theory of gift giving and other prosocial behavior, see Dovidio et al. (2006).

Designing giving

The benefits of having a culture of charity and gift giving in a virtual economy are many. Reciprocal exchange of gifts between users strengthens social ties and helps turn acquaintances into friends, which makes users less likely to leave the system. The search for good items to give can drive usage as well as virtual goods sales (gift wrapping makes for a good premium item). Helpful attitudes can also reduce maintenance costs: if users who find themselves in sudden need or trouble can successfully seek help and redress from other users, they are less likely to burden customer support staff with their petitions. Old users can delight new users with gifts and material assistance, giving the new users positive experiences and old users something meaningful to spend their time and wealth on. In libertarian thinking, voluntary giving is also presented as a complete alternative to government redistribution.[15] However, economic theory suggests that relying on voluntary giving alone to balance a game would run into trouble with the free-rider effect (people giving less than what is required) and suboptimal distribution (donations not necessarily going to where they are needed).

There are several ways designers can promote gift giving. The most obvious is to highlight occasions in which different cultural institutions call for gift giving, such as friends' (or friends' avatars') birthdays, weddings, Christmas, and various door-to-door begging (Halloween) and coming-of-age rituals around the world. Suitable goods and materials for gift giving should also be visibly promoted. Where possible, the giver should have the option of customizing the present in some way so as to make it more personal for the people involved. To promote help giving in games, game designers should lay out their worlds in such a way that old and new users come into frequent contact.

In addition to promoting the supply of gifts and help giving, designers can also try to increase the demand for gifts and help. The more people seek help and assistance, the more it is naturally granted. On average, men are more reluctant to request help from others than women are. This may be because in our culture, the ideal man is often painted as independent and self-sufficient, and men face pressure to conform to such expectations. Research on help-seeking behavior among MMO players suggests that this gender disparity is imported into virtual spaces: male avatars are less likely to seek help than female avatars.[16] However, men are quite willing to seek help using indirect means and expressions, such as casually mentioning a grievous problem in a conversation without expressly petitioning the other party for help in solving it. Such

15. See the previous section.

16. Lehdonvirta et al. (2012). There is a large literature in game studies and cultural studies that deals with gender and sexuality in games. This is an important topic of study, because many gaming communities struggle with discrimination, particularly of the type directed against women gamers.

indirectness allows masculine types to seek help while maintaining face. Because text-based communication lacks nonverbal cues, indirect expression is more difficult. To compensate for this, designers could create emotes and gestures that allow avatars to communicate trouble and need nonverbally. Other designs that promote help seeking and gift seeking are wish lists and tip jars.

A couple of caveats to gift culture should be mentioned. First, public begging for gifts causes negative externalities in the form of irritation and can end up decreasing the total amount of gift-giving activity. Most help-seeking behavior should be directed toward users' own social networks (friends, guild members, and so on), which have the means to discourage it with social punishments (i.e., telling the beggar off) in case it turns bothersome.

Second, if old users give new users too much virtual wealth, the newbies will miss the challenge and spending opportunities of gathering that wealth by themselves. This is sometimes a problem in games and services like *Habbo* that have no level or similar restrictions on what items users can give each other and use. An old veteran who decides to quit the service and dumps all of their stuff on an unsuspecting newbie can ruin not only the newbie's journey but also that person's potential value as a customer. One design that discourages such dumping is to allow quitting users to transform their possessions into a permanent "hall of fame" score that will remain as a nostalgia-inspiring record of their time in the system. We return to this in chapter 11.

Table 9.4 shows some data on gift-giving behavior in the teenage virtual world *Habbo*. The great majority of users in all of the countries surveyed had given a virtual gift at least once. Note that almost all of these virtual goods (or "furni" as they are known in *Habbo*) are premium goods that someone originally had to pay for (for examples, see chapter 10).

Crime

Crime is not an institution as such, although criminal activities can become institutionalized as ongoing rackets or gangs. But crime is clearly one way in which wealth changes hands outside the control of markets. People rob, steal, burglarize, extort, and defraud goods instead of obtaining them through exchange. We therefore finish this chapter on nonmarket allocation mechanisms with an economic perspective on crime. In chapter 8, we approached crime as a kind of pollution that results from perfectly legal activities like alcohol sales. Here we focus on the individual level, looking at criminal decision making and the sometimes surprising effects of crime on its victims in a virtual economy.

Earlier in this chapter, we framed crime as an attempt to gain a personal benefit at the expense of others by transgressing institutional norms. Indeed, economists who study crime often model it as an economic decision-making situation: every person is a

Table 9.4
Survey data on virtual gift giving in *Habbo*

Have you ever given furnis as a gift to someone?				
	United Kingdom	Japan	Spain	Mexico
Yes	86%	64%	71%	67%
Who was the recipient of your last gift?				
A friend	77%	86%	74%	64%
A random new user	12%	3%	14%	21%
A date or romantic interest	9%	8%	6%	10%
A member of my team, gang or similar group	2%	3%	6%	4%
Other	1%	1%	1%	2%
What was the reason for the gift? Select all that apply				
To help the recipient	33%	47%	48%	43%
To thank for something	31%	22%	24%	22%
A special occasion	30%	20%	19%	19%
To give a good impression of myself	19%	15%	13%	14%

Source: Habbo Socioeconomic Survey 2007 (described in Lehdonvirta 2009b). *N* = 5,288.

potential criminal who weighs the benefits of perpetrating a crime against its costs. The most prominent cost is the risk of getting caught and suffering a punishment. Another cost is the opportunity cost: Is there something more worthwhile that the person could be doing instead of crime? Suffering from bad conscience can also be seen as a cost. If the expected benefits of committing a crime exceed these costs, then the crime will be committed. In practice, it turns out that this model is bad at predicting violent and sexual crimes, but better at predicting economic crimes. Professional burglars and fraudsters really do weigh the potential consequences of their misdeeds against the expected benefits. Crimes of temper and passion follow different processes.

Let's assume that we're dealing with economic crime that follows the model we have set out. It follows that if a government wants to reduce crime, it must increase the cost of perpetrating it. This can be done by increasing the likelihood of getting caught (more police) or increasing the punishments given to those who are caught (longer sentences). It can also be done by providing people with better things to do (jobs), which increases the opportunity cost of crime. The government can also try to increase the social and psychological costs of crime by promoting the meta-institution of good morals. But all of these actions cost money. A rational government will weigh the benefits of crime reduction against its costs and reduce crime only as long as the benefits exceed the costs. There is unfortunately an *optimum level of crime* in society, which is reached when the marginal benefit of crime reduction equals its marginal cost.

A type of economic crime that is regrettably common in virtual economies is account hacking. In a typical case, a professional computer criminal uses fradulent e-mails, key-logging programs, or other malware to obtain passwords to a large number of online game accounts and then sell the virtual goods and currencies contained in those accounts to other players on online marketplaces. One insider of the Chinese third-party gaming services industry estimated that at one point, as much as 20 percent of the game currency sold on unsanctioned secondary markets was obtained through account hacking.[17] Game publishers fight against account hacking by implementing stricter authentication protocols, educating players about the potential dangers, and increasing real-time monitoring by staff—at least to the extent that the benefits of these actions justify their costs to the publisher and the players.[18]

Designing crime

The hard-working miners, haulers, and traders of the *EVE Online* universe are subject to constant attacks by space pirates. Pirates seek to plunder the tradesmen's wealth through a variety of means: stealing containers, capturing and ransoming ships (see box 9.3), and destroying ships and looting their cargo. The cost of preventing these injustices would be negligible because computer-controlled space police are highly effective and highly inexpensive. Yet *EVE*'s designers have chosen to provide police protection for only some parts of the universe. Why?

In this book, we need to go beyond textbook criminology and also consider the potential benefits of crime. The economic effect of space piracy is to make mining and trading riskier. Some shipments are taken over by pirates and never arrive. Those that do are sold at a higher price, because supply is scarcer and traders must recoup losses from lost shipments. In effect, trading starts to resemble a gamble: the merchant stands to lose everything or make a big profit. In purely economic terms, risk is a cost that makes markets less efficient at allocating resources to those who most desire them. But from psychology and game design, we know that risk, or variation in the outcomes of actions, makes things more exciting and potentially addictive. By allowing pirates to roam, *EVE*'s designers not only allow some players to pursue the thrilling career of a space buccaneer but also make other players' mercantile careers more exciting.

You could make the argument that account hacking also makes life riskier for players. You'll never know if your items are still there the next time you log in. Yet players don't seem to be very excited about this type of crime. What is so different about these two variations of theft? You could say that one happens within the rules of the game and the other doesn't, but this is not the right answer. We could make a game where

17. Lehdonvirta and Ernkvist (2011).
18. To dig deeper into the economic analysis of crime and law enforcement, see Nicholas and Medema (2006, chapter 4).

Box 9.3
Transcript of a pirate attack in *EVE Online*

Hello, one or more members of The Tuskers are prepared to destroy your vessel. Should you wish to pay a ransom to save your ship, please do the following immediately:

1. Turn off all modules and recall all drones. Stop your ship.
2. From the time a ransom amount appears below, you will have 30 seconds to pay the amount specified. Right-click the picture of the pirate stating our demands and select "give money" to do this.

If you do not comply immediately, we will re-open fire on your vessel.

Tressin Khiyne > howdy
Tressin Khiyne > we will require 40 mil for the ship, sir
Tressin Khiyne > you can pay to me
Shillowska > i dont have that much
Tressin Khiyne > how much do you have?
Shillowska > about 20 mln
Tressin Khiyne > 20 will do, please stop shooting
Tressin Khiyne > pay to me and you'll be set free
Shillowska > done
Tressin Khiyne > have fun sir
Bourreau > thank you sir
Bourreau > /emote tips his hat

Source: Adapted from http://thebaldbuccaneer.blogspot.com/2010/07/exitiale-you-know-i-enjoy-tuskers-i.html.

account hacking is permitted, but it would still fail to be fun. The right answer is that a risk is enjoyable and addictive only if it satisfies the following criteria:

• *Users feel in control of when they expose themselves to risk.* Random misfortunes are not exciting. Misfortunes that happen as a result of users doing something they knew was risky are much easier to accept. The feeling of danger on entering a low-security area in *EVE Online* can be exhilarating. Escaping once more to a police-protected area is a relief. In contrast, living under constant threat of account theft is depressing.

• *Users feel in control of how much risk they expose themselves to.* A wealthy user can afford to lose more than a poor one can. There are also psychological differences in how risk averse people are. In *EVE Online*, risk-averse players can stick to high-security zones, and risk-loving players venture out to pirate-infested regions. In the event of a pirate attack, the most that a player can lose is the ship that they currently ride on, including cargo. If a pirate tries to ask for more ransom than what the ship is worth, a player can simply decline and accept destruction. "Don't fly what you can't afford to lose" is a common saying among the pilots. In contrast, having one's account hacked can happen to anyone and usually results in the loss of all of the user's marketable property.

• *Higher risk comes with a higher potential payoff.* A higher risk feels unfair unless there is also a bigger potential upside involved. In *EVE Online*, paucity of competition on the most dangerous trading routes means that they tend to yield the best profits. The possibility of having your account hacked has no corresponding upside.

Crime that fulfills these criteria has the benefit of making the economy more exciting. At the same time, such crime retains its negative effects: despite any passive excitement, no merchant is happy when cargo is actually stolen. The task of the designer is to find a sweet spot between too much crime (unhappy users) and too little crime (bored users) and implement just enough law enforcement to keep the crime level at this optimum. Any crime that doesn't fulfill the three criteria listed above and thus lacks any positive benefits should be eliminated as far as it is economically feasible.

Besides excitement, another potential positive effect of virtual crime could be that it creates bonds among those who are victimized. Usually crime tends to break communities rather than build them, as victims withdraw from public life. But studies in the sociology of crime are now testing the hypothesis that crime could create solidarity among members of a community when the crime is perceived as an attack against the community rather than against individual members.[19]

19. Hawdon, Räsänen, and Oksanen (2013).

10 Money

Money is ubiquitous in today's societies. In virtual economies, however, this assumption does not always hold. Money might not exist, or it might come in forms that are rare in national economies. In this chapter, we take a step back and examine the fundamentals of money: what money is, what it is needed for, what makes good money, and what types of money there are. We also look at how designing money for a virtual economy differs from designing money for a national economy. We touch on the macroeconomic aspects of money, but leave detailed discussions of monetary policy to chapter 12.

The fundamentals of money

What is money, and what is it used for?

To understand what money is and what its purposes are in an economy, we first examine an economy that has no money. For many years, the virtual economy of *Habbo Hotel* did not have an official currency. Anyone who got bored with the furniture in their virtual room and wanted to redecorate it would try to exchange the items with someone who had a different set of furniture. A user might walk into a room and announce that they wanted to exchange the tenant's dining table for a sofa and a shower curtain. This kind of trade without currency is called *barter*. It works fine as long as the needs of the two persons happen to coincide. But if the tenant did not want a sofa and instead asked for a Victorian wardrobe, the person with the sofa would now have to find a third person with a wardrobe and an interest in sofas. Needless to say, trading by barter is laborious. In economic terms, such trade involves high transaction costs.

To reduce the transaction costs of trade, *Habbo Hotel*'s participants made a spontaneous innovation that people facing similar circumstances have made throughout economic history: they started to use one commodity as a *medium of exchange*. Instead of saying, "I want a Victorian wardrobe and a green shower curtain for this dining table," the seller would say, "I want eight Plasto chairs for this." The Plasto chair was a readily available staple item that formed the basis of many room layouts. Even if the seller did not need Plastos, they could be confident that many other people did, and that eight Plastos would be sufficient to buy the wardrobe and the shower curtain from someone. In basic terms, this is the definition of money: a good or a record that is generally accepted as payment for goods and services in a given cultural or social context. Thus, Plasto became the de facto money of *Habbo Hotel Finland*.

Besides acting as a convenient medium of exchange, money often has two other uses as well. The first of these is that it is used as a *store of value*. Storing your wealth in the form of ordinary physical goods has various drawbacks. Apples decay and lose their value, for example, and automobiles are costly to store. It is often better to store your excess wealth in the form of money, usually a durable commodity that is easy to store. Virtual goods need not have the same kinds of storage problems as physical goods do, but their designers often build some into them anyway in order to achieve macroeconomic design goals. For example, in *Habbo Hotel*, virtual automobiles disappear forty-eight hours after ignition, and there is a limit on the number of items that users can access through their inventory.[1] For such reasons, money is often used as a store of value in virtual economies as well.

The third use of money is as a *unit of account* in business deals, accounting, and administration. Instead of talking about how many tons of steel a factory consumed and how many cars it produced, accountants measure profit, loss, assets, and liabilities in monetary terms. This makes it possible to compare businesses that produce completely different goods and also to levy equal taxes on them. Sometimes the money that is used as an accounting unit is different from the money that is used as a medium of exchange. In medieval and early modern France, coins used in everyday commerce came and went as tides turned in war and commerce: the écu, Louis, teston d'argent, denier, double, franc, and various other currencies were all circulated at one time. However, accountants and bankers needed to write their books and loan certificates in a unit that would stand time. For centuries, they stuck with one unit: the livre tournois, or Tours pound. It mattered little that this coin had not been minted since the thirteenth century and was practically extinct. The rate of conversion from the various circulating currencies to this accounting unit was set by royal decree. A few centuries later, when France was in the process of joining the European monetary union, a similar situation arose once more: the euro was adopted as the accounting unit, but the franc coins and notes were used as the medium of exchange until the new euro notes and coins could be rolled out.

In *Habbo Hotel*, the same Plasto chairs that were used as the medium of exchange were also used as the unit of account. Sellers would quote prices in Plasto, that is, use the Plasto as their accounting unit. But they would not necessarily insist on receiving

1. We discuss money sinks in chapter 11 and monetary policy in chapter 12.

Table 10.1
The three uses of money

1. Medium of exchange: facilitating trade
2. Store of value: preserving value over time
3. Unit of account: providing a standard measure of value

Plasto chairs as payment—they might accept any items as long as the items' total value was approximately equal to the number of Plastos quoted. Self-professed market analysts observed trades taking place in the halls of the hotel and published up-to-date Plasto-denominated market values for hundreds of different items. Using these values as a guide, traders could accept almost any item of suitable value as payment. The Plasto was thus first and foremost an accounting unit, and only secondarily a medium of exchange.

The three uses of money are summarized in table 10.1. These three uses are really what all money is fundamentally about. From coins minted by princes of the past to today's commercial bank money, and from game money to private digital currencies created by contemporary cyberlibertarians, all ultimately owe their existence to the need to facilitate trade, preserve value, and measure value. Money designers may also have other objectives in mind (like providing privacy and replacing government-issued money; see box 10.2). But if a money fails to address these basic needs, it is unlikely to win much adoption. Money need not be metal: anything can be called money if it fulfills these uses.

What makes a good money?

Can anything at all become money? Not quite. There is one attribute that any object or digital record absolutely must have if it is to be used as money: it must have exchange value. Something that no one is willing to give anything in exchange for is obviously not a viable medium of exchange, and it cannot store any value (beyond its possible personal utility to the owner) or function as a yardstick of value.

Habbo Hotel's Plasto chairs are an example of *commodity money:* money whose exchange value is based on the value of the object from which the money is made. Plastos are frequently used in decoration in *Habbo*, so there are always people willing to give something in exchange for them. But the same applies to many other *Habbo* commodities as well. Why was only Plasto adopted as money? In fact, several commodity moneys are sometimes used in parallel. Once it happens that one money becomes more popular than the others, people start switching to the popular one because a money used by a larger number of people is more useful than a money used by few. A positive feedback loop ensues, and soon it may be that everyone uses the same money. In economic terms, the choice of money exhibits positive network externalities. The fact that Plasto ended up as the currency of choice was thus somewhat a matter of chance. In the British version of *Habbo Hotel*, the market tipped in favor of not the Plasto chair that was used in Finland but a different commodity, known as the Club sofa.

That being said, the choice of commodity used as a money is by no means completely arbitrary. Both the Plasto and the Club sofa had properties that made them better suited for use as a money than many other items in the virtual hotel. In general, it is possible to identify a set of attributes that make something a good medium of exchange, a good store of value, and a good unit of account. Let's start by examining the attributes that make a good medium of exchange:

• A medium of exchange should be *fungible*, that is, any one unit of the currency should be as good as the other—interchangeable. If individual units are different, people assign different values to them and they no longer function as a neutral medium. Standardized commodities such as 18-carat gold or white rice are very fungible, as one measure of either is for all intents and purposes equal to another measure of the same size. Unique objects such as large diamonds or valuable paintings are not fungible at all. Virtual goods tend to be extremely fungible: one virtual item is an exact copy of another item of the same type, unless quality differences have been expressly programmed in.

• A medium of exchange should be *divisible*, that is, capable of being divided into smaller units without loss of value. This makes it possible to convey the correct amount of value in a trade: not too much, not too little, but "exact change." Rice and gold are very divisible, but diamonds and paintings are not: if they are cut in half, the two halves are together less valuable than the whole was. It is usually not possible to cut virtual goods into pieces, but *Habbo Finland*'s Plasto currency was reasonably divisible in that one chair represented only a small quantity of value, like a grain of rice. For the most expensive items, one had to dish out hundreds of Plastos. In contrast, the Club sofa used as a currency in *Habbo UK* had a much bigger unit value. To improve divisibility, a subunit quickly emerged: one Club sofa was equated with approximately 75 rubber ducks, in the same way as $1 equals 100 cents.

• A medium of exchange should be *easy to transport and handle*. In a physical currency, this means that the currency should have a high value in relation to its weight and volume, so that market participants can carry their money in a purse rather than a cart. Virtual goods don't necessarily have weight and volume, but an analogous concept in many game economies is inventory space. Club sofas provided high value per inventory slot, whereas expressing the same amount of value in Plasto chairs took up several times as many slots. Dragging all those chairs to a trading window was a chore, so superunits emerged. One superunit, the Turntable, was equated with approximately 250 Plastos. In games that implement an inventory mechanic where items of the same type can be stacked on top of each other, the emergent commodity money tends to be a stackable item.

• A medium of exchange should be *verifiably countable*, that is, it should be possible to easily ascertain the quantity, weight, size, or other measure on which the value of the medium depends. Coins made of precious metals are often milled with a reeded edge, so that any removal of the metal from the coin will be easy to detect. Virtual goods tend to be easily countable.

• A medium of exchange should be *recognizable*, that is, not easily confused with other objects. Sometimes market participants try to cheat each other by passing objects off as something they are not. Virtual goods can look confusingly similar, but participants can usually access metadata that make it crystal clear what the object in question is.

A good store of value has the following attributes:

• A store of value should be *durable*, that is, it should not deteriorate, expire, or otherwise lose its utility over time. Being digital records, virtual goods can in theory be extremely durable. But virtual goods are sometimes programmed to disappear after a certain time, which limits their usefulness as stores of value.

• A store of value should have *low demurrage*, that is, the cost of owning and holding it should be low. Gold can cost a lot of money to store safely. Digital money is cheap to store, though not free. It costs around \$.10 per month to store 1 gigabyte of data in the cloud with Amazon S3. If one virtual good is a 1 kilobyte record, the cost of storing it in the cloud is a measly 1/100,000 of a cent per month. But large databases are more expensive to use, maintain, and analyze. The publishers of *Ultima Online* even experienced server failures because players were hoarding millions of items. Many publishers thus limit the number of objects storable in user accounts. *MapleStory*, a side-scrolling 2D massively multiplayer online (MMO), passes the cost of storage down to players by charging a fee for extra inventory slots. In such circumstances, stackable items can make a good store of value. They are easier on the database, so publishers may place fewer restrictions on their possession.

• A store of value should be *difficult to steal*. Small physical objects are obviously easier to hide and store securely than large and conspicuous ones. Traveler's checks and so-called registered instruments are registered to a named individual. Because they are in principle worthless in others' hands, they are inherently more secure against theft.

• A store of value should *retain its exchange value* against other goods over time. Goods that have a limited supply and steady demand are good candidates. In *Habbo Finland*, the turntable was considered a very safe store of value, as only a limited number had been issued as part of a one-off campaign in 2002. But in 2006, the publisher started a new campaign and issued more turntables to the users. The turntables' exchange value against other goods fell sharply, seriously hurting the net worth of avatars who had been hoarding them.

• A corollary to the previous point is that a store of value should be *resistant against counterfeiting*. In principle, counterfeiting is not possible in virtual economies unless such a feature has been expressly programmed in. In practice, all software tends to contain bugs and vulnerabilities, and attackers have sometimes been able to exploit these to achieve an effect similar to virtual counterfeiting. Early MMO game economies, such as *Asheron's Call*, *Ultima Online*, and *Lineage 2*, suffered from "dupe bugs," or bugs that allowed unscrupulous players to duplicate items and money. This destroyed the value of official currencies and led to the spontaneous adoption of commodity currencies, made from goods that were not subject to the dupe bug and thus retained their value.

A good unit of account has only one important attribute: its value against other goods should remain stable over time. A store of value is good as long as its value doesn't fall, but in the case of a unit of account, we don't want its value to grow significantly either. The reason is that if the value of a unit of account rises or falls significantly, it ceases to be the same measurement stick that it used to be, forcing a costly reevaluation of all values expressed in the unit. Price tags in shops have to be changed, numbers in accounting books become incomparable with past numbers, and business deals may have to be renegotiated. All this is costly and tiresome, and it reduces the efficiency of the economy.

Special considerations for digital money

When a physical currency such as coins, banknotes, or gold ingots is used as the medium of exchange in a transaction, that transaction is in principle known only to the buyer and the seller. Cash changes hands, but no record of the transaction is left behind unless one of the parties decides to record it in a receipt or an accounting book. In contrast, electronic transactions almost always involve a third party, and often more than one of them. For example, when you use a credit card to buy something from an online store, your payment request first goes to a credit card processing company, which forwards it to your credit card company, which authorizes the payment, after which the processing company eventually notifies the seller's bank, which credits the money to the seller's account. All of these third parties retain a digital record of the transaction, sometimes indefinitely.

Records are useful to authorities in that they allow transactions to be investigated afterward in case a crime such as tax evasion, drug trade, money laundering, or fraud is suspected. Criminals can falsify their own accounting books, but they cannot change or erase records maintained by third parties. For this reason, criminals prefer to use forms of money that are *unaccountable*, that is, not observable by third parties. If we completely eradicated physical currency from society and replaced it with debit cards, mobile payments, and other accountable means, that would deal a devastating blow to organized crime.

However, the flip side of accountability is the loss of *financial privacy*. Privacy is considered a fundamental need in many cultures and very often recognized as a legal right. Even if we don't have anything in particular to hide, we prefer to have curtains in our bedroom windows and go to the bathroom behind a closed door. More important, privacy in one's papers and communications makes it possible to develop and hold opinions that differ from those of one's parents, boss, community, or government without having to fear social pressure or punishment. Privacy, at least some degree of it, is therefore fundamental to democracy.

Privacy must also extend to financial transactions. The fact that one has paid the subscription fees of a queer culture magazine or the membership dues of a local union or social democrats' club can be just as sensitive information in some contexts as private letters. On a more mundane level, you wouldn't want your spouse to know in advance what you bought for them as a surprise birthday present, and you might not want to reveal your salary to everyone. Accordingly, the third parties that process our payments traditionally uphold bank secrecy, meaning that they promise not to reveal balances and transactions to outsiders. However, this secrecy is not absolute. In a democratic society, courts can force banks and credit card companies to provide investigators with access to the records of persons implicated in criminal cases. In this way, commercial bank money attempts to balance between privacy and accountability.

Of course, there is no moral reason to stop people from breaking their financial privacy themselves when they so desire. This attribute of money might be termed *flauntability:* the ability of the money's owner to voluntarily and selectively break their financial privacy to reveal balances or transactions to others. Flauntability is important for two reasons. First, there are situations in which people need to be able to prove how wealthy they are, such as when applying for a loan. Second, besides its exchange value, money also carries great social value: it affords access to social circles and attracts admirers and marriage partners. In contemporary consumer culture, people usually display their wealth through consumption styles rather than by directly exposing their bank statements, but throughout history, money has also been flaunted directly: the seashell necklace, the jingle of coins in the purse, and the fat wallet bulging in the pocket.

Electronic savings account balances can be flaunted through the rather unsexy balance certificates issued by banks, but many digital currencies and online game currencies are almost unflauntable. All other avatar attributes, from experience points and skills to armor and equipment, are often freely observable to others, but money is almost never so. Game developers have apparently strongly internalized the idea of financial privacy. In *World of Warcraft*, players use the one-to-one trade screen to show their gold to others, but this can be done to only one person at a time. They can take a screenshot of their purse and post it online if they need to impress a larger number of people, but screenshots can be faked. We consider this a little flaw in current virtual currency implementations.

Table 10.2
The 14 attributes of a good money

---

1. Valuable: can be exchanged to other goods and services
2. Fungible: any one unit of the currency is as good as the other
3. Divisible: capable of being divided into smaller units without loss of value
4. Verifiably countable: quantity of the money can be easily ascertained
5. Recognizable: not easily confused with other objects
6. Durable: retains its utility over time
7. Constant value: neither significantly gains nor loses exchange value over time
8. Easy to transport and handle
9. Low demurrage: inexpensive to own and store
10. Resistant against theft
11. Resistant against counterfeiting
12. Private: balances and transactions are not observable by third parties
13. Flauntable: privacy can be voluntarily and selectively broken by the owner
14. Accountable: privacy can be broken by legitimate authority to enforce laws

---

The attributes of a good money

We are left with no fewer than fourteen attributes desirable of a system of money. Of these, eleven are general attributes, and three are attributes that come up particularly in the context of digital money. These attributes are summarized in table 10.2.

What makes money valuable?

In the previous section, we posited that the most important attribute of money is its exchange value—in other words, the fact that people are willing to give other goods and services in exchange for it. We mentioned that *Habbo Hotel*'s Plasto chairs are an example of commodity money: money whose exchange value is based on the value of the object from which it is made. Commodity money can be contrasted with *fiat money*, such as banknotes, which are worthless as objects but accepted as payment because of government decree. In this section, we examine the different bases of value that a money can have and discuss the pros and cons of each type.

Commodity money

Commodity money is the earliest type of money in history. Gold, silver, and other metals have been used as currency around the world since ancient times. Medieval Japanese measured wealth in rice, and ancient Finnish hunter-gatherers used squirrel pelts. In many languages, the very word for money refers to a commodity that was used as money: for example, German *geld* (gold), French *argent* (silver), and Finnish *raha* (animal pelt). Commodity money is not just an ancient phenomenon. In World

War II prisoner-of-war camps, cigarettes emerged as a currency. In modern US federal prisons, smoking is banned, so inmates have started to use plastic-and-foil pouches of mackerel fish filets as a form of money.[2] In online games, virtual commodities like magical reagents are frequently adopted as a currency.

Precious metals are by far the most common type of commodity money in history. They are valuable, divisible, recognizable, and durable. However, one big problem with using pieces of metal as money is that their purity can vary a lot: one nugget of gold can have less than half the gold content of another nugget of the same weight. This limits the fungibility and countability of metal-based money. This problem was addressed by the introduction of coinage, first invented in the eastern Mediterranean countries or possibly India. A wealthy prince or merchant would take a large quantity of metal of uniform purity and strike or cast it into uniformly sized pieces, or coins. The coins would feature a distinctive mark that distinguished them from coins of other sizes and purities. Assessing the quantity and therefore the value of the metal present in a transaction becomes a simple task of identifying the coins and counting them. Thanks to this convenience, markets actually value coins slightly higher than the equivalent quantity of unshaped metal.

Representative money

Coins made of soft metals such as gold are vulnerable to gradual erosion. In part this is due to natural wear and in part due to fraudsters shaving off tiny bits from each coin before passing it on. Other commodities, such as grain, are impracticable to circulate due to their low value-to-weight ratio. These problems were addressed by the invention of *representative money*: certificates that have little value in themselves but legally entitle the bearer to a valuable good stored elsewhere. In ancient Egypt, farmers deposited their grains for safekeeping in royal warehouses and received written receipts specifying the quantity deposited. The receipts could be redeemed later for the grains. Similarly, in the United States in the late nineteenth century, banks and individuals deposited gold with the government and received gold certificates that could be used at any time to withdraw an equal amount of gold; the certificates were thus considered "as good as gold." Both the grain receipts and the gold certificates obtained the exchange value of the underlying commodity and were used as a convenient form of money in place of the actual commodity.

The national currencies of major Western countries and Japan have at various times been officially pegged to gold or silver, but the last such arrangement, the Bretton Woods system, ended in 1971. Today, representative money lives on on the Internet, where a handful of companies operate private digital gold currency systems. In such a system, the operator holds gold bullion in a vault and maintains a database that links

---

2. Scheck (2008).

every ounce of that bullion to an owner, a username. A user who wants to send some gold to another user simply instructs the operator to update the ownership information in the database entry referring to the gold. The actual gold stays put in the vault.

Representative money can also point to other valuables besides commodities. Medieval kings of England issued tally sticks, each of which represented the right to collect taxes due to be paid by a subject at a later date. The kings used these sticks to pay their creditors when the crown treasury was low on gold. The creditors could either collect the taxes or use the sticks to pay their own taxes to the crown. The sticks also changed hands and were used as a medium of exchange.

Fiat money

Although the exchange value of a given gold coin or gold certificate is rooted in the allure of the underlying commodity, their practical day-to-day value is based on the fact that they are widely accepted as payment for goods and services. Ancient rulers found that they could strike coins from an inferior metal with the same markings as the gold coin and make it a law that the new coins must be accepted as payment in the same way as the old coins were. Similarly, US governments began to issue more paper certificates than they held gold in their vaults, requiring by law that the paper be accepted as payment. Thus, money was divorced from any underlying commodity, and its new basis of value became the government decree, also known as *fiat,* that mandated its acceptance. A currency declared in this way to be a legally mandated payment instrument in a country is called *legal tender.*

Rulers have often had selfish reasons for introducing fiat money. By producing coins that were inexpensive to produce yet carried a significant face value, ancient monarchs could earn significant income. This income, the difference between the commodity value of a coin and its legally mandated face value, is called *seigniorage.* Governments have likewise often printed paper money for the sake of earnings. This seemingly free money is not without a cost, however. Every new note printed by the government diminishes the purchasing power of all the existing notes held by the government and its subjects. (See box 10.1.) The effect of printing money is therefore to take purchasing power away from the subjects and give it to the government or whoever receives the new money. Printing money can thus be a crafty form of taxation—an invisible capital tax.

Fiat money requires considerable political power to set up. The issuer must be able to force or otherwise coax people in the planned currency area to accept symbols that have no intrinsic value as payment. The issuer must also be able to enforce a strict monopoly on the issuance of that currency, because otherwise someone else reaps the benefits (competing issuers, even if their notes or coins are physically indistinguishable from the original ones, are called counterfeiters). In contrast, commodity money such as gold coins is accepted without any political pressure, and new gold

Box 10.1
Quantity theory of money

According to the quantity theory of money, the prices of goods depend on the amount of money in circulation in the economy. If the amount of money in everyone's pockets increases, prices will increase in the same degree (inflation); if money in pockets decreases, prices will fall (deflation). This relationship is more precisely expressed as

$M \times V = P \times Q$,

where M is the amount of money in circulation, V indicates how fast the money circulates (how many times on average each unit of money is spent during the time period), P is the price level, and Q is the volume of transactions during the time period. Assuming that the circulation velocity and transaction volume stay the same, changes in the amount of money will result in corresponding changes in the price level. Total purchase power is not affected: all the money spent buys the same amount of goods as before. The value of money, however, is affected: the more money there is in circulation, the less value one unit of money has in terms of the goods it can buy. Merchants will have to adjust their price tags upward. This is known as *inflation*.

coins can be minted by anyone without affecting their value (as long as they are of equal purity). In games, publishers are usually able to force players to use a particular currency. For example, the "gold coins" of *World of Warcraft* can be described as fiat money. These so-called virtual gold coins have no real function as a commodity; one cannot, for example, fashion rings or necklaces out of them. Their value is instead based on the fact that many transactions in the game cannot be conducted through any other medium. The robotic masters of the auction houses will accept bids only in gold coins, for example.

From the end user's perspective, a significant drawback with fiat money is that if the political force mandating its use weakens or disappears, fiat money may quickly cease to be accepted as a means of payment and lose its value. Interestingly, there are some rare cases in which fiat money has continued to enjoy a stable exchange value even in the absence of any government decree or other formal rule. For example, "Swiss dinar" banknotes continued to be used as a currency in the Kurdish regions of post–Gulf War Iraq even after the government officially renounced them. The value of the notes was upheld purely by a collective belief in their value. This can be called *community fiat money*.

At the same time, there are also good reasons that end users of money might prefer fiat over other forms. One reason is that fiat money is not vulnerable to physical erosion and shaving. A note is worth the same amount no matter how worn out it is. In this way, fiat money is similar to representative money.

Another reason that fiat money can be preferable to both commodity and representative money is that it allows the quantity of money in circulation, the money supply, to be better managed. In the previous section, we identified constant exchange value as an important attribute of a good money. But the value of a commodity can vary significantly from one day to another. For example, the price of gold is influenced by new discoveries, developments in extraction methods, and demand for gold in industrial processes. In recent years, the value of gold has more than tripled, which would have been highly inconvenient if gold ounce was used as a unit of account (imagine, for example, the value of your mortgage tripling). In contrast, fiat money can be created or destroyed at will, making it possible for benevolent governments to stabilize its exchange value and thus the prices of goods (see box 10.1). We return to this topic in chapter 12, where we discuss monetary policy.

In the case of virtual economies, fiat money does not necessarily have to have any advantages over commodity money. Virtual commodities can be made to be immune to erosion and shaving. They can also be created and destroyed at will, making it possible for a system operator to manage the exchange value of a virtual commodity money in the same way as central banks manage the value of fiat money. On the other hand, in a typical virtual economy, commodity money hardly has any advantages over fiat money. If the operator of a centralized virtual economy folds or the system crashes, virtual commodity money disappears just as surely as virtual fiat money does. The distinction between fiat and commodity is not very important in a virtual economy.

Token money

Tokens are records or objects that obtain an exchange value due to the fact that someone has pledged to redeem them in exchange for money, goods, or services. Consider a $10 Amazon gift card. Although no one else except Amazon has promised to accept the gift card, many people would accept it as payment for a $10 or $9 debt, since they know they can always redeem it at Amazon. Other examples of tokens are casino chips and arcade tokens. In Finland, supermarkets redeem empty 1.5-liter plastic bottles for .40 euros each. Tokens are different from representative money in that each token is not backed up by a corresponding good in storage. Tokens represent a promise that may or may not be fulfilled. Accepting tokens requires trust in their issuer.

In environments where cash is scarce, such as the frontier areas of nineteenth-century America, tokens frequently end up fulfilling the functions of money. A token passes from one person to another and might never be redeemed by the original issuer. This is highly beneficial to the issuer, as every token adopted as currency and never redeemed is pure profit. Tokens known as scrip, issued by logging companies to their employees and redeemable at the company canteen or store, continued to be used as currency between logging camp dwellers well into the twentieth century.

Most fiat currencies actually have a partial token basis for their value: even if everyone else suddenly ceased to accept dollar bills as payment, you could still use them to pay any taxes you owe to the US government. In this sense, the value of the dollar is in fact "backed" by taxes. Similarly, many kinds of small taxes and fees that players encounter in *World of Warcraft* are payable in virtual gold coins, backing the coins' value.

Facebook Credits were tokens: companies that develop applications for Facebook accepted Facebook Credits as payment from consumers only because they knew that Facebook would redeem the credits for US dollars. However, Facebook made it impossible for the developers to pass the credits on to anyone else. Consequently, Facebook Credits could not be used as money in the way that logging company scrip was. Developers couldn't use them to pay wages, for example. This is not an attribute of the money itself but of the *markets* set up by Facebook. We discussed this aspect of market design in chapter 5. While Facebook is already phasing out this system, Amazon has recently set up a new one with similar attributes, the Amazon Coin (for a radically different type of digital money, see box 10.2).

Box 10.2
Bitcoin: The new digital gold?

Most digital currencies are records stored in a central database controlled by the company issuing the currency. To conduct a payment, a user must send a request to the company, which checks that the user is authorized to carry out the transaction, and then updates the payer's and payee's balances in the database accordingly. This applies to game currencies as well as to dollars and euros stored on bank accounts. Bitcoin is different: it is a *distributed digital currency*. Instead of being stored in a central database, a complete copy of Bitcoin's records is stored on every user's computer. The computers are connected to each other via a peer-to-peer network. Conducting a payment involves essentially announcing the transaction to every other computer in the network. Clever use of cryptographic technology ensures that users can spend only their own money. If a user attempts to spend money to which they lack access keys, other computers in the network will refuse to pass the message along.

Bitcoin's proponents sometimes compare it to gold because both exist in a strictly limited quantity. A maximum of twenty-one million bitcoins exist in theory, of which 11.1 million have been discovered at the time of writing. Bitcoins are discovered by "mining": running a computationally demanding algorithm that examines millions of numbers, trying to find ones that fulfill certain criteria. As more bitcoins are uncovered, finding more gets progressively more difficult. Because of these gold-like qualities, Bitcoin is particularly favored by libertarians and others who distrust central banks and dislike their power to manage the amount of money in circulation. No one can manage the amount of bitcoins in circulation: it is predetermined by design.

However, unlike gold, which can be used in jewelry and electronics, bitcoins have no intrinsic uses. They have value only as long as someone is willing to accept them as
(Continued)

payment for goods and services. Many merchants currently accept bitcoins as payment for a variety of goods and services. But if they should lose faith in the currency's value or be forced to stop accepting it by authorities, then bitcoins would become as worthless as discontinued paper money. In this sense, bitcoin is most accurately classified as fiat money, specifically community fiat money. Its value depends on the strength of its community.

Internet entrepreneur and investor Jason Calacanis called Bitcoin "the most dangerous project we've ever seen." Although Bitcoin's complete transaction history is public, it is quite feasible for a participant to obfuscate their identity and transactions using a variety of means. This results in an extremely high level of financial privacy, which is a good thing. But in some cases this privacy can be so strong as to prevent even legitimate authorities from gaining access to records—like a Swiss back account, but stronger. Because of this lack of accountability, bitcoins are already used in tax evasion and to pay for illegal goods and services such as drugs and gambling. In this sense, Bitcoin shares qualities with cash, except that since it's digital, it can be moved rapidly around the globe with ease. Given that Bitcoin is a peer-to-peer technology, it would be very hard to shut it down. Should governments be afraid?

Probably not. In a rather poetic way, Bitcoin's main strength is also its biggest weakness. Since no one manages Bitcoin's supply, its exchange value changes purely in response to demand. In the short run, this has led to speculative price bubbles, fueled by media attention. In the long run, this means that Bitcoin is inherently deflationary: the more the currency is used, the more a single unit will be worth. For example, if bitcoins replaced just 10 percent of the euros used in the economy today, one bitcoin would have to stand in for over 50,000 euros. To reach this value from its current value of around 80 euros ($100), bitcoin would have to appreciate approximately 62,500 percent, or double in value almost ten times over. But this kind of deflation is self-defeating: it encourages hoarding instead of spending and thus prevents the currency from reaching widespread use in the first place. Both usage statistics and our personal observations suggest that most people who buy bitcoins simply hold on to the currency in the hopes that it will gain value rather than use it in transactions. For transactions, they continue to use national currencies, which are inflationary.

Despite its flaws, Bitcoin has a lot to teach to other money systems, both national and virtual. In contrast to national money, it offers an easy way for software developers to integrate all sorts of money-related features into their applications, providing a great platform for money-related innovation. It also facilitates intense competition between financial providers, resulting in things like fast and inexpensive cross-border money transfers. And compared to other digital currencies, its main attraction is its decentralized database, which means that users don't have to trust their money to a single entity. Even if Bitcoin itself is destined to remain a minor currency favored perhaps more by the network's shadier side, its innovations and initial victories have already inspired a next generation of digital money projects, which we will certainly be hearing about in the future.

Table 10.3

Types of money and their sources of value

---

1. Commodity money: valuable thanks to being useful for something else besides exchange

2. Representative money: valuable thanks to representing a claim to something valuable

3. Fiat money: valuable thanks to being generally accepted as payment for goods or services, because of decree or convention

4. Token money: valuable thanks to someone pledging to redeem it for something of value

---

Real versus virtual currency?

In examining the question of what makes money valuable, we identified four different types of money, summarized in table 10.3.

What about virtual money? Is it not one type of money? In the previous sections, we saw that *Habbo*'s Plasto chairs are commodity money, digital gold currencies are representative money, *World of Warcraft*'s gold coins are fiat money, and Facebook Credits were token money. But are these not also virtual money, as opposed to being real money?

What is the difference between real and virtual money? The difference is obviously not that one is digital and the other is not. Some virtual currencies come in the form of physical cards or tokens, and most dollars and euros today exist only in the form of digital records in banks' accounting systems. No difference there. A reader might intuitively suggest that the fundamental difference is that real money is more trustworthy than virtual money. After all, real money is issued by governments and banks, whereas virtual currencies are typically issued by Internet companies and other smaller institutions. As a general rule of thumb, this may be true, but it is not a fundamental difference. National fiat currencies have the same potential to completely lose their value as virtual currencies have. And this does happen: most recently, the Zimbabwe dollar, a "real money" according to conventional understanding, began to experience rapid inflation in 2005. The inflation exceeded 200 million percent in 2008, and the currency was abandoned in 2009. During these four years, almost any "virtual" currency would have been a more reliable store of value—even virtual gold coins in an online game! What we are really describing is the difference between public money and private money—between government-issued money and privately issued money. But if we took to calling private money "virtual," then gold coins struck in a private mint would be virtual money.

Contrary to popular belief, there is no fundamental difference between "virtual currency" and "real currency." Both US dollars and *World of Warcraft* coins are fiat money. The major difference between these two moneys is in the size of their *currency areas.* Economists define a currency area as a geographic area in which a given currency is accepted as a means of payment. It can also be understood as the total set of different goods and services payable with a currency. The US dollar is accepted as payment for many kinds of goods and services in a wide variety of places and stores. It competes with the euro for the title of the biggest currency area in existence. But one place where you cannot pay with dollars is the *World of Warcraft* (*WoW*) auction house. In contrast, *WoW* gold coins have a very small currency area. You can buy virtual goods and services inside *WoW* with them but not much else. People are known to sometimes sell non-*WoW*-related goods and services for *WoW* gold, but we know of none who would sell housing, food, or residential tax credit for *WoW* gold. For this reason, US dollars and other national currencies remain the preferred way to receive one's salary—not because they are somehow more "real." Differences in the sizes of the currency areas are only differences of degree, not of any fundamental quality. In some cases, a virtual currency may even have a currency area that rivals small national currencies in size, as perhaps is the case with China's Q coin, described in chapter 1. When the People's Bank took action against this digital currency, it was not because of its virtuality, but because of its reality, its real economic influence. When we use the terms *virtual money* and *real money* in this book, you should consider them shorthand for, respectively, "money with a small currency area" and "money with a large currency area." Nothing more.[3]

Designing money for a virtual economy

In the previous sections, we outlined the design space for money. Any object or record that is to be used as money must at the very least have exchange value, and we outlined four strategies for achieving this (table 10.3). We also identified thirteen other attributes that a good money should possess (table 10.2). How should these be applied in designing money for a virtual economy? A textbook economist would simply seek to maximize all the attributes, because the better the money, the more efficient the market. If you are designing a currency that will be used on a market that allocates naturally scarce resources like attention, or on a market where the publisher sells virtual goods to users to earn revenues, then making the currency as good as you possibly can is a great idea because you want these markets to operate efficiently. Simply take the list of attributes and use it as a checklist, making sure that your currency performs well on each of the dimensions.

But these are not the only situations in which virtual currency is used. In many cases, the currency you are designing will be used in user-to-user transactions on a virtual market whose main objectives are to engage and entertain, not necessarily to

---

3. To dig deeper into the history, uses, types and characteristics of money, a good source is Galbraith (1975). John Kenneth Galbraith was an economist and public intellectual influential throughout late-twentieth-century North America. On electronic and alternative money systems, see Zorpette et al. (2012), North (2007) and Ingham (2004).

be highly efficient. To support these objectives, it may be necessary to turn textbook economics on its head and design *bad money* rather than good money.

Designing bad money

In 2006, *Habbo*'s Plasto chair was the best money *Habbo Finland*'s users had, but in all fairness, it was not a very good money. It was valuable, fungible, and durable, but it also had several drawbacks. It was slightly lacking in divisibility, meaning that exact change was difficult to give. It was difficult to handle, as payers had to drag chairs one by one to the trade window. It took up a lot of inventory space. The number of chairs in the trade window or in one's inventory was not displayed anywhere and had to be counted manually, giving rise to errors. The basic chair used as money could be confused with an extremely rare but similar-looking variation, the army chair. Being commodity money, the value of Plasto against other goods was in constant flux, necessitating regular reevaluations of prices expressed in Plasto.

In 2007, *Habbo*'s publisher, Sulake, introduced changes that essentially made it possible to use a new money in user-to-user transactions: the Habbo Credit. The Habbo Credit was already being used as a money in the publisher-to-user market, where users bought new items from Sulake's catalogue. It was a token money: it obtained its value from the fact that it could be redeemed for items in the catalogue, and its exchange value against these goods was thus perfectly stable. Being a carefully designed official currency, it was superior to Plasto in every aspect, especially in convenience (see table 10.4). As it became possible to use credits in user-to-user trade, it soon replaced Plastos as the currency of choice among users.

Table 10.4
Comparing the old and new money of *Habbo Finland*

	Plasto chairs	Habbo Credits
1. Valuable	Yes (commodity)	Yes (token)
2. Fungible	Yes	Yes
3. Divisible	Somewhat	Yes
4. Verifiably countable	Somewhat	Yes
5. Recognizable	Somewhat	Yes
6. Durable	Yes	Yes
7. Constant value	Somewhat	Yes
8. Easy to transport and handle	No	Yes
9. Low demurrage	Somewhat	Yes
10. Resistant against theft	Yes	Yes
11. Resistant against counterfeiting	Yes	Yes
12. Private	Yes	Yes
13. Flauntable	Yes	Yes
14. Accountable	Yes	Yes

Better money results in a more efficient market, which means that different contents are allocated to those who value them the most. Having to hand-drag dozens of chairs to the trade screen was a terrible chore, and eliminating that made trade smoother. Yet some of the inefficiencies that the better money eliminated were themselves a form of engaging content. The whole business of valuating different goods in Plasto and arguing over differences in valuations was an important activity for some users. The introduction of credits made this activity redundant for items listed in the catalogue. The lack of divisibility and the resulting inability to give exact change meant that users had to negotiate and haggle to complete their deals. The introduction of a more divisible currency reduced the need for such discussions.

In *Habbo*'s case, the positives of the new money probably outweighed the negatives. The efficiency update was important for heavy traders such as builders and collectors, to whom trading was a means rather than an end in itself. But the moral of the story is that money designers need to be mindful of the trade-off between efficiency and engagement and understand that efficiency is not automatically the best option. For example, a clever money designer might deliberately make a currency vulnerable to theft or counterfeiting, and in this way introduce new elements of risk and trust to the game. This new content might well offset the fact that virtual goods would then be allocated less optimally. The very value of a virtual good to a user is often in the challenge of obtaining it rather than in its actual possession. From this perspective, money should be so bad as to make trade stimulatingly challenging, but good enough to keep the challenge reasonable. Crime and trust were discussed in chapter 9. Some other ideas follow for designing bad money that is entertaining and promotes social interaction.

Money that's not very fungible

What fun could there be in forcing a currency on your players that lacks fungibility? Consider the history of coins. One euro coin today is exactly the same as any other, and this makes trading smooth, since you don't have to pay attention to each coin you're giving or receiving. But back in the days of gold and silver coins, one coin could actually be worth less than another supposedly equivalent coin, because someone might have shaved some of the gold off or the coin might simply be worn out. Unless you had the skills and equipment to measure coins, you risked being shafted every time you dealt with coins.

Imagine introducing this mechanic into a game. There are two types of coins: good ones and bad ones. They look identical, but the bad ones are less useful, because non-player characters (NPCs) won't accept them. Only some players can tell them apart. This introduces a whole new element of trust into the economy. Do you trust your friend to give you good coins? Do you trust that NPC? If you do happen to end up with bad coins, do you try to pass them on to some other poor sucker, or do you do the right thing and have them recast into half as many good coins? The economy of the game is suddenly much more social.

Money that's not very recognizable

Accidentally giving away your super-rare item instead of the piece of currency that you intended to give is not much fun. But if designed on purpose, lack of recognizability could also be a fun feature. In every fantasy game today, like *Skyrim*, no matter how exotic a culture you meet, the currency always consists of round metal coins, which the player character immediately recognizes as money. But if you look at the history of coinage, cultures throughout history have produced many imaginative designs that through today's eyes are not recognizable as money at all. For example, the ancient Chinese coins known as knife money were shaped like a small knife. A slightly later Chinese metal money resembles a bicycle key. In a more challenging adventure game, players would discover all kinds of objects exchanging hands, and it would be up to their anthropological acumen to figure out which of the objects are actually used as currency in the culture they are visiting.

Money that's not very easy to transport

What could be fun about wealth being troublesome to move, like gold being really heavy? The challenge this provides might in itself be fun—or it might not be. Designers can also add potentially fun features to help players overcome the challenge. For example, in *EverQuest*, one could acquire a magical bag that would render anything placed in it weightless.

One potentially very useful aspect of heavy money that to our knowledge has not been explored in game design is this: weight could be an alternative or complement to sinks in balancing the economy. A common problem in game economies is that long-time players eventually become so rich that no matter where they go, they can simply buy everything that they see, spoiling the game for themselves and potentially for new players as well. Making it difficult to move large amounts of money over significant distances could address this problem without imposing heavy sinks that players hate. Like Scrooge McDuck, players could have vast amounts of money stored at home, but when adventuring in faraway lands, their buying power would be limited to what they can carry themselves.

Money that's not very durable

The virtues of a perishable currency are explained in this quote from fifteenth-century Spanish historian Anghiera:

Oh, blessed money which yieldeth sweete and profitable drinke for mankinde, and preserveth the possessors thereof free from the hellish pestilence of avarice because it cannot be long kept or hid underground.

He is talking about cocoa beans, which native Mexicans used as money. Spanish colonists found the idea crazy, because cocoa beans spoil in a few months. But Anghiera argued that this is perfect, because it prevents people from hoarding money and encourages them to use it instead—if for nothing else, then to make hot chocolate! While durable money makes for a great store of value, sometimes we would like to encourage spending instead, and less-than-perfect durability is one way to achieve that. Note, though, that it also has an impact on the currency's fungibility because different units will be at different stages of decay.

Money that's not very private

We already discussed the benefits of flauntability, which means that users can selectively reveal their account balances to others. What if money was completely public, so that everyone could see your net worth? A negative (or positive, depending on how you look at it) consequence is that publicity can make you vulnerable to theft. A more interesting consequence is that it promotes social interaction and trade. In *Team Fortress 2*, other players can see your inventory through various third-party tools. If someone finds that you have a lot of money of the type that they want, they will often contact you and offer to sell all kinds of stuff. And you can't brush them off simply by saying you can't afford it because they know exactly what you can afford.

As the examples demonstrate, by understanding what makes money good and then turning this understanding on its head, it's possible to create money that's broken in many interesting ways. Let us conclude with a word of warning, though. There is a limit to how bad money can feasibly be. If the currencies available on a user-to-user market are too inefficient or costly to use, the users may adopt a national currency as their medium of exchange instead. When counterfeiting (duping) destroyed the value of the official currency in *Ultima Online*, many users found it most convenient to trade very large assets such as castles in US dollars instead of using one of the commodity currencies available. Not all unsanctioned real-money trade is motivated by a desire to cheat; some is motivated by a desire to be efficient.

11 Macroeconomic Design

So far in this book, we have dealt with different components that make up a virtual economy: agents and their behavior, goods, markets, institutions, and money. In this chapter, we are ready to consider how these components combine to form a virtual macroeconomy. Along the way, we also introduce two more sets of building blocks that are crucial to almost any virtual economy: faucets, which introduce new goods and money into the economy, and sinks, which remove goods and money from circulation.

Macroeconomic metaphors: Wheels and pipes

In our economics studies, we learned a conceptual model for the entire economy that was supposed to help us understand how the government's activity influences markets and trade. It was called the wheel of wealth. As students of virtual economies, however, we have learned that developers and managers use different words to speak conceptually about their work. They use words like *faucets* (also known as sources) and *sinks* (also known as drains). We have taken the liberty of naming this the pipes model. Each model focuses on different aspects of the macroeconomy.

The wheel model

In the wheel of wealth model, at the top are companies—the entities that make things. At the bottom are households—the entities that buy things and consume them. Goods flow from the companies to the households. To pay for the goods, money flows from the households to the companies. All this is happening on the right side of figure 11.1.

At the same time, on the left side of the figure, the households and companies are involved in another transaction that mirrors the right side. Here, labor flows from the households to the companies, while the money is flowing from the companies to the households as wages. The real stuff flows clockwise around the wheel, while the money flows counterclockwise.

The wheel is useful for thinking about some basic facts in an economy. First, in some deep way, the money does not matter. The economy is really about people working,

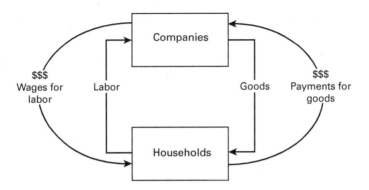

Figure 11.1
The wheel of wealth, c. 1990

making things, and then consuming them. The money just facilitates the working and consuming in better or worse ways. In practice, though, we tend to fetishize money and ascribe a social value of its own to it. Second, it shows that *companies* and *households* are just labels for *people*. There's no necessary conflict between companies and households; both are inhabited by the same human beings, just in different roles. The laborer is the consumer, and the boss is the customer is the boss.

Third, the wheel points up one of the most complex problems for economic management in the real world, which involves *size*. This basic wheel works as it does at any scale. It could be one household trading potato-picking labor to itself in return for pebbles, which it then pays itself to buy the potatoes to eat. But it could also be 7 billion people working in an uncountably vast number of ways to create massive value for others, which is purchased using dozens, if not thousands, of forms of money. How do you grow the wheel? Economists continue to debate this; no one has an answer that always works.[1]

The pipes model

People who design virtual economies have developed a different model of the macroeconomy, the pipes model. In the pipes model, stuff flows into the economy via a faucet at the top, whirls around inside for awhile, and then flows out of the economy via a sink at the bottom. This is illustrated in figure 11.2.

The pipes idea illustrates nicely the remarkable difference in scope of control between national and virtual economy managers. National economy managers deal only with the wheel in the middle. Virtual world managers can deal with the wheel if they want,

---

1. For a comprehensive introduction to the wheel (circular flow) model of a national economy and to the multitude of theories on economic growth, consult a standard macroeconomics textbook, such as Mankiw (2009).

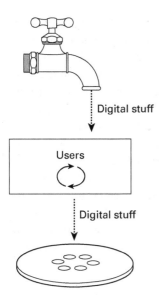

Figure 11.2
The pipes of wealth, c. 2010

but they can affect what the wheel gets to play with as well. Virtual world managers can turn up the faucets or close the sinks, changing the rate at which things flow through the economy. National policymakers mostly can't affect the sinks or the faucets: they neither create nor destroy. The world is what it is. But virtual world managers can create and destroy things at will, costlessly. It is a very big difference in perspectives and scope of action.

The pipes model allows us to see how much we, as virtual economy managers, can actually control. We can change how rapidly items are produced by the world. We can also, through application design, change how useful different items are. We can enter the economy as an actor if we wish, but we can also make computer-driven surrogates, "merchants" and "stores" that seem to do their own buying and selling but actually operate according to artificial intelligence routines that we design. We can tax things, but we can also determine how rapidly they decay. The pipes model helps us see this tremendous scope of action.

In the following sections, we go into detail on how to use different components to design a wheel and pipes that constitute a virtual macroeconomy.

Constructing the wheel

The wheel is the internal part of the virtual economy. It encompasses everything that happens from the point that virtual money and goods enter the system through faucets up to the point that virtual money and goods leave the system through sinks. In some virtual economies, this is not much. An arcade game where players purchase power-ups between levels and then consume them does not have a wheel to speak of; the only thing between the faucet and the sink is the player's inventory. But in an online community where participants use virtual points to reward each other for their contributions or a multiplayer game where virtual commerce is part of the game content, the wheel can be a complex system that consists of many different components.

Let's assume that a designer has defined a set of agents, goods, and possibly also currencies that they want to use for building a virtual economy. The ingredients that need to be added to this mix to construct the wheel are user-to-user markets and institutions. Markets and institutions create flows of goods and currencies between the agents. They are chosen according to what the designer wants the wheel to do. Let's first consider markets. The design and functioning of different kinds of markets were discussed in detail in chapters 4 through 8. Summarizing the different strands of discussion in these chapters, here is what user-to-user markets can be used to achieve:

• *Providing content.* On a personal level, user-to-user markets can be great content in themselves. Some people buy and sell stuff on eBay or at local flea markets as a hobby. Markets for virtual goods can provide the same kinds of pleasures: the thrill of the search for a bargain, the joy of discovery, the excitement of haggling and negotiating, the gratification from a purchase, the satisfaction from making a sale, and the delight of having happy customers. Dealing with real humans makes virtual economic activities feel more meaningful than activities carried out in a purely single-player economy.

• *Facilitating user-created content.* On a higher level, markets tie users' activities together, making them mutually interdependent. This can be a constant source of dynamism and novelty in the economy, giving rise to strategies and counterstrategies as different groups compete and collaborate while vying for market power. On the other hand, competitive user-to-user markets can also be associated with negative experiences: playing to earn rather than to enjoy, having rewards for your favorite activity cut due to competition, and playing with numbers rather than with people.

• *Supporting different tastes.* Different users naturally prefer different types of content. User-to-user markets allow virtual goods to be allocated to the users who prefer them the most, while keeping the goods scarce. Markets also reward experience in a particular skill or trade, supporting specialization among users. For example, in a game, user-to-user markets are a natural companion to a class system, where each class specializes in producing one type of good and purchases other goods from other classes.

• *Incentivizing user contributions.* In economies that involve user-created goods such as expert knowledge, level designs, or virtual items, user-to-user markets allow users to reward each other for contributions that they find worthwhile, creating an incentive to contribute more. Users can also present buy offers or "bounties" for desirable content that does not yet exist, creating an incentive for someone to create it. Similar mechanisms apply to commodities and public goods that will be available to all once produced, as well as to bespoke items like forum signature graphics that go to a single buyer.

• *Allocating scarce resources optimally.* When we use a word like *optimal*, we open something of a can of worms. At the broadest level, the idea of pursuing economic optimality can set off alarm bells in some readers' minds. There is plenty of scope for philosophical dispute on what the word *optimal* means. A society of maximum wealth? Total equality? Minimal environmental impact? At a narrower level, however, the idea of optimal allocation is less controversial. It simply means "making sure that resources go where they are most valued by people." Regardless of overall objectives for human society, all would agree that people who desire to eat cucumbers should be able to acquire cucumbers at a price that roughly reflects the cost of growing cucumbers and bringing them to market. All would agree that wasting resources is a bad idea; if you are going to irrigate, don't start with the desert.

Besides flowing through markets, goods and money also flow between users via institutions and other nonmarket allocation mechanisms. These were discussed in detail in chapter 9. Summarizing earlier discussions and adding some elaboration, we find that institutions can be used to achieve the following things:

• *Providing content.* Like markets, nonmarket institutions can be great content in themselves. Creating a new organization, working closely with other people, advancing in the ranks, being part of something bigger, participating in a local custom, or simply helping out others with material support can all directly yield meaningful and pleasurable experiences.

• *Facilitating user-created content.* Like user-to-user markets, user-to-user institutions make users' activities mutually interdependent. Individuals seeking to grow their organizations, overlapping institutions struggling against each other to assert their power, and individuals struggling to break free from the grip of coercive institutions act as constant engines of dynamism and novelty. Practical manifestations of such dynamism are guild and alliance politics that occupy many users in massively multiplayer online (MMO) games, for example. On the other hand, institutions can also be the source of negative experiences: pressures to conform, participating out of obligation instead of fun, and becoming overly dependent on others.

• *Improving user engagement and retention.* Since institutions create duties and obligations, they can increase the frequency and length of user participation in a service. First-time users are more likely to return to a service if they are immediately socialized into an institution that creates an obligation, such as receiving a gift that they feel must be paid forward to another user. Users who become members in an organization feel pressure to show up regularly so as not to let their colleagues down. Organization leaders sometimes continue logging into a service long after they have lost interest in its content for the sake of fulfilling their duties in the organization. The flip side is that virtual organizational duties can require so much time and engagement as to sometimes result in personal crises.

• *Compensate for gaps in design.* There are many examples of a user-created institution stepping in to compensate for a serious problem in a virtual economy's design or implementation. Prominent examples are virtual tourism offices to improve new user experiences and virtual commodity money to replace hyperinflated official currency.

Putting together the wheel

Let's use markets and institutions to put together a simple wheel. Imagine a game economy that has two classes of player agents: Dragonslayers and Armorers. There are also two types of goods: dragon scales and dragon armor. There is also a currency: gold. Now let's put in place two markets: one for dragon scales and another for armor. In practice, both markets can be implemented with a single auction house that allows both types of goods to be traded. The wheel works as follows. The Dragonslayers produce dragon scales, which they sell to the Armorers. The Armorers turn the scales into armor and sell it to the slayers who use it as protection. Goods change hands; money circulates. From the point of view of design, the purpose of the two markets is to provide something to do for the players and make their virtual economic activities seem worthwhile, as there are real people demanding their products.

Let's add an institution: clans. Clans in this economy are essentially mutual insurance schemes that provide assistance from the clan treasury to members who go down on their luck (having their equipment destroyed by dragon fire). Starting grants are also provided to new players joining the clan. To replenish the treasury, every member is expected to pay a tithe. A handful of clan officers are responsible for collecting the tithes and distributing the grants. From the point of view of design, this institution enhances the new player experience, smoothes out chance-based game mechanics, and creates social bonds and obligations that improve engagement and retention.

But there's more than meets the eye in the clan institution. Because a bigger clan means more financial security for its members and more prestige for its leaders, clans naturally start competing against each other. Alliances are made. Promises are broken. A new type of content, clan politics, emerges in the game. The ostensible reason for the clans' creation, mutual insurance, might be just a pretext. The designer might have intentionally created this need in order to give rise to clans and clan politics.

The wheel that we put together for the Dragonslayer economy is depicted in figure 11.3.

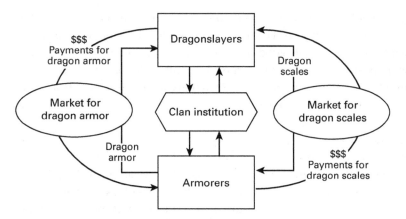

Figure 11.3
The macroeconomic wheel of the Dragonslayer economy

Constructing the pipes: Faucets and sinks

In the previous section, we looked at how to make goods and currencies circulate in an economy, but we didn't say anything about how they entered the economy and at what point they possibly exit it. In theory, a virtual economy could have a fixed stock of virtual material that just keeps on circulating. In practice, this is difficult, because it means that any bottleneck in one part of the wheel will cause the other parts to grind to a halt too. The designers of *Ultima Online* discovered this the hard way. Some of their users started hoarding goods, which resulted in less material circulating in the economy, which prompted users to hoard even more, driving the system toward standstill. As a result, *Ultima Online* was switched to the model that most virtual economies today use: having faucets that add new stuff into circulation and sinks that remove it.

Faucets and sinks are used for several purposes: adjusting the rewards and difficulty level of a game, adjusting the amount of stuff in circulation to correspond to changes in the user base, earning revenues by selling virtual goods and currencies to users, incentivizing specific actions, and so on. We will return to these objectives in the next chapter, where we discuss how to balance faucets and sinks as part of the overall operations of a virtual economy. In this chapter, we introduce in very practical terms the main types of faucets and sinks used in games and other virtual economies and briefly consider their pros and cons.

When choosing faucets and sinks to put into an economy, there are three dimensions on which to evaluate them. The first is efficacy: their ability to do the job of adding stuff into the economy or removing it. The second is adjustability: how predictably the operator can adjust their flow. The third is user acceptance. Users rarely appreciate

it if you make it harder to gain stuff and easier to lose it, even if you do it in the interest of the economy's long-run health. The most effective and adjustable sinks are often
the least acceptable to users. A really good sink, though, can be not only acceptable but
even fun to the users, forming a valuable part of the content. Most virtual economies
use a mix of several types of faucets and sinks to achieve a good level of efficacy and
adjustability while upholding acceptance.

Faucets for goods and money

The quintessential faucet in classic MMO games is the *drop:* an item or a quantity of
currency created out of thin air and given to the player as a reward for killing a monster. Items and currency are also given as quest rewards. In other types of games, such
as mobile and tablet games, the drop takes different forms, such as income obtained
from a virtual building or plants gathered from a virtual field. The basic mechanism
remains the same: new goods or currency in exchange for gameplay actions. This faucet can be adjusted in three ways. The first way is to make the gameplay action more
difficult to carry out—by making the monsters stronger, for example. The second way
is to adjust how often players have the opportunity to carry out the action—by making
the monsters spawn less often, for example. The third way is to adjust the "loot table,"
or the likelihood at which the action yields potential rewards. Small adjustments to
these parameters can be largely undetectable to users. But the challenge in adjusting
these parameters is that they can affect different types of players in different ways.

In social and mobile games as well as nongame services, virtual goods and currencies are also given to users as *incentives* intended to encourage actions not directly
related to gameplay, such as inviting a friend to try the service, logging in every day,
or taking up on an offer from an advertising partner. In terms of our three objectives
of virtual economy design, these rewards are intended to drive up user acquisition,
retention, and monetization rather than contribute to the substance of the experience.
The challenge is to balance these objectives against the need to keep the substance of
the economy compelling, which often means exercising restraint in setting the reward
level for nongameplay actions.

In some virtual environments, it is possible for users to design new virtual goods
from scratch. Examples introduced earlier in this book include *Second Life, IMVU,* and
Team Fortress 2. In *Second Life,* any new design created by a user becomes an actual
object in the economy and can even be duplicated indefinitely if the creator allows
it. *Second Life* thus gives much control over scarcity to its users. Those intent on making money from selling their creations usually opt to keep their items scarce. In *Team
Fortress 2,* players' designs don't directly turn into actual objects in the economy. If a
design is approved, objects that are instances of it will start appearing in the economy
through normal faucets—in this case drops. In other words, user-created content can
be implemented as an actual faucet or as a design feature without any automatic faucet

attached. The latter is usually the safest option for game economies, as it retains control over scarcity with the publisher. For nongame services, the former may be a more interesting option.

From a business perspective, the most important faucet in today's free-to-play (F2P) games and online services is the publisher-to-user market, where the publisher sells virtual goods and currencies to the users. The design and functioning of such markets were examined in detail in chapters 5 and 6. In this chapter, we discuss only their role in the pipes. So-called *cash shops,* where the publisher sells goods and currencies for real money, are sinks for the users' dollars and euros but faucets for virtual money and goods. Their flows can be adjusted by adjusting the prices and availability of goods. In the teenage online hangout *Habbo,* collectible items are often available for only a limited amount of time, from hours to weeks, after which they disappear from the catalogue. Such limits excite users, but they can make it tricky to predict the quantity sold, as the excitement may create a spike in demand. Another way to control the flow is simply to put up a limited quantity for sale and stop selling once that quantity is reached.

Publisher-to-user shops where users pay in virtual currency rather than in national currency are faucets for goods but sinks for virtual currency. From a balancing perspective, such *virtual shops* are tricky. Adjusting the entry flows of goods by changing the shop's prices will have the side effect of also changing currency exit flows. Depending on the elasticity of the demand, raising the prices can lead to either more currency leaving the economy (as people pay more) or less currency leaving the economy (as people buy less). This highlights the importance of having several different faucets and sinks available for effective control.

When users sell virtual goods back to the publisher to obtain virtual currency, as happens in MMOs when players sell worthless items to nonplayer characters (NPCs), this acts as a sink for goods and as a faucet for currency.

Finally, *new user endowments* are a small but important faucet for both goods and currency. New players in games typically start with a small amount of cash and some basic items. New users in Quora, a knowledge exchange platform, start with 500 Credits that they can use to reward other users for their insights.

Sinks for money

If you forget to put faucets in your economy, the lack quickly becomes obvious. Not having enough sinks in the economy is a more subtle problem. At first, users may even be happier without them. Problems start accumulating only after some time as things pile up. For publishers that sell virtual goods or currency for real money, sinks are also ultimately what generates their revenues, as sinks ensure the need for repeat purchases. In our consulting engagements, probably the most common advice we give to virtual economy designers is to consider adding more sinks. Coming up with more sinks is usually not a challenge. The challenge is to come up with sinks that users don't get up in arms about.

Essentially every price, tax, and fee that users pay to the publisher and its representatives, like NPCs, is a sink. One obvious money sink is the publisher-to-user market, where the publisher sells things to users. Depending on the currency used, publisher-operated shops can be sinks for any currency, from real money and "hard currency" purchased for real money to "soft currency" earned through gameplay. From a balancing perspective, the problem with relying on the publisher-to-user market as the sole money sink is that it is also simultaneously a faucet for items. A virtual economy that also has money sinks that are independent of the item stock provides more room for adjustment.

Common virtual currency sinks not related to publisher-to-user item sales include *payments for services, time-based fees,* and *transaction taxes.* Payments for services include such things as virtual equipment repair costs and aerial transport fees in *World of Warcraft*, paying to have more people see your questions in Quora, and paying to get more visibility for your social networking profile in Finnish social network IRC-Galleria. Time-based fees refer to such things as monthly premium membership fees and virtual goods maintenance costs. Transaction taxes are taxes that the operator levies on user-to-user virtual goods trade. From a user acceptance perspective, it is natural to charge taxes and fees on transactions conducted through exchange mechanisms that involve an institutional intermediary, like an auction house. Charging taxes and fees on direct one-to-one transactions might meet with less acceptance and is usually not done.

Transaction taxes are structured differently on different platforms. In *World of Warcraft*, auction houses take a 5 or 15 percent cut from each sale, depending on the house. In *EVE Online*, all trades through the bourse-style market interface incur a 1.5 percent sales tax. An additional broker's fee of under 1 percent is payable if a user leaves a new sell order or buy order instead of taking up an existing offer. In Habbo, the buyout house style Marketplace involves a 1 percent sales tax as well as a fixed listing fee.[2]

Currencies can also have a *limited lifetime.* Many games and online hangouts feature seasonal currencies, like Snowflakes at Christmas, that can be earned and spent in a limited number of ways until a specified date when the whole campaign ends. A more sophisticated system that could be run on a permanent basis would involve each piece of currency having its own expiration timer. This kind of perishable currency was introduced in chapter 10. There are several historical examples of perishable

---

2. A fixed listing fee is easier on traders of large, thinly traded items and hits harder on traders of small, frequently traded items. Interestingly, the exchange mechanism used by Habbo Marketplace, *buyout house,* is better suited for small, frequently traded items than large, thinly traded items. There appears to be a slight mismatch in the design. Exchange mechanisms are discussed in detail in chapter 7.

commodities like cocoa beans and eggs being used as currency, but in virtual economies, they are almost unheard of. The main feature of such currencies is that they cannot be hoarded for long, which encourages spending. But the problem with perishable currencies is that they lack fungibility: a fresh egg and a month-old egg nearing its best-before date are not equal in value. This makes payment complicated. There are also historical examples of paper money that must be stamped every year to remain valid but loses some of its face value in each stamping in order to encourage spending. This is essentially the same as a yearly property tax that removes a certain percentage of money from circulation. This would be an easy money sink to implement in a virtual economy and a highly efficient one, but user acceptance might be hard to win.

Sinks for goods

Developers have come up with a large variety of clever and interesting ways of removing goods from circulation. They vary significantly in how acceptable they are to users, although acceptance ultimately depends on the context. Next we introduce a selection of the most common and interesting sinks, as well as a couple of our own designs:

• *Items have a limited lifetime.* Cyworld, a Korean social networking site that pioneered the virtual goods revenue model, sells virtual profile decorations that expire after ninety days. This is a simple solution for removing goods from the economy that works predictably and is highly adjustable. However, user acceptance may be a problem, and willingness to pay for the items may decrease. Having goods expire rules out collectability as a purchase motivation, prevents the emergence of valuable "virtual antique" items, and makes it easier for users to switch to a competing service. Limited lifetime is also used as an item sink in the material economy, where it is known to economists as "contrived depreciation" or "contrived durability."

• *Items deteriorate or are expended when used.* In *Ultima Online*, many tools and items gradually wear out through use until they eventually disappear. This ensures that there is always demand for items crafted by players. In mobile arcade games, purchasable power-ups are often single use, after which they disappear and must be repurchased. Thanks to this, arcade games can monetize successfully despite featuring a very small selection of items. This sink has similar advantages and drawbacks as limited lifetime. From a user acceptance perspective, it works best with items where the wearing out or expendability is consistent with the game's fiction—tools, bombs, food, and so on.

• *Items become obsolete.* This is an implicit sink that consists of having the item remain fully intact and usable, but changing things around it so as to make it lose its value to the user. Recall from chapter 3 that virtual goods tend to obtain their value from how they are positioned relative to other goods or the environment. In a player-versus-player combat game, a publisher might give players a new, superior weapon that makes their old ammunition stores obsolete. In a teenage avatar dress-up community, a publisher

Box 11.1

Virtual pet maintenance in *Habbo*

The following is an excerpt from the introduction to *Habbo Pets* from teenage hangout *Habbo*'s website:

You'll need to take care of your pet to keep it happy and healthy. The Pet Accessories section of the Catalogue offers different kinds of accessories that will help satisfy all your pet's needs. Your pet becomes hungry several times a day. Food can be bought as single portions or in an economy package of six portions. The food will take your pet a while to eat. A healthy pet will need to eat just one portion per day. When your pet is hungry or thirsty, it searches for food or a water bowl. If it finds some, it will eat or drink it until it's full. If there isn't any food in the room, it will come to your *Habbo*, begging and trying to catch your attention. Your pet cannot get flu or any kind of virus. The only time it'll show signs of illness, is if you don't take care of it. If the pet is starving, it will get weak and sad and sleep all the time.

---

might promote a seasonal fashion cycle that makes apparel stylistically obsolete every three months. Although obsolescence doesn't destroy items directly, the idea is that users then dispose of these items willingly in response to other sinks, such as limited inventory sizes and recycling opportunities. This item sink is also frequently used in the material economy, where it is known to economists as planned obsolescence.

• *Items have a maintenance cost.* This is both an item sink and a money sink. User must pay or surrender goods in a regular manner in order to keep holding a valued object or in order to maintain some attribute or statistic. If the user fails to pay, the object or attribute is lost or degraded. The user may also voluntarily give up the object in order to stop paying. In general, maintenance costs are not popular with users. A typical maintenance cost is buying food for a pet (see box 11.1), but maintenance costs can also be more subtle, like having to buy more fuel for a starship when carrying lots of cargo.

• *Limited inventory size.* Users can fit only a limited number of items in their inventory, after which they have to dump an old item for every new item they acquire. This will effectively limit the number of items in circulation, but it may also discourage new purchases and other activities aimed at acquiring items. The limit can also be "soft," in that users are given the option of purchasing more inventory space or paying a maintenance cost for items that exceed the limit. Limited inventories are found in many games, and it is an accepted convention among players. Compared to other sinks, limited inventories can encourage "twinking" (advanced players giving powerful items to new players or characters), which is usually not desirable.

• *Publisher buys items back from users.* In MMOs, NPC traders often buy low-value items from players in order to make their activities feel more meaningful.[3] This is obviously

---

3. Using NPCs as buyers and sellers to make markets more fun is discussed in chapter 5.

highly acceptable to users, but it creates a new money faucet into the economy, which has to be balanced out with corresponding money sinks. In F2P games, the publisher could buy real-money items back from users for a fraction of their original purchase price or accept old items as trade-ins for new purchases.

• *Users can recycle old items into new items.* Users have the option of giving up a number of old items in exchange for a smaller number of new items. As a result, the total number of items in circulation decreases. For this deal to be attractive, the new items must obviously be something desirable that cannot otherwise be easily obtained. This sink is essentially a type of transformation, described in the previous section, but one designed to remove the maximum number of objects from circulation. Recyclers exists in three variations. In the *transparent recycler*, users know what outputs they will get in exchange for a given input. In practice, this could mean crafting items from raw materials or bartering with an NPC. In the *mystery recycler*, input-output mappings are initially not known to users but can be discovered through experimentation. This is like mixing magical reagents to discover new potions. In the *Monte Carlo recycler*, input-output mappings are probabilistic, not fixed: the better the output item is, the lower the probability is of getting it (see box 11.2). This is like playing the lottery with items instead of money. Publishers with experience in the matter suggest that suitably adjusted Monte Carlo recyclers are the most efficient in getting users to dispose of their items. This is not surprising, as probability-based rewards appeal to the human appetite

Box 11.2
Ecotron, the virtual recycling machine

In 2007, *Habbo* introduced the Ecotron, a virtual recycling machine. Users would insert pieces of virtual furniture and other real-money items into its massive input funnel. After processing the items for one hour, the machine would yield one neatly packaged new item as a reward. The initial Ecotron was a transparent recycler: there were five possible rewards, and users could insert either ten, twenty, thirty, forty, or fifty items to obtain the reward that they wanted. In 2009, Ecotron was reprogrammed into a Monte Carlo recycler that takes five items as input and yields one item as reward, chosen at random from a changing selection according to a probability table. The quality of the inputs has no bearing on the output. Below is the probability table excerpted from *Habbo*'s website. The "Urban Legend" level items became highly sought-after among users.

Level 1—Common (These items are most likely to come up)

Level 2—Uncommon (You have a 1 in 5 chance of getting one of these)

Level 3—Arcane (There is a 1 in 40 chance of getting one of these items)

Level 4—Phenomenal (There is a 1 in 200 chance of getting this item)

Level 5—Urban Legend (There is a 1 in 2000 chance of getting this item) for gambling. Mystery recyclers offer good content for players as they compete and collaborate to discover mappings.

• *Abandoned user accounts*, that is, "dying with your gold buried." Users who leave the service and abandon their accounts effectively remove from circulation any items that they had left. This is a passive sink that should be taken into account when calculating economic indicators.

• *Users can redeem virtual items for external benefits.* Sometimes users who are leaving a service bequeath their virtual possessions to friends and newbies instead of taking the goods with them to virtual oblivion. This is usually not desirable, as it deprives the recipients of the need to obtain those goods themselves. Providing leavers with a way to cash out their virtual possessions can help avoid this. This can be done as follows: in exchange for giving up their virtual riches, users are given something valuable outside the virtual economy as a reward. This could be entry to an online hall of fame, a gift card provided by an advertising partner, a pledge from the publisher to donate a commensurate amount of real money to charity, or even a 3D print of the users' late avatar.

Transformations

Some processes in a virtual economy are simultaneously sinks for one thing and faucets for another. We call these *transformations*. We have already discussed publisher-to-user shops, which transform currencies into goods. In game economies, lots of transformations can also be found in so-called crafting systems: simulated production processes like baking and metalcrafting. For example, in *World of Warcraft*, a character with suitable crafting skills can transform one Copper Ore into a Copper Bar. They can also transform one Copper Bar with a Tin Bar into a Bronze Bar, and a Bronze Bar together with two Tigerseye crystals into Flying Tiger Goggles. In transformation chains like this, some objects are removed from the economy and other objects are introduced. The net effect of the whole transformation chain can be found by using what economists call an input-output table.

Table 11.1 shows an example input-output table. It's based on *World of Warcraft*'s Flying Tiger Goggles, but we've added coal as an ingredient to make things more interesting. The table works as follows. The designer estimates how many final goods of each type the users want and enters this information into the "Final Demand" column. The designer then enters the material demands of each type of final and intermediate good into the "Intermediate Demand" section. The "Grand Total Demand" column then tells the designer how many raw materials of each type will be needed. In this example, we've estimated that users will want 1,000 pairs of Flying Tiger Goggles to protect their eyes and 500 Tigerseye Crystals to use as gifts and ornaments. The table tells us that, among other things, 4,000 units of coal will be consumed in the process of creating these goods. Coal faucets should be prepared accordingly.

Table 11.1
An example input-output table

Supply	Final demand	Intermediate demand								Grand total demand
		Flying Tiger Goggles		Bronze Bar		Tin Bar		Copper Bar		
		Material demands per unit	Total material demands	Material demands per unit	Total material demands	Material demands per unit	Total material demands	Material demands per unit	Total material demands	
Flying Tiger Goggles	1,000									1,000
Tigerseye Crystal	500	2	2,000							2,500
Bronze Bar		1	1,000							1,000
Tin Bar				1	1,000					1,000
Copper Bar				1	1,000					1,000
Tin Ore						1	1,000			1,000
Copper Ore								1	1,000	1,000
Coal				2	2,000	1	1,000	1	1,000	4,000

Table 11.2
Faucets and sinks for virtual goods and currencies

	Virtual currency	Virtual goods
Faucets	Drops, incentives, cash shops, users selling goods back to publisher	Drops, incentives, cash shops, virtual shops, transformations
Sinks	Virtual shops, payments for services, transaction taxes, time-based fees, maintenance costs, limited lifetime, property tax	Limited lifetime, deterioration, expending, obsolescence, maintenance cost, limited inventory size, publisher buy-back, recycling, redemption, abandoned accounts, transformations

Table 11.3
Faucets and sinks in the Dragonslayer economy

	Gold coins	Dragon scales	Dragon armor
Faucets	Drops from dragons	Drops from dragons	Transformed from scales
Sinks	Transaction tax	Transformed into armor	Destroyed by dragons

Assembling a virtual macroeconomy

The faucets and sinks that we introduced above are summarized in table 11.2.

Let's return to our Dragonslayer economy that we began to design earlier in this chapter. We got as far as building the wheel. Now let's add some faucets and sinks to complete the design. The theme of the game suggests that we have dragons that drop dragon scales. Let that be our first faucet. We have also already established that Armorers have the skill to transform dragon scales into dragon armor. This transformation is a sink for scales and a faucet for armor. Finally, we need to have some way for armor to exit the economy, preventing it from piling up and losing its value. The most logical sink seems to be to have dragons occasionally destroy armor worn by Dragonslayers. We now have exactly one faucet and one sink for each type of good in the economy.

We also need a faucet for gold coins, the currency that players use to trade scales and armor between each other. The simplest way is to have dragons drop it. After all, dragons since Tolkien's Smaud and before have been known to hoard gold. As for sinks, let's use a transaction tax on the user-to-user market to suck gold out of circulation. We now have exactly one faucet and one sink for each type of good and currency in the economy, the minimum viable set of pipes. They are summarized in table 11.3.

Our macroeconomic design is now complete. The whole design, consisting of the wheel we designed earlier and the pipes we just laid out, is depicted as a flowchart in figure 11.4.

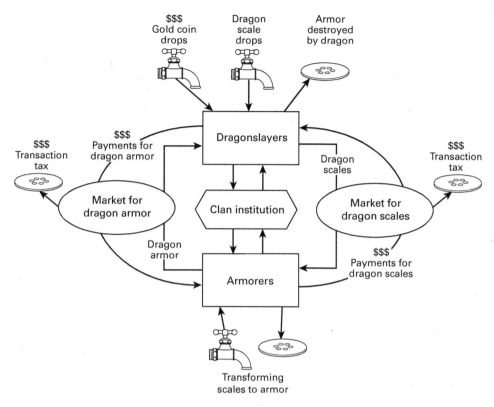

Figure 11.4
The complete macroeconomic design of the Dragonslayer economy

Note that that this is a bare-bones design. A real game like this would typically have a bigger set of faucets and sinks. It would, for example, give every new user a small endowment of goods and currency. It would have an NPC shop that buys old, worthless pieces of armor from users. And it would certainly have a larger variety of goods and character classes, resulting in a bigger wheel. With such additions, it becomes increasingly difficult and less illustrative to depict the whole economy as a detailed flowchart, as we have done here (although not impossible, and we have seen developers with huge, mind-boggling flowcharts). This is not a problem. The most important in points in the method that we have just introduced do scale. They are:

1. *Breaking down the task of macroeconomic design into components.* The overall design can be broken down into the wheel and the pipes. The wheel can be broken down into markets and institutions. The pipes can be broken down into faucets and sinks. Thinking in components makes the overall task manageable. In the most complex

virtual economies, it can also be useful to break down the economy into subsystems and design those separately using the methods described here. Flowcharts too can be illustrative on the subsystem level.

2. *Understanding what role each component is intended to fulfill in the big picture.* Markets, institutions, faucets, and sinks can be used to aim for a variety of goals, which ultimately boil down to creating content, attracting users, and monetizing. When each component is put in place with a specific purpose in mind, it is possible to later evaluate whether it is doing its job. We return to this in the next chapter.

In this chapter, we've covered the steps required to put together a whole economy. The wheel represents transactions that make money and goods flow around the economy. The pipes represent the rate of overall growth and abundance of the economy's components. In the next chapter, we discuss numbers: how to manage a live virtual economy and how to balance faucets and sinks.

12 Macroeconomic Management

In the previous chapter, we showed how to build a virtual macroeconomy by combining various building blocks. In this chapter, we look at how to manage a live virtual economy. The main issues that we need to deal with are how to measure the status of a virtual economy, how to steer it in a desired direction, and how to know what that desired direction is in the first place. Along the way, we look at some of the ways in which national economies as well as corporations are measured and managed.

Performance management

First let's consider virtual economy management from the perspective of how the performance of any corporate enterprise should be managed. Here we can draw on accounting and management studies, where this question is examined under the topic of performance management frameworks, the best known of which is the *balanced scorecard*.[1] The first thing that this literature tells us is that in order to manage something, we need to have objectives: concrete statements of what we are trying to achieve. In chapter 1, we outlined the most important objectives of virtual economy design. To recap, these objectives are:

1. *Creating content.* Virtual economy features can form part of interesting single-player content or act as a framework for the generation of user-created content. Virtual economy features can also be used to provide direct incentives for users and third-party developers to contribute new content. Virtual economy features, especially suitably defined virtual property rights and markets, can also be used to ensure that scarce resources such as content and attention are put to the most valuable uses possible.

2. *Attention: attracting and retaining users.* Virtual economy features can be used to give out some content for free in order to attract users while reserving other contents for

---

1. Kaplan and Norton (1996). Robert Kaplan is an American management professor, and David Norton is an American consultant and business author.

paying users. Virtual goods and currencies can also be used to reward users for referrals and loyalty. Virtual goods tend to create lock-in, where users are discouraged from switching to a competing service because in doing so they would lose the time and money invested in their virtual possessions.

3. *Monetizing.* Virtual economy features can be used to translate content and attention into revenues by selling virtual goods and currencies for real money. In services that use some other revenue model, such as subscriptions or advertising, the virtual economy can contribute to revenues by regulating the rate at which users gain access to content. If content is revealed too sparingly, users get bored and leave. But if content is revealed too rapidly, fresh content runs out quickly and memberships are short.

The focus varies from economy to economy and publisher to publisher, but these are the main categories under which most purposes for running a virtual economy are likely to fall. So once we have set our objectives, how do we find out how well the system is performing in relation to these objectives and identify ways in which performance could be improved? The performance management literature tells us that each objective must be associated with at least one *measure* (also known as *metric):* a source of concrete data that can be used to assess performance in relation to the objective. For example, attention could be measured by the number of hours users spend in the service in a week. The measure may not capture every aspect of the objective, but it is much better to have a partial measure and be aware of its limitations than to fly completely blind. Each measure should also be associated with a *target:* a particular level of the measure to which performance is compared. For example, we might learn from a market report that the typical weekly amount of time users spend in services similar to ours is 5.5 hours and decide to set our target to 10 hours.

How, then, do we identify ways to improve performance? The literature tells us that we should spell out *causal chains* that lead to good performance. For example, good performance in total attention is caused by, among other things, good performance in new user acquisition. Good performance in new user acquisition is caused by, among other things, good performance in referrals. New user acquisition and referrals are thus subgoals of attention. This causal chain shows us that if we want to improve new user acquisition, we can focus on improving referrals. To make things concrete, each of these subgoals needs to be associated with its own measure and target. For example, performance in referrals could be measured by the number of times users tap on the "invite a friend" button. But there is often a time lag before improved performance on one objective translates to improved performance on the next one. Thus, we say that the number of invitations sent by users is a *leading measure,* while the number of new users acquired is a *lagging measure* (or that invitations lead acquisition, acquisition lags invitations). This knowledge allows us to anticipate changes in the top-level measures before they happen. Top-level measures, like weekly new users, are sometimes called *key performance indicators* (KPIs). Each measure and target should also be associated with an *initiative*: a strategy or action plan intended to nudge the measure toward the target. In macroeconomics, this might be called an intervention.

The virtual scorecard

By identifying objectives, measures, targets, and initiatives and spelling out the causal links between them, we can create a performance management framework for a virtual economy—a "virtual scorecard." Figure 12.1 shows an example of such a scorecard, loosely aimed at the Dragonslayer economy described in the previous chapter. For brevity, our example includes only one measure per objective and omits targets and initiatives. The scorecard starts from three top-level objectives: content, attention, and monetizing. Several relevant subobjectives are then added that are believed to contribute causally to the top-level objectives. These subobjectives are hypotheses: they are based on theories and experiences presented in this book, but to what extent the causal links work in a given implementation can be confirmed only by trying them out. This same framework could naturally also accommodate things like paid advertising to produce a full picture of a digital content business, but in this example we have focused narrowly on the virtual economy–related aspects.

Our example scorecard has three top-level objectives. It is in fact possible to draw a causal link from content to attention, and from attention to monetizing, to create a single hierarchy with monetization at the top. After all, good content leads to attention, and attention tends to increase revenues. However, to what extent we should focus on monetizing as the ultimate objective depends on the publisher's strategy. Focusing too much on revenues at the expense of quality content and customer relationships can hurt the publisher's long-term prospects and damage other firm success factors, such as recruitment, that are not included in our model. The top-level objectives and their relative priorities are thus matters of firm strategy and vision rather than something that can be derived from a model.

The measures used in our example scorecard mimic typical measures used in mobile and online free-to-play (F2P) games. For example, revenues are measured as user lifetime value, the total earnings from one user over his or her period of active use, and as average revenue per user (ARPU), earnings from one user over a period such as one month. Costs are typically measured similarly, as user acquisition cost, or how much money needs to be spent on advertising to acquire one new user. These are tried-and-true measures in F2P publishing. But they can be even more useful if you can think of ways to measure them in *marginal* rather than in average terms. The reason goes back to chapter 2 of this book. There, we explained that rational action involves balancing marginal benefits and marginal costs. The right question is not, "How much net money are my users bringing in on average?" but, "How much money did my last user bring in, and how much money did it cost me to get them in the door?" The revenues and

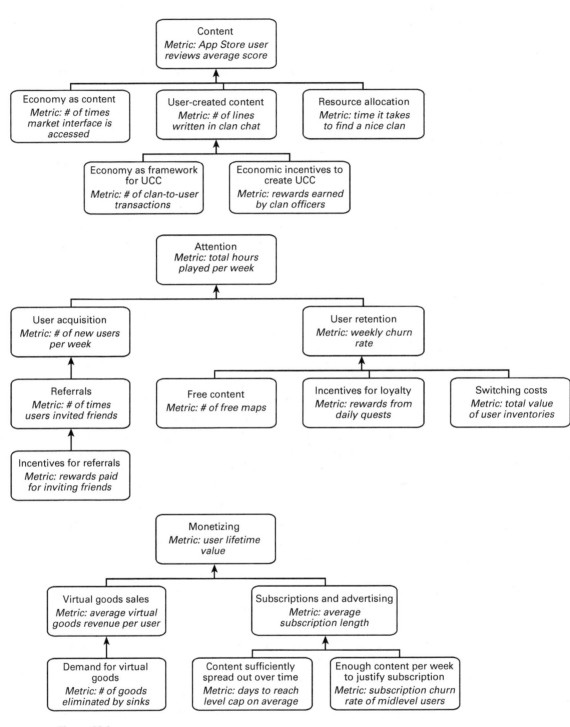

Figure 12.1
A virtual scorecard example

costs relating to users who are on the edge about staying in your platform are far more important than revenues and costs about people who are surely sticking around. Metrics should therefore pay special attention to new users and users who have recently exited.

The same reasoning also leads to the recommendation that you should collect data on features and the cost of making and deploying and managing them. What was the marginal effect of the most recent feature on costs? How does that compare to the effect on revenues, before and after the feature was introduced? By comparing the marginal cost of the feature to its marginal revenue, the designer can judge whether to push the feature more or to cut it back.

Beyond managerial measures

The virtual scorecard provides a great starting point for understanding the management of a live operation, but it is not the full picture of managing a virtual economy. The reason is that complex virtual economies are not the same thing as firms with hierarchies and chains of command. Nor are they simply e-commerce websites with customer-supplier interactions that can be accurately captured with measures such as ARPU and time spent. Virtual economies are economies, which means that they can play host to complex networks of interactions not easily captured by the kinds of measures normally used in performance management and web analytics.

An important case in point is measuring and acting on the extent to which the virtual economy is providing users with fun experiences (what we call *content*). In the virtual scorecard example, we measured the time spent in the market interface and assumed that more time spent implies more entertainment gained from the economy. A better measure would be a regular survey that asks a panel of users to rate how much fun they are having in the economy. This is more expensive but still doable and part of standard performance management. But here's the real problem: What if the measure shows that satisfaction with the economy is going down? How do we know what is going wrong and where to intervene?

We could always just ask the users where the problem is and apply a fix there. For example, new users in the online community *Gaia Online* were complaining that they didn't have enough virtual currency to afford the items traded on *Gaia*'s user-to-user marketplace. The publisher heard the complaints and responded by giving the users more currency. But all this meant was that there was now even more currency competing for the same number of items, driving goods prices even higher. New users were left almost as disappointed as before.

A better way to manage the health of a complex virtual economy is to track *economic indicators*, understand their causal relationships with each other as well as with KPIs such as user satisfaction, and carry out interventions where appropriate. Economic indicators are measures that describe an aspect of an entire economy as a number.

Economic indicators can also be calculated for specific segments of the economy, such as certain user cohorts or goods categories. In the following sections, we draw on macroeconomics, national accounting, and studies of virtual economies to introduce the most important economic indicators in a typical virtual economy: indicators relating to money, goods, inequality, and experience. We also introduce concrete methods of intervention using faucets and sinks, and finally we examine some practical issues related to data management and analysis.

Monetary policy

In chapter 10, we discussed money in terms of its microeconomic functions and affordances as an object, and only touched on its macroeconomic aspects. Here we focus on the macroeconomic aspects of money and the management of money in an economy. The total amount of money available in an economy is called the *money supply*. Actions that aim to adjust the size of the money supply are called *monetary policy*. We first consider the objectives of monetary policy (Why adjust the money supply?). We then introduce practical measures of money supply size and inflation. Finally, we present a method of adjusting money supply size by adjusting the faucets and sinks for money.

Objectives of monetary policy

In national economies, central banks are tasked with managing the money supply with two main objectives in mind. The first objective is price stability, which we began to discuss in chapter 10. By adjusting the amount of money in the economy, the central banker can influence the general price level. This link is expressed in the quantity theory of money (box 10.1): create more money, and the price level increases as more money chases after the same quantity of goods (inflation). Remove money from the economy and the general price level falls, as every remaining coin must do more work (deflation). Another way to say this is that increasing the money supply decreases the exchange value of a single unit of money, while reducing the money supply enhances the exchange value of a single unit of money. Prices of goods and value of money are just two sides of the same coin.

Why attempt to keep the value of money stable? In chapter 10, we introduced some reasons. For a currency to be a good store of value, it shouldn't lose its value over time. This means that significant inflation is not desirable. For a currency to be a good measure of value, it shouldn't gain much value either, because if the measuring stick changes, every price and value must be reevaluated. This means that significant deflation is not desirable either. Besides these quite practical reasons, a more theoretical argument is that mainstream economists generally believe that price stability is important for economic growth. Deflation is seen as harmful to economic activity because it encourages hoarding rather than spending. If you know that your money is going to be worth more at the shops tomorrow, why spend it today? Inflation can destroy trust in the money altogether if it gets out of hand, but slight inflation can be beneficial in encouraging spending. Consequently, the European Central Bank attempts to keep the value of the euro almost but not quite stable, falling at a rate of slightly less than 2 percent per year. The US Fed follows similar policy.

Besides price stability, the other objective of monetary policy is to manage the rate of economic growth directly. During boom times, the central banker can tighten money supply to attempt to prevent a bubble from forming. During recession, the central banker can attempt to encourage spending by increasing the money supply. Often this objective and the price stability objective are in perfect alignment, but not always. Economists sympathetic toward the monetarist tradition, rooted in the work of Milton Friedman, tend to argue that price stability is the most important objective. Economists aligned with the New Keynesian school, rooted in the work of John Maynard Keynes, tend to argue that active monetary policy can be used to offset shocks even when this creates the risk of a temporary departure from price stability. The New Keynesian view is supported by recent results in behavioral economics, which suggest that in practice, prices are sticky: they do not reflect changes in the money supply as directly as the quantity theory of money would suggest.

These two objectives, price stability and managing the rate of economic growth, are a good starting point for thinking about monetary policy in a virtual economy as well. In a virtual economy, many prices are often fixed: prices in the publisher's item catalogue, prices charged by nonplayer character (NPC) merchants, wages in the monster killing industry, and any other prices in markets where the publisher has a monopoly often remain constant over time by design. In simpler virtual economies with no user-to-user markets, all prices can be like this. In such cases, price stability is obviously not an issue. But the other side of the same coin, the value of money, remains very much an issue. If the Sword of Intransigent Compromise is sold by the publisher at a fixed price of 1,000 gold, but the money supply inflates to the point where every user now holds millions of gold, then that sword ceases to be a very rare item. Managing the money supply is a way of managing the difficulty level (and thus speed of content consumption) of a game with fixed prices.

If your economy has only unregulated market prices and no fixed prices at all, then changes in the price level and value of money are not quite as dangerous for the design. Still, keeping the value of your money relatively stable over time allows the money to function as a good store of value and an easy measure of value, making the economy more user friendly. Of course, if you think that your users might like that kind of excitement and challenge, you might do the very opposite and attempt to make the price level fluctuate as wildly as possible.

In terms of practical money supply management, keeping prices stable means ensuring that the money supply remains constant in relation to the amount of economic activity. Since more users generally mean more economic activity, the simplest thing to do is to track money supply per capita (or per character level gained) and keep that as constant as possible. When the economy is just starting out or recovering from a major crisis (such as a bug or a public relations disaster), it can be a good idea to let the money supply grow a bit even if this creates some inflationary pressure. This ensures that the economy has enough liquidity and gives it a nice jump start because everyone has some money in their pockets.

Measuring the money supply

To be able to control the money supply, we must be able to measure it first. In a modern national economy, measuring how much money is available is far from straightforward. This is because money comes in so many different varieties: coins, notes, traveler's checks, different types of bank deposits, and various other assets of varying degrees of liquidity. Anything that is used as medium of exchange or as a store of value is to some extent money. Economists thus have to make somewhat arbitrary decisions regarding what is included in their money supply measurements. Several measurements of varying scope are commonly used in parallel. For example, the European Central Bank (ECB) reports 5,233 billion euros worth of "narrow money," or M1, circulating in the euro area in April 2013, and as much as 9,819 billion euros worth of "broad money, or M3. ECB's narrow money includes only cash and overnight deposits, while broad money also includes many sorts of securities that can be used as money.

In a virtual economy that has an official currency, measuring the money supply is usually simpler. There are no private banks creating new money through deposits and loans.[2] In many cases, money exists in only one variety: virtual central bank account balances. These may be called "gold coins in your purse" or "credits in your universal communicator," but all the same, they function like electronic checking accounts in a single bank. Measuring the total money supply is thus a simple matter of adding up all the users' account balances. As with many measurements in a virtual economy, the only difficulty is in deciding which users to include: everyone or only those who are active. When calculating economic indicators, it is wise to include only reasonably active accounts. What counts as active depends on the service. One login per month is a typical definition.

In some virtual economies, the official currency comes in a number of varieties, just like euros. The creators of *Habbo* introduced a line of items, such as gold bars and sapphires, that could be easily converted into Habbo Credits and back at a fixed rate. Users therefore used these items as money in their transactions, just as they would

---

2. The most likely reason for this is the lack of a legal system that could enforce debt payment. See chapter 9.

use credits. The only catch was that in order to buy something from the publisher's catalogue, users had to use actual credits, and a small tax was charged in the conversion process. The items were therefore slightly less valuable than what their credit face value suggested. In terms of real-world equivalents, *Habbo*'s gold bars and sapphires were thus similar in effect to traveler's checks that cost money to redeem. Highly liquid instruments like this should certainly be included in all but the narrowest money supply measurements.

Many virtual economies, especially games, have several official currencies. If conversions between these currencies are possible and cheap, then it makes sense to consider them as part of the same money supply and simply add them up. But in many cases, games operate what are in effect two or more distinct economies. In such cases, the money supplies should be measured and adjusted independently. What if the economy has a user-created commodity money, like early *Habbo* did? Simply measure the quantity of the commodity in circulation.

Measuring inflation and deflation

Besides keeping track of the money supply, it is a good idea to also measure changes in the general price level directly. It can take a long time before changes in the money supply are reflected in prices, and prices are also influenced by other factors.

A common method to track changes in the general price level is the consumer price index (CPI). You can create a CPI for your economy as follows. Decide on a basket of goods that represents roughly what an average user would be buying in a week, for example. In the Dragonslayer economy, the basket might contain one sword and one piece of armor. Then simply begin to note down how much it would cost to buy that basket on the market at regular intervals, say weekly. The CPI for a given week is calculated as follows:

CPI = Cost of the basket this week / Cost of the basket in the base week × 100

The base week is the first week when you started the data collection, or any other week that you want to use as the baseline. The CPI figure for the base week will be 100. If the CPI figure for the current week is 125, this means that the price level has grown 25 percent. This is a significant amount of inflation, so you might want to tighten the money supply.

In many economies, consumption behavior is highly stratified. For example, in a fantasy game where players advance in levels, new players buy low-level items, whereas more advanced players compete for high-level goods; wizards buy wizard gear, while warriors buy warrior items. In such economies, it may make sense to construct separate indexes for different strata and analyze their price stability separately. For example, you might have the Wizard Price Index and the Warrior Price Index. (We discuss measuring inequality in more detail below.)

An issue separate from stratification is technological development. Over time, you may be introducing new items into the economy that make old ones obsolete. For example, whereas previously all the new players used to buy the Sword of Questionable Value, now they are buying the Sword of Better Marketing. The basket should be updated accordingly, so that it continues to reflect approximately what people are actually buying.

Implementing monetary policy with faucets and sinks

For national central banks, adjusting the size of the money supply is complicated because of the many varieties and sources of money involved. Most money is not created by the central bank itself, but by commercial banks in the process of taking deposits and lending them out again. When a bank takes a deposit of $100 from a person and then lends 70 percent of that to another person, the total account balance increases to $170. The money supply grew by $70. Consequently, one of the main ways in which central banks attempt to control the money supply is by adjusting the lending ratio: the percentage of deposits that banks are legally allowed to lend out instead of holding on to them to satisfy withdrawal requests.

The more straightforward way in which central banks can control the money supply is by creating new money by themselves or removing it from circulation when necessary. This is the main approach used by today's virtual economy managers. In this section, we describe a method of controlling the money supply per capita—what game designers refer to as *balancing the economy*. It is suited for both setting initial parameters before the economy is live, as well as for adjusting the parameters once the economy is running.

The basic idea of our method is simple: measure or estimate how much money your faucets create in a period of time, such as a day or a month, and compare that with your measure or estimate of how much money is erased by the sinks during the same period. Faucets and sinks were described in detail in the previous chapter. The difference between the faucets and the sinks is the net change per capita. If the net change is not what you wanted it to be, adjust the faucets, sinks or both until the desired result is achieved (see box 12.1). The trick, if there is any, is how to estimate the inflow and outflow.

The Dragonslayer economy that we designed in the previous chapter had one faucet for money: drops from dragons. Let's say that we've decided that each dragon will drop 100 gold on average. How do we estimate the total inflow from this faucet before the economy is live? We do that by taking the expected behavior of the player—how many dragons the average player is expected slay in a month—and multiplying that number by 100 gold. How do you know what the expected behavior is? If your game designer is up to the task, they should have some idea. Perhaps the dragons are intended to be rare bosses slain only once per month, or perhaps they are something that the player slays

Box 12.1

Stocks and flows

In macroeconomics, two types of measures are used to track money and goods around the economy: stocks and flows. To illustrate these concepts, let's look at an analogy where we substitute water for money. A stock is a quantity of water in some container at a given point in time. For example, in this picture, stock S is the quantity of water in the tub. It is measured in liters. A flow is a measure of the *movement* of water in or out of a stock. In this picture, flow A measures water pouring into the tub through a faucet, and flow B measures water pouring out of the tub through a sink. They are measured in liters per second (or per minute, per hour) because they measure the rate at which water is moving rather than the quantity of water at a given point in time. By comparing flows A and B, we can determine whether stock S is growing or diminishing. For example, if water is flowing into the tub at a rate of 0.5 liters per second and flowing out of the tub at 1 liters per second, then the net change is -0.5 liters per second, indicating that the stock is diminishing. The same approach can be used to examine changes in stocks of money and goods held in various parts of an economy.

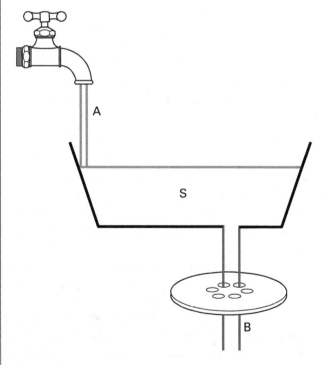

Figure 12.2

An inflow, a stock, and an outflow

Table 12.1
Monthly inflow of money in the Dragonslayer economy, per player

Faucet name	Effect and driver	Expected behavior per month	Resulting inflow per month
Drops from dragons	100 gold / dragon slain	10 dragons slain	1,000 gold
Daily login bonus	10 gold / daily login	25 daily logins	250 gold
		Total inflow per month:	1,250 gold

Table 12.2 A
Monthly outflow of money in the Dragonslayer economy, per player

Sink name	Effect and driver	Expected behavior per month	Resulting inflow per month
Transaction tax	5 gold / sale	10 sales	50 gold
		Total outflow per month:	50 gold

Table 12.2 B
Monthly outflow of money in the Dragonslayer economy, per player (adjusted)

Sink name	Effect and driver	Expected behavior per month	Resulting inflow per month
Transaction tax	5 gold / sale	10 sales	50 gold
Purchases of mounts	1,200 / mount bought	1 mount bought	1,200 gold
		Total outflow per month:	1,250 gold

a dozen of every day. Let's say the expected behavior is 10 dragons slain monthly. To make things more interesting, let's add a second faucet—a daily login bonus of 10 gold. Let's say the average player is expected to be playing on 25 days of each month. Table 12.1 shows a calculation where these numbers are put together to yield an estimate of the total inflow of gold per month.

Next, we do the same exercise for sinks. Only one sink has been planned—a transaction tax of 5 gold per each sales transaction. We expect players to sell things ten times per month on average. The resulting estimate is presented in table 12.2A.

According to our estimates, it looks as if each player will be bringing in 1,250 gold to the economy every month, while losing only 50 gold to sinks. The net change will be an increase of 1,200 gold per player per month. What should we think of this? If the game is yet to be launched and the economy is starting from scratch, it doesn't hurt to have some surplus to provide liquidity and let the money supply grow. However, a surplus of 96 percent of the inflow is just too large. In the interest of price stability, we need to reduce it.

A cheap way to reduce the surplus would be to turn down the faucets, but since we still have some development budget left, let's add a new sink. Let's add flying mounts that look cool but cost the moon to buy. Players much prefer to have a new way of spending currency rather than having their income slashed or taxed. In economic terms, the inflow per capita can be called *income*, while income that is left for purchases after more or less mandatory sinks like taxes can be called *discretionary income*. The adjusted outflow estimate is shown in table 12.2B.

The inflow and outflow are now equal, so the expected net change per capita is zero. The money supply per capita remains constant. If new players join, the total money supply will grow, but so will economic activity. In theory, our economy is now balanced. In practice, there are many complications. One is that users may hoard currency, causing deflation and liquidity crises. Active monetary policy in response to observed changes in CPI helps deal with this. Another complication is that different user segments, such as different character levels in a fantasy massively multiplayer online (MMO), may experience radically different inflows and outflows. We deal with this issue in the section on inequality later in this chapter. First, let's move from money management to managing the other thing that circulates in an economy, goods.[3]

Production and economic growth

In a virtual economy context, production means any act that brings a new good into being. This can happen through any of the goods faucets described in the previous chapter: crafting, harvesting a resource node, killing a monster, buying an item from the publisher's virtual store, and so on. When a new good enters the system by any means, it has been produced.

In national economies, production is famously measured with the gross domestic product (GDP). The truth is that this is not a very important measure in virtual economies, especially in simpler ones. However, it provides a good starting point for teasing out some important theoretical issues in understanding production, growth, and well-being in any economy, which is why we will focus on it first. Later in the section, we discuss more practical ways of measuring and managing production in a virtual economy, including faucets and sinks.

Gross virtual product
Gross domestic product measures the value of a country's total production of goods and services in one year. More generally, we can speak of gross product (GP): the total

3. To dig deeper into monetary policy, consult a macroeconomics textbook, such as Mankiw (2009, chapters 4, 19).

money value of everything produced in a given period in a given region, whether a country, a village, or a virtual economy. Soviet economists measured total production by the quantity of goods produced. The problem with this was that not all goods are equal: some are more important to people than others. GP addresses this problem by measuring money value instead of raw quantities.

The formula for GP is

$$GP = \Sigma_{i=1 \text{ to } N} (p_i \times q_i)$$

This says, "take the N goods that were newly made in the economy in this region and time period. Take the quantity, q, of the good that was produced. Multiply that quantity times the good's price. This gives the total money value of production of that good. Then add up these money values across all the goods in the economy. This produces the total money value of goods produced in this location in this time period."

For example, the GDP (i.e., country-level yearly GP) of Ukraine was approximately $127 billion in 2010. This means that $127 billion worth of stuff was produced in Ukraine during that year. If we divide this dollar amount by the number of inhabitants in Ukraine, approximately 46 million, we get the country's GDP per capita, which is approximately $2,761.

GP measures should include only the value of *final* goods—those that are ultimately consumed rather than used in the production of other goods. For example, an apple pie sold to a consumer is a final good, but the apples that were sold to the bakery are intermediate goods, and thus not included in GP. This is because the value of an apple pie already includes the value of the apples that went into its production. Including both the apple pie and the apples in GP would be counting the apples twice. But if the consumer buys an apple directly, then it is a final good and must be included in GP.[4]

Why would we want to measure GP? In national economies, GDP per capita is used as a measure of material well-being. Other things being the same, nations that produce a lot of stuff relative to their population are able to provision for the needs of their inhabitants better than nations that produce little. Nations with a high total ("aggregate") GDP also have an edge in wars, because it means that they are potentially able to churn out more tanks and bombs than their rivals.

A concept closely related to production is *economic growth*, which is usually defined as the percentage change in GP from one period to the next. The change in GP measures the change in the size of the productive economy (see box 12.2). An economy

---

4. It is possible to include goods that were produced but not (yet) sold in GP. Just apply the market price to every final good that is made, whether the maker sells it or not. That is, use the market data to assign a value to goods that do not go to market. This is quite easily done if the unsold goods are very similar (or exactly the same) as sold goods. It is much more complicated, though, if some of the goods people produce are never marketed. In this case, a price must be imputed, but it is a specialized technique beyond the scope of this book.

Box 12.2

Real versus nominal figures

From 2007 to 2008, Ukraine's GDP grew from $142 billion to $180 billion—a whopping 27 percent increase. Unfortunately this does not mean that Ukraine was suddenly producing 27 percent more goods and services than before. GDP depends on both the quantity and the prices of goods. During the year, the prices of goods went up as raw materials became more expensive. In other words, the country experienced inflation. To find out how much production really changed during the year, we should calculate the 2008 GDP using 2007 prices:

Real GDP = Quantity of goods in 2008 × Prices of goods in 2007

This is called a *real GDP*. A real GDP is calculated using the prices of some chosen reference year, in this case 2007. A GDP figure that uses current prices is called a nominal GDP. In the case of Ukraine, our real GDP in 2008 turns out to have been only $140 billion. In other words, real production measured in US dollars actually decreased by a couple of percent from 2007 to 2008.

that experiences economic growth, so defined, is producing more this period than it did last. Growth in per capita GP indicates that this economy's members are more productive. The absolute and per capita growth measures can be very different. An influx of new members (immigrants, new users) will almost always make the economy grow in absolute terms: more people producing things means more things are produced. But if the new members are inexperienced, the value of what they produce individually may be low, meaning that per capita GP falls. In the brick-and-mortar economy, rising GP is often referred to as "boom" and is treated as good times. Falling GP is called "recession" and "depression" and is associated with bad times.

Everything left over from production after consumption and depreciation (e.g.,, armors destroyed by dragon fire) is added to the economy's total stock of *wealth*. If the economy produces more than what is destroyed in the same period, then its wealth grows and it becomes richer. In some ways, it might seem that the more intuitive meaning for the term *economic growth* would be growth in wealth rather than growth in production, but the latter is the established use in economics.

Table 12.3 summarizes the indicators discussed above, using the language of performance management. In national policymaking, the targets are clear: the more production and wealth, the better, other things being the same. Let's call the gross product of a virtual economy its gross virtual product (GVP). Are GVP per capita and virtual wealth good proxies for well-being in a virtual economy, in the same way as GDP per capita and material wealth are in a national economy? If so, we have identified an easy way to make users very happy. Just make it easier to produce everything, including

Table 12.3
Production-related measures and objectives in a national economy

Measure	Objective that it is a measure of	Target
GDP	Country's economic power in relation to other countries	Maximize
GDP per capita	Material well-being	Maximize
Wealth	Material well-being; production capacity; reserves	Maximize

money, and watch the GVP grow. Or add a button that says, "Make me rich." Boom! Happy users. Right?

MUDflation

In the days of multiuser dungeons (MUDs), designers created virtual items very simply: A Knife. A Hat. A Hairdo. A player who did whatever it took to create or harvest the item possessed it. Inventory space was more or less infinite. The item never went away. Over time, players would get items and give them to their friends or sell them; new players constantly came in; old players told new players how to get stuff, so there was no time or learning delay in obtaining items; the designers constantly made new powers and abilities for the players to retain their interests, thus allowing them to get more stuff more quickly. All of these practices and habits and design decisions meant that two things happened: first, more and more items were entering the economy at a growing pace; second, every player's inventory became filled to the brim with every item in the world. The textbook economist would call these two things economic growth and wealth and congratulate the designer for a job well done. But the designers called this situation *MUDflation*, and they hated it.

First, let's think about wealth. Why might massive wealth be a problem in a virtual economy? Recall from chapter 3 that virtual goods tend to be positional goods: their value depends not so much on their intrinsic qualities but on how they rank in relation to other goods and the environment. That Level 100 Dagger of Doom? It was once owned by only three players out of 400,000, making it a unique and powerful item. But now everyone and their pet imp has one. If everyone owns everything, there's nothing special about owning anything anymore. Moreover, since you own the most powerful item in the game, there are no more challenges to look forward to. The game is finished. All the content is consumed. Time to move on.

Now let's think about GVP and economic growth. To some extent, high GVP per capita can actually correlate with user well-being or even exhilaration. A high level of production can mean that the users are constantly gaining new goods, which are giving them new powers, access to new areas, and other joys. In other words, a high level of production can mean that users are experiencing content at a rapid pace. To some extent, GVP per capita thus reflects the rate at which users are consuming content. In chapter 1, we showed why it is important to control this rate. If it is too slow, users get bored. If it is too fast, users zip past content without fully enjoying it and the publisher's content budget runs out before they are able to turn a profit. The implication from this is that unlike national policymakers, virtual economy managers usually do not want to maximize GVP. Instead, they want to balance it, to keep it at a sweet spot that represents their desired trade-off between the intensity and the duration of the experience.

However, GVP per capita is not a perfect measure of content consumption and user well-being. The reason is that it doesn't necessarily go down when fresh content runs out. When the economy reaches the "wealthy" (i.e., fully spent) state described above, production can still continue. Already have the Dagger of Doom? Have another one! Have three! Measured in virtual currency units, the value of the economy might be growing. But the value of those virtual currency units to the user might be falling as users lose their interest in the economy. In this situation, the GVP gives a false impression of the state of affairs.

Converting virtual figures into real money

GVP is not a very good measure of user well-being because it is expressed in virtual currency, and the value of that currency to the user might vary or even disappear. Could we convert a GVP into national currency, say, US dollars? That would also allow us to compare the productivity of a virtual economy to the productivity of a national economy.

GDP figures from different countries are frequently reported in US dollars to facilitate cross-country comparisons. In the example above, we reported the GDP of Ukraine in dollars, even though the National Bank of Ukraine originally calculated it in the local currency, the hryvnia. We converted the hryvnia into dollars by using the foreign exchange market rate: the rate at which central banks, businesses, and speculators are willing to trade hryvnia to dollars. There are two problems with this, however.

The first problem is that foreign exchange rates do not accurately reflect differences in countries' living standards. Two dollars are worth over 15 hryvnia in the foreign exchange market. Two dollars is not enough to buy a Big Mac hamburger; 15 hryvnia can buy that hamburger. And even though $2.00 is certainly not enough to buy a ticket to a good classical music concert, 15 hryvnia are. If Ukraine's GDP is converted to US dollars using the foreign exchange rate, the result is an overly pessimistic view of Ukrainians' material well-being.

The second problem is that foreign exchange rates fluctuate depending on movements and moods in international trade and financial markets. In 2007, one unit of the Ukrainian currency hryvnia was worth 20 cents; by the end of 2008, its value had dropped to 13 cents. The consequence is that although in local currency terms Ukraine's real GDP actually grew a couple of percent from 2007 to 2008, it seems to have decreased in dollar terms. This dollar-value decrease does not necessarily reflect any actual changes in Ukraine's production and material well-being. The foreign exchange rate is therefore not a very good way to make GDP figures comparable.

A better way to convert GDP figures into US dollars is to use a so-called purchasing power parity (PPP) exchange rate. A PPP rate is calculated as follows. First, decide on a hypothetical basket of goods that contains different kinds of final products and services, from food to diapers and haircuts to housing. Second, measure what that same basket would cost to buy in each country using the country's local currency. The PPP exchange rate between two currencies is the ratio of the cost of the basket in one currency to the cost of the basket in the other currency. The World Bank's PPP rate for hryvnia and dollar is currently around 0.5. This means that 1 hryvnia buys you about the same amount of stuff as 50 cents.

One of us (Castronova) famously calculated in 2001 that the dollar value GDP per capita of *EverQuest*, an MMO, was between that of Russia and Bulgaria. The method he used to convert virtual production into US dollars was similar to the foreign exchange market method: he used prices from secondary market sites where *EverQuest* assets were traded for US dollars as the conversion factor.

Unfortunately this approach has the same shortcomings as the foreign exchange market method: the prices on real-money markets are shaped by factors that don't always reflect conditions in the game's internal economy. Why didn't he use the PPP method instead? The reason is simple: it is impossible to construct a basket of goods that would be available in both the United States and *EverQuest*. *EverQuest*'s game items are not direct substitutes for any material or immaterial goods traded in the national economy, and nothing traded in the material economy can directly substitute for a weapon or fancy hat in *EverQuest*. This makes it almost impossible to compare the purchasing power of *EverQuest*'s platinum coins with the purchasing power of US dollars.

Virtual economies and national economies are not substitutes or alternatives to each other, so comparing them is ultimately not that fruitful. Trying to compare GVP figures between two different kinds of virtual economies is likewise problematic. For the most part, we are best contenting ourselves with using GVP as a measure of virtual value only, remembering that it may not always reflect how users feel about the economy. In a game where a vibrant and complex virtual economy is a key part of the experience, such a measure can be useful. It can be used to examine changes in activity over time in response to design changes and other shocks, and it could even be used to compare the economic prominence of different virtual nations within the same virtual economy. But other measures and tools are needed to manage user well-being and content consumption on a more finely grained level.[5]

5. To dig deeper into the conventional economic measures of production and growth, consult a macroeconomics textbook, such as Mankiw (2009, chapters 3, 7–9).

Managing production with faucets and sinks

In the previous subsections, we examined production and wealth through the lens of modern macroeconomics, in which production is measured in terms of its market value, not in terms of raw quantities. The rationale behind this approach is that using monetary values makes it possible to add up the production figures of different kinds of goods into a single aggregate figure. If we used raw quantities, we would have to decide how many apples one orange is worth or examine each good separately. In the GP approach, we let the market determine the relative values of everything for us and added everything up. In this section, we are going to be more like Soviet economists, who favored measuring production in terms of quantities rather than in market value. Like economic planners, game designers often believe they know what quantity of a given good or category of goods results in an optimal experience, and they want to ensure that such quantities are produced in practice. For example, they want to ensure that rare status items remain scarce and that basic crafting materials are available in sufficient quantities. The overall goal is usually not to maximize production and accumulation, but to balance them in such a way as to make the economy entertaining (providing content) and maximize revenues (monetization).

Our approach to achieving these objectives is to track the quantities of different goods or categories of goods circulating in the economy and adjust the faucets and sinks that create and destroy these goods when necessary. In economic terms, faucets are equivalent to production and sinks are equivalent to consumption and depreciation. Their difference equals wealth accumulation.

The method of adjusting faucets and sinks for goods is exactly the same as the method we used to adjust the faucets and sinks for money earlier in this chapter. List the faucets and their effects, multiply the effect by how many times per time period each faucet will be triggered, based on expected user behavior, and sum up the results to find out the total inflow (see table 12.1). Do the same for sinks, and compare the results to find out the net change per capita. Do this separately for each type of good, set of close substitutes, or broader category of goods, depending on what is meaningful and feasible with your goods lineup. As you start to obtain data on actual user behavior, change the estimates to real data and play with your model to see how changing the effects of different faucets and sinks would influence the net change.

In chapter 5, we approached similar objectives from the perspective of market structure. We showed how the publisher's involvement in markets as an omnipotent buyer or seller could be used to create price floors and price ceilings that keep market prices within acceptable parameters. The approach presented here differs in two ways. First, the focus here is on active management rather than stark boundaries resulting from static design. Second, we focus on managing quantities rather than prices, although on a market, one will affect the other. The two approaches are complementary. The faucet-and-sink approach tries to ensure that the economy stays in the desired balance. The market structure approach ensures that even when things do get out of hand, damage is limited by design.

Managing production by adjusting utility

In any economy, the effective economic demand for an item depends on how much utility people experience from it. In chapter 3, we discussed the various reasons that people experience utility from virtual goods. Many of these sources of utility are such that within certain bounds, it is possible for the virtual economy manager to alter them—in gamer parlance, to "nerf" or "buff" an item. This opens up another avenue to managing the quantity of an item produced.

For example, human psychology dictates just how much fun a ZX-4000 Railgun may be and to how many people. But the designer can easily change how powerful the gun is in the context of a game. Making the ZX-4000 a better zombie killer will raise its demand. In the short run, this will only raise its price relative to other guns. But then more users will try to make or harvest this gun, and in the long run the price spike will moderate. Higher quantities of the gun will be present in the economy. In short, if you want more players to have the ZX-4000, give it more bullets.

Inequality

In addition to measures of money and goods, economists are interested in measures of inequality, that is, differences between people in the degree to which they obtain and possess things like money and goods.

The desirability and consequences of inequality in virtual economies, especially game economies, were discussed in chapter 9, in the section on redistribution. To summarize, in order to provide a good play experience, it usually makes sense for game designers to try to offer equal rewards to participants showing the same level of skill and effort and higher rewards to participants who have better skill and show more effort. Thus, Ice Wizards and Fire Wizards are expected to have the same ability to earn money, but wizards on different levels are expected to have different earnings. It may also make sense to provide some kind of "social security" for players who lose their virtual possessions to avoid locking them out of the economy and prevent churn.

Besides providing an enjoyable experience (i.e., content), virtual economies are also expected to make money. Sometimes this monetization objective is implemented in such a way that it is in conflict with players' sense of fairness and equality. For example, being able to buy one's way to success is often perceived as unfair and detracts from players' experience of the economy. However, what is perceived as fair and appropriate depends entirely on the product and audience. Casual mobile gamers might consider quite acceptable some virtual item purchases that competitive PC F2P gamers would be absolutely against. Thus, it is up to the designer to figure out what kind and degree of inequality is part of the design and what kind or degree of inequality is inappropriate and must be addressed.

In the following sections, we first discuss general methods of measuring inequality and then introduce one additional economic indicator that is particularly relevant when we talk about inequality: unemployment.

Measuring inequality

The most obvious way to track inequality is to divide the user base into segments, based on whatever variables are relevant for equality purposes in your economy. In a game, this could be character class and level, and in a nongame service, this could be sign-up year and weekly logins. Then simply calculate the different measures discussed earlier, such as money inflow (income) per capita, separately for each segment. Express the results in percentages in relation to one segment and compare. For example, you might find that the average Ice Wizard's income is only 72 percent of a Fire Wizard's income.

The problem with this approach is that we don't always know beforehand what dimensions inequality might grow along, or it might not follow any of our preexisting dimensions. Ice Wizards and Fire Wizards might be equally rich, but there might instead be a growing chasm between 1 percent of wizards who grab most of the loot and 99 percent who get little. Once they appear, such dynamics can be self-reinforcing: money begets money. To address this, we also need a way of measuring inequality in any given variable X to see if it is within the acceptable range and track how it develops over time. Fortunately, there are several standard metrics.

One simple way to look at inequality is to estimate not only the average of X but also its standard deviation. In a normal bell curve distribution, most users should have values of X within two standard deviations of the average value. If two standard deviations above and below X take us quite far away from the average, this means there is much inequality.

Many economic variables do not follow a bell curve, however. Rather, they follow the power law, such that the top 10 percent of the population accounts for 50 percent of the variable in question, with declining shares as one goes down the distribution. Metrics to capture the power law include the 80/20 distribution and the 90/10 distribution. This indicates what proportion of X is owned by the bottom 80 or 90 percent of the population and what is owned by the top 20 or 10 percent. The pattern of such numbers can be summarized into a single metric, the Gini coefficient. The formula for Gini coefficient is beyond the scope of this book, but in summary, the Gini measures in one number the average deviation of a variable from a perfectly equal distribution. A Gini of 0 indicates perfect equality. A Gini of 100 means that one person owns everything. The Gini coefficient for income in most developed countries, historically speaking, has been between 30 and 40.

A rising Gini coefficient means that smaller numbers of users are eating bigger shares of the pie. Changes of five or more points in the Gini are rare and would be considered massive. A regular reporting of the Gini for key measures can be a good way to tell if things are starting to go wrong.

Unemployment and unused capacity

In a national economy, unemployment is one of the most important economic indicators and a significant predictor of inequality. However, it seems to have little analog in virtual economies. The brick-and-mortar version of this number comes from survey data. A number of working-age people are asked whether they currently have work. Those who say no are asked whether they are currently looking for work. The total of workers plus those looking for work is called the *labor force*. The *unemployment rate* is the percentage of the labor force that is not working but looking for work. Since people in virtual economies typically do not have "work" in this sense but rather seek their own fortunes, this statistic is not likely to make sense in most virtual economic contexts.

Unemployment is critical in the real world because of both economic and psychological reasons. An unemployed person has no income and thus cannot buy things; when fewer people buy things, the economy contracts. But more important, an unemployed person has no vocation, which can have a devastating effect on their sense of well-being. Being unemployed is a huge predictor of dissatisfaction.

Economic analysts are concerned about unemployment for a third reason, this one relating to efficiency. People who have no work but want work are, in the economic sense, wasting time. They have the ability and the desire to produce things of value for others but are not able to do so. In this, unemployed workers are similar to an empty factory or an unplowed field: a resource that the economy could use but does not. Unused capacity is a sign of economic inefficiency. When large numbers of assets (human and material) are not being used, people are going without goods and services that could be made available.

From this perspective, we can see that even if unemployment as such is not a very relevant measure in a virtual economy, the wider concept of unused capacity can still be relevant. To what extent do users have things that they do not use? To what extent has the system provided inputs and resources that are not being used? While virtual economies usually do not have jobs, they certainly do have meaningful activities. "Unemployment" could be interpreted as "unable to find meaningful/fun tasks to do." Or it might be "unable to find a good way to get income." Understood this way, unemployment is just as important for virtual world designers as real-world policy analysts. Unemployment makes people very unhappy in the real world, which means that those who are unemployed in the virtual economy will rapidly get bored or frustrated and quit. Simple surveys could be used to determine whether users (and which ones) are having difficulty finding a vocation or calling in the virtual economy.[6]

Progressive and regressive policies

Inequality is addressed and adjusted through the use of progressive and regressive policies. The terms *progressive* and *regressive* are taken from the world of tax policy and refer to the way that tax burdens differ between rich and poor people. A progressive tax is higher for rich people and lower for poor people. A regressive tax has the opposite pattern. Subsidies can also be progressive or regressive; a progressive subsidy gives bigger gifts to poorer people, while a regressive subsidy helps the rich more than the poor. In virtual economy design and management, inequality in a given measure, such as currency, can be addressed with progressive and regressive faucets and sinks pertaining to that measure.

Another advantage of progressive and regressive policies is that they can help catch anything weird. Suppose the managers have a problem that some users are trafficking money through their system. Dirty money is used to buy gold pieces, the gold pieces are transferred from one user to another, and then they are sold for real money, which is now clean. Any such operation would make sense only if it were conducted in massive amounts. A progressive tax that takes 99 percent of trades above a certain amount would make such trafficking senseless. Similarly, anyone who managed to hack a system and create large amounts of anything can be caught by a generally progressive penalty system—for example, a system that charges immense fees for storage of very large amounts of anything in inventory.

Experience

We have now covered the main areas of managing a virtual economy: money, goods, and inequality. Here we introduce a handful of additional measures that can be used to track participants' satisfaction with and commitment to an economy. These can be used alongside measures introduced earlier to complement our view of the objective material state of the economy with an understanding of its subjective, mental state. This is especially important in a virtual economy, where most, if not all, of the value produced is mental in nature.

Well-being

The whole point of an economy, whether national or virtual, is to provide well-being to people. Economists are increasingly reaching beyond income and wealth to attempt

6. To read more about unemployment and unused capacity, see Mankiw (2009, chapter 6).

to measure subjective states of happiness more directly. The most common well-being measure in this area is "life satisfaction." Life satisfaction data comes from simply asking people to rate on a scale from 0 to 10 how satisfied they are with their life. A virtual economy designer may apply this measure by building in a regular survey (of a sample of users, not all of them) asking directly how satisfied the user is with life within this virtual economy. Like the Gini, life satisfaction does not move much on average. It tends to average about 6 to 8 for most populations; a change of more than 0.5 in a time period is a powerful signal that something very good or very bad is happening.[7]

Confidence

One metric that is often used by market analysts and less frequently by scholarly economists is survey-based assessment of consumer confidence. Like life satisfaction, this is a frankly psychological measure: people are asked how confident they feel about their economic future and their plans to buy things over the next few months. Indexes of consumer confidence are taken to be leading indicators of economic growth. This is because confidence (and its lack) is in some ways self-fulfilling. A nation of people worried about the economy will not buy as much, which harms the economy. A nation buzzing with consumption excitement will go buy things, thus animating the economy and confirming the confidence.

In a virtual context, surveys of users about their attitude toward the world and the economy would yield similarly forward-looking data that might be useful in some contexts.

Investments

Investments are an objective measure that can be used as an imperfect proxy of commitment and confidence in much the same way as economists use income as a proxy of happiness. An investment is a commitment of valuable resources (time, money, goods) in the hopes of a future return. For example, a user may spend considerable time building a virtual barn that produces a small stream of benefits that continue indefinitely. The cost of the time that went into the barn is an investment, and it makes economic sense only if the builder either enjoys building for its own sake or hopes to reap those future benefits for some time. By measuring the value of expected future returns from existing investments, designers can get a sense of the degree to which users are locked into the economy, awaiting with joyful hope the benefits that are on the way.

7. For more ways to measure people's subjective well-being, see Layard (2006). Richard Layard is a distinguished labor economist who later in his career became interested in the question of what all the economic variables mean for actual happiness and helped to launch the field of happiness economics.

Disinvestment, like selling, is a sign of waning attachment. To disinvest is to sell a benefit stream in return for current cash. A user who is trying to turn investments into money right now may be on the way out and should be flagged for attention.

Wages

In a national economy, wage data is used to measure productivity and opportunity, as well as the value of time. The wage is defined as income per hour. Hourly employment statistics deliver this number immediately. For salaried employees or the self-employed, the common practice is to obtain hourly wages by taking the weekly, monthly, or annual income and dividing by the number of hours worked in that period.

The wage tells us what an employer is willing to pay someone to do this work, and since employers are not assumed to be giving away money for nothing, we can assume that the value of the worker's output is at least as high as their wage. The wage thus represents a measure of the productivity per hour in an economy or a sector of an economy. Because of this, wages should be closely related to the GVP per capita per hour, another measure of productivity.

Wage data indicates something about opportunity because they tell us how much extra income a person can get from working for an hour. Inequality in wages means that even though all people are given the same twenty-four hours per day, some people have to work many hours to get the income that a highly paid person gets in one hour. Wage inequality, especially among people who perceive themselves as equally qualified, is a predictor of great dissatisfaction.

The third use of wage data is as a measure of the value of time. The idea is that a person facing a choice of spending time in an activity could always, if they wished, go do an hour's worth of work instead. For that hour, they would receive their normal wage. And thus the cost of doing the activity, its opportunity cost, is the hour's wage that they did not get. Using wages as a measure of the value of time allows governments to estimate the cost of traffic congestion: all of those people caught in all of those cars for all of those hours do lose something, and the best way to estimate what they lose is to use the value of their time. The labor market is a place where people trade their time for money, and the wage is the price of that time.

As with unemployment, these concepts do not translate all that well into a virtual economy setting, since there is rarely a labor market with hourly wages. Yet the idea of salaried or self-employed people having implicit wage rates translates very well. In the virtual context, one would take the income a person has earned in a time period and divide by the number of hours they have spent in income-producing tasks. This yields income per hour. It is not exactly a wage rate, but it does capture the virtual productivity of the person's time, and it gives a sense of the relative income-earning opportunities that the person has in the virtual economy.

The time-value aspect of wages is quite critical for many virtual economy applications. Most often, the primary user input to a system is his time. It is important to know how much this time investment is worth. It is wonderful to know that users spent $100,000 on premium items, but what does it mean when they spent 35,000 hours using them? How invested are these people overall, as compared to a competitor's user base that spent $20,000 but 120,000 hours? What is an hour worth? In order to make sense of the investment of time into the application, it is necessary to estimate the money value of the users' time. There are two methods: survey a sample of users about their real-life wage rates or estimate their in-world hourly productivity and then use exchange rates to attempt to express that in terms of the national currency.

Wages are a sign of health or illness in an economy because people with low wages can be presumed to be unhappy. Wage stagnation is a problem in that users are not experiencing growth in the hourly purchasing power. And as we have mentioned, wage inequality leads to dissatisfaction.

Data collection and analysis

Table 12.4 presents a summary of all the economic indicators that we have discussed in this chapter. The indicators' relationships to each other are described in the language of performance management: which indicator leads or lags which other indicator.

Table 12.4
Economic indicators in a virtual economy

Indicator	Description	Relation to other measures
Monetary policy		
Narrow money supply (M1)	Amount of virtual currency available in the economy. Also measure per capita.	Leads CPI
Broad money supply (M2)	Amount of virtual currency and items that can be used as currency, measured using their monetary value. Also measure per capita.	Leads CPI
Consumer price index (CPI)	Indexed cost of a defined basket of goods. Change in CPI is inflation/deflation. Several parallel indices/baskets can be used to measure prices for different user segments.	Lags M1 and M2
Total money inflow	Total amount of money created in a period. Also measure per capita (income). In the case of premium currencies, a measure of current revenues.	Leads M1 and M2
Total money outflow	Total amount of money destroyed in a period. Also measure per capita. In the case of premium currencies, leads revenues.	Leads M1 and M2 (inverse relation)

Term	Description	Note
Discretionary income	Per capita inflow left after mandatory sinks like taxes.	Better proxy for well-being than income
Foreign exchange rate	Exchange rate of the virtual currency at real-money markets.	Lags CPI (inverse relation)

Production

Term	Description	Note
Gross virtual product (GVP), nominal	Total monetary value of all goods produced in a period, measured using current prices. Also measure per capita. Change is nominal economic growth or contraction.	Leads wealth; correlates with CPI
Gross virtual product (GVP), real	Total monetary value of all goods produced in a period, measured using prices from a reference year. Also measure per capita. Change is real economic growth or contraction.	Leads wealth
Wealth	Total monetary value of all goods in the economy. Also measure per capita.	Lags GVP
Total goods inflow	Total number of goods of a given type or category created in a period. Also measure per capita.	Leads market price
Total goods outflow	Total number of goods of a given type or category destroyed in a period. Also measure per capita.	Leads market price (inverse relation)
Market price	Average price of a given type or category of goods in a period.	Lags inflow and outflow; correlates with CPI
Unused capacity	The percentage of a given resource, such as a mineral harvesting opportunity, that is not being used.	Leads GVP (inverse relation)

Inequality

Term	Description	Note
Relative income or other measure	Income, or any other per capita measure pertaining to a user segment expressed as a percentage of that of another user segment.	Unfair or extreme inequality leads dissatisfaction
Standard deviation	A basic measure of inequality in a given measure, such as income.	
Gini coefficient	An advanced measure of inequality in a given measure, such as income.	
Unemployment	Percentage of users who have not found a meaningful activity to pursue in the economy.	Leads inequality and dissatisfaction

Experience

Term	Description	Note
Satisfaction	0 to 10 subjective assessment of satisfaction with one's (virtual) life.	A measure of well-being
Confidence	A measure of people's beliefs regarding their economic situation or spending in the next period compared to this period.	Leads GVP, inflows and outflows
Investments	Amount of wealth (virtual or otherwise) tied up in assets as opposed to being in a highly liquid form. Measures commitment.	Change is a proxy for confidence
Wages	Monetary value of an hour of a user's time, in virtual or national currency.	Proxy for well-being

Using these relationships, you can integrate relevant indicators into your performance management framework, or virtual scorecard. The next time there is an issue with user satisfaction, monetization, or some other aspect of the economy, you have a causal chain that suggests where you need to intervene to address the issue on a foundational level.

That said, in a complex economy, the different indicators and the concepts that they measure are interlinked in numerous ways, and their relationships vary over time as the economy changes and evolves. Virtual economy management is thus never simply about maximizing a given measure. It's about monitoring a variety of measures, seeing if they continue to influence each other in the way we think they do, and being ready to update our understandings and our intervention strategies when the economy moves to a new era. Virtual economies that have been successfully managed for over a decade, like *Habbo*, *EVE Online*, and, soon, *World of Warcraft*, have in many ways been rediscovered and even redefined several times over the years.

It may be useful to think of virtual economy management as two parallel but distinct functions. The first is day-to-day operations, aimed at maintaining a certain balance and maximizing certain measures based on the current understanding of the economy. The second is economic analysis, which is aimed at understanding how both our models and measures of the economy, as well as the economy itself, could be updated and improved. The knowledge created in the analysis function can be used to improve the current service, but it can also be used as the foundation for developing new, even more successful services in the future. This applies to both games and other virtual economy applications, such as currencies and incentive systems. In the remainder of this chapter we present some practical advice concerning data collection and analysis in a virtual economy.[8]

Dealing with big data

A virtual economy can easily produce vast reams of data. Social scientists have started to refer to these kinds of detailed data on many people's choices and behaviors as "big data"—opening up entirely new possibilities in research and policymaking, but also in intrusive surveillance.[9] For virtual economy managers, big data presents a practical challenge: how to store and manage such vast amounts of data for deriving useful insights. We briefly present the most typical issues and solutions below.

8. Some general advice on conventional macroeconomic data is also available in Mankiw (2009, chapter 2).

9. For an accessible introduction to big data and their societal implications, see Mayer-Schönberger and Cukier (2013). Viktor Mayer-Schönberger is a professor of Internet governance and regulation, Kenneth Cukier is a data journalist. For a practical example of big data research, see Bollen, Mao, and Zeng (2011).

Consider virtual item purchase data, for example. The raw data consists of millions of lines pertaining to items like "Level 47 Sword of Fire with an Emerald Gem." But how many economic management decisions will swing on the buying of this particular sword? Very few. To get the bigger picture of how the market is performing, we need to augment the raw data with metadata. For example, the metadata for this sword could be Level 47; Level 45-50; Slashing; Sword; Has Effect; Effect: Fire; Has Power-up; Power-Up: Emerald. Metadata allow us to start analyzing the market from a number of angles. Having a metadata framework in place from the beginning avoids the arduous task of applying it later, after already accumulating a lot of data and changing the database layout a few times. Too often big data is simply a big mess.

Having a metadata framework not only helps with analysis, but also suggests an easy way of reducing the data that need to be stored for analysis. Probably the most important piece of metadata above (judging from our experience of games with swords) would simply be "Weapon." We can imagine someone being concerned about the market for weapons and even level 45 to 50 swords in particular, but we have a harder time imagining an actionable concern about level 47 Emerald-Enhanced Slashing Swords specifically. To reduce storage requirements, you could simply record the total number of items of a certain category purchased by a user within a period rather than each individual transaction with a precise time stamp. However, the downside with this is that if in the future you get an idea for a new, interesting way of slicing the data, you won't be able to apply it retroactively.

Data storage is actually less of an issue today with modern distributed storage systems. But retrieving and analyzing vast amounts of data is still very hard. Imagine that you wanted your designers to have a quick point-and-click interface for looking into your data. For that kind of use, a quick response time is essential. Depending on the nature of the queries and analyses being performed, operations on a huge data set could take from minutes to days.

Brick-and-mortar economic statisticians handle this issue using samples. If you want to know the general trend of a variable over time at such-and-such a scale, you don't need to get every observation and take the average of that very large column. We don't have to measure the weight of every Bavarian to get a sense of how heavy Bavarians are in general. Given the population (12 million), only 1,000 people need to be put on the scale to produce a reasonably accurate estimate. Statisticians can help a team decide how many data points need to be sampled, but as a general rule, once the sample size gets into the thousands, it can accurately estimate trends for populations many orders of magnitude larger. A sample obviously won't allow you to use data mining techniques to identify individual users across the population, but there shouldn't be any need for that kind of analysis in management that is concerned with developing and measuring economic indicators.

It is true that using samples will always result in some error. However, the error margins involved (2 to 4 percent) are as large as the errors that occur whenever one tries to work with all the data. In the United States, a debate has smoldered for some time over the accuracy of the Census. The Constitution requires a *count*—not a sample—of the population every ten years. Because some people are hard to find, there are always errors in the counting. Statisticians argue (and can mathematically prove) that the data collection would be more accurate if sampling were used. (It would also be a lot less expensive, but that's another matter.) Vast collections of digital data may at first glance seem immune to such errors—the computer finds everybody—but the data must eventually be used by humans, where size and scope surely lead to time delay costs and simple mistakes.

In conclusion we can say that despite the opportunities offered by big data, in practical virtual economy management, there is usually no need to collect everything, and often it is better to collect less—if for no other reason than to safeguard users' privacy. The more important virtual economies become, the more personal and sensitive virtual economy data should be considered. On the other hand, virtual economy data can also be used for more forward-looking analysis, even scholarly work. For these uses, more data is usually better, but they should still be collected and stored within a framework that addresses ethical concerns.

The importance of theory

With large amounts of data, multiplied by many ways of slicing them, comes the possibility of finding huge amounts of connections between things. "Aha! People who wear black pants spend more than $40 monthly on our game!" Some correlations reflect real causal relationships between the measures in question; some correlations are caused by a third factor that influences both measures; some correlations are artifacts resulting from the way the data is collected or managed; and some correlations are simply random chance. To derive actionable insights from an observed correlation, we need to know which type it is.

What is it about black pants that links people to greater spending? This is not a data question; it is a theory question. Theories are models that try to explain the data we see. When we introduced our economic indicators, we described causal mechanisms that provide plausible explanations of how they might be linked to each other. Thus, if we observe that both CPI and money supply in our economy are growing fast, we know that there are good reasons to expect that money supply growth is causing CPI growth and act to tighten the money supply. In the case of black pants and spending, however, we are hard pressed to come up with any plausible theory, especially one that would be supported by earlier research and experience. Yet this kind of correlation does come up. We can always make a wild guess and say that black pants somehow causes greater spending and focus our efforts accordingly. But when our data is revealing dozens or even hundreds of connections like this, it is obvious that we need some method of separating the real ones from the spurious and the superficial from the fundamental. Theory is that method. That's why, even in the age of data mining and big data, when we can see everything that happens in real time, we still teach and develop abstract economic and social theory.

Making data public

Theory is never finished. As we write this, economists debate the nature and strength of the link between money supply and prices in today's economies. New observations help to test, elaborate, and redefine the theory. We conclude this chapter with an appeal to virtual economy designers to publish their data or measures in some form.

There are several quite selfish reasons that a designer might want to publish their data. Analysis by scholars, students, or the users themselves might reveal insights that help designers improve the service or design their next offering. Data can also make the economy run better. National governments have become persuaded over the centuries that the best policy is to make economic data publicly available (and honest). Actors in the economy rely heavily on these data to make key decisions. Hiding the data adds to anxiety and fuels crises. Hiding data is also a sign that the people running the show are afraid or incompetent, not a message that most administrators want to send. One of the duties of *EVE Online*'s lead economist, Eyjólfur Guðmundsson, is to publish data and analysis to the game's players.

Several factors limit designers' ability to publish virtual economy data: cost of publication, business-sensitive data such as earnings, data that spoils gameplay, and data that compromises privacy. Publishing aggregate economic indicators instead of raw data, just like governments do, goes a long way toward solving most of these issues. Publicly accessible indicators about virtual economies are increasingly important to everyone, not just users, because of the bumping and scraping that occurs whenever economic forces encounter one another. Real and virtual economies are linked to each other in myriad ways. National policymakers already publish a lot of data. We will all be better off if managers of virtual economies do the same.

13 Policymaking

In this chapter, we discuss practical questions involved with implementing an economy in a virtual world. The issues are the same as in the offline environment, although the powers of a virtual economy designer are greater. The great power of virtual economy owners is not as helpful as one might think, however. Merely being a dictator does not make it easier to govern well. There is much more to good policymaking than rolling out new code.

We saw in chapter 12 that there are many tools for managing a virtual economy. Those tools by themselves do not tell a manager what to do. Recall the basic objectives of virtual economy design: content, users, and monetization. Determining whether these objectives are being met is difficult, especially with populations of thousands or millions of users. So far, we have discussed how to do things like lower the price of a virtual good. But how does one determine that the price of a virtual good is too high? And how does one handle the politics of changing the price? It may be controversial: How can managers convince the users that the change is a good one?

The topics of the chapter include how to determine the sorts of policy the economy needs, how to design those policies, how to implement them, and how to assess their effects. We conclude with a discussion of classic economic policy problems and how they play out in a virtual environment.

How policy differs from design

At first glance, the policy process and the design process might seem quite similar. You begin with a broad notion of what a system needs; then you think about a series of rules and mechanics that might meet that need. You craft the rules and mechanics in more detail; then you implement them in code. While a team does perform all these steps whether it is working on design or policy, the critical difference is that with policy, the user community is at the center of the process. Some designers in fact see users as the center of their design process, in which case there is no real difference between design and policy. Policymaking begins and ends with the user.

The user plays several roles. In the offline world, the "user" is a citizen of a jurisdiction. That citizen has a number of ways to express their concerns about what the government is doing. Through these expressions, the people in government develop some sense of what the citizen wants. In principle, the government then goes about designing a response to these needs. In practice, the government actors pay close attention to their own interests and resources, and the hope is that the system of governance encourages a wide overlap between the citizen's needs and the political actor's incentive to meet those needs. In any case, a policy is eventually adopted and rolled out to the citizens, who then take stances on it. If the citizens are happy, the policy has been a success.

The interests of the public are thus constantly in the mix as policy is conceived, designed, and implemented. Furthermore, policy is constrained by whatever policy-making process is in effect. Critically, the interests of the public can change or defeat a policy effort. Therefore, managing changes to rules and mechanics as policy changes is a way to mitigate the risk of failure.

Problems of interest aggregation

The policy process begins with a method of discovering what the affected public wants or needs. Good politicians sometimes have a sixth sense about the public's preferences, but most people aren't that lucky. Instead we must rely on different ways that the broad interests of the public may be known. Some sort of interest aggregation is necessary for policy to be successful; you have to not only find out what people want or need, but how much and for whom. It is a nontrivial problem, and policy analysts have not come with a perfect system to date.

Public opinion surveys

Sometimes the interests of the public can be collected broadly through surveys. A survey might ask people what they think the biggest problem facing the community is or if they favor or oppose a particular policy step. While this may seem like a simple and direct way to find out what the public wants or needs—just ask them—surveys in practice can be quite problematic.

One problem with surveys is that people answering them are offering a free opinion. There is no reason to answer accurately or truthfully. At times, people will answer a survey simply to "send a message" or they will answer in a way that they think is most likely to produce a survey result that they prefer. For example, a person asked how much they would have to be compensated to accept a sewage treatment plant in their neighborhood might respond, "100 million billion dollars," because they really don't want the sewage plant nearby. Or responses may be affected by an issue in the news that day. These kinds of unserious answers can distort the meaning of survey results.

Another survey problem is nonrandomness. A random (i.e., representative) survey costs money to conduct, and many surveys are "convenience samples." An example is a survey sent to everyone on a certain e-mail list. You may discover much about the policy interests of people on that list, but if those people do not represent the average person in the community, the information is skewed.

Finally, survey results can be very hard to interpret in terms of practical consequences. If a survey shows that the number 1 problem facing the community is "crime," that does not necessarily mean that the community would be in favor of having more police. Even specific policy questions, such as, "Do you favor policy X over policy Y?" can be distorted if the respondents do not have good information about the policies. One kind of bias is when you compare a policy that exists to one that is only hypothetical: "Do you prefer the current speed limit of 30 mph or a faster speed limit of 90 mph?" If people have not experienced what things would be like with a 90 mph speed limit, they must try to imagine it, and those imaginary pictures may be wrong.

Media

Another source of public interest information can come from media reports. Those who write stories about policy problems may be in touch with public interests, especially if they go out and directly do stories with lots of research. Unfortunately, such stories will always depend on a small number of interviews. You can never tell whether the people in the news story are really representative of the whole.

Another problem with media reports is that they are usually light on specifics and responses. They are helpful for discovering that people are unhappy but not what to do about it.

Nonetheless, the images projected through media are important to pay attention to because they can affect how other people feel about the policy.

Public commentary

Some policy processes involve open meetings where the public is invited to share their thoughts. In online communities, this sort of situation is always available on the forums related to the product or game.

Public commentary is extremely hard to evaluate and should be treated with caution. The people who speak at events and on forums are logically the most passionate and dedicated people about the topic. If the speakers represent a broader community, their opinions are informative. If they represent fringe groups, which is often the case, their opinion is not very important. Yet heated public commentary can, as with media, affect how the broader community feels about a policy.

As with the media, public commentary is not usually helpful in determining what to do. Even the most informed public commentators are unaware of the constraints that policymakers face. Often they discount costs that fall on others and highlight benefits that come to themselves.

Voting

Sometimes policy options are stated as direct questions on election ballots. While the act of voting is free, and so is subject to some of the possible biases of survey questions, the fact that people know their vote will become actual policy at least has a chance of making their responses more serious.

Voting also serves as interest aggregation when politicians represent policy platforms and then stand for election (see box 13.1. for a virtual example). The policies are often vague, however, and some politicians have been known to mislead the public about what they will actually support if they are elected.

Behavior

Behavior is like "voting with your feet" or "putting your money where your mouth is." Behavior is probably the best overall source of information on aggregate interests.

Box 13.1

Interest aggregation in *EVE Online*: The Council of Stellar Management

CCP Games has a unique approach to player interest aggregation. Every twelve months, *EVE*'s half a million players elect from among themselves a Council of Stellar Management that represents the views of the players to CCP. This fourteen-member council is empowered to bring players' wishes and grievances directly to the developers' attention through special online channels and regular physical meetings. To get their voice heard, individual players can petition council members on a forum provided for the purpose, support the election of candidates who share their views, and stand for election themselves. A degree of party politics based around in-game alliances also takes place. CCP gives the council credibility by showing that it takes its recommendations into account in its decision making, and also supports the council financially by flying its members to Reykjavik, Iceland, for physical meetings. The minutes of the meetings between the Council of Stellar Management and CCP are public.

This system of player representatives benefits CCP's developers in several ways. It deflects a great deal of the lobbying and hate mail that they would otherwise face themselves, but also gives the developers a good idea of what players want. It also functions as a sounding board for the developers' own ideas, and helps in winning players' support for new features and policies. It also appeases players by giving them an official process through which to vent their frustrations and express their dreams.

In October 2013, the council was in its eigth session and had advised CCP's developers on hundreds of issues and initiatives, ranging from small user interface fixes to major economic adjustments.

Behavior is not free, like survey answers, but costs real time and money to perform. Behavior is also a pattern that the entire community, not just a few reporters or public forum posters, creates.

It can usually be assumed that behavior moves toward things that most people like and away from things that most people dislike. Sudden interest in a product or service should result in an increase in profit for those who provide the product or service and an increase in its price and quantity too. Conversely, if people move away from something, the commerce that surrounds that thing will flatten and decay. Profits (and things like attendance, clicks, and likes) are a strong and reliable sign of aggregate interest.

The problem with behavior as a method of determining public interest is that it rarely says anything directly about policy options. For example, say the price of beans suddenly rises. That's a broad-based behavior, and it certainly says something genuine about the supply of and demand for beans in the community. With some investigation, you might be able to determine that the price rose because there was a sudden increase in the demand for beans. Does that mean anything for policy? It's not clear. Maybe people just like beans. Maybe the new price, while higher, is still "okay," that is, people can still get all the beans they need. Or perhaps the rush into bean buying happened because beans were discovered to be the only way to prevent a terrible illness. Just because you can observe broad behavioral surges in a population does not mean you can easily learn what to do about them, if anything.

Special interests

In any system of interest aggregation, the data from voting, public commentary, media, behavior, and the rest must be collected and then reported to the people who make the decisions. This is necessarily a bureaucratic and organizational process: someone is in charge of getting the data and then explaining what they mean. The people who do this interest aggregation will invariably become the target of people who have a special interest in the policy outcome. They will attempt to lobby for one outcome or another using every persuasive means at their disposal. Sometimes the information that a special interest brings to bear can be quite helpful. For example, a convenience survey may have overlooked an important population, and a representative of that population may enter the interest aggregation process through the media or public commentary, or through direct personal access to decision makers, to give voice to their concerns. Sometimes this can improve the information that decision makers have.

However, special interests are known to cause severe bias in information aggregation. One form of bias involves concentration of interest. Most policies affect some people more than others. Indeed, most times, a policy change hurts some people and helps others. How those helps and hurts are concentrated can have a huge effect on

Table 13.1
Examples of concentrated and diffused interest groups

Policy area	Concentrated interest group	Diffused interest group
Old age insurance	Retired and elderly persons	Working people
Defense spending	Defense industry employees	All citizens
Advanced game content	Elite gamers	Casual gamers
Social network design	Frequent contributors	Occasional visitors
Multiuser online environment	Current users	Potential users

whether policies get enacted. Policies that have large positive effects on a small group of people and small negative effects on a large group of people encourage the small group to organize quickly and speak out loudly in favor. Meanwhile, the vast majority of people perceive only a tiny cut to their well-being, so they say nothing. This creates a bias in policymaking if the decision makers pay too much attention to the people who speak the loudest (as they often do). Because of this bias, governing can become a process of handing out benefits to small, organized, vocal interest groups that are paid for by the large and disorganized mass of citizens. This may make policymakers popular with the small groups, but it is not healthy for the whole community. Possible examples are given in table 13.1.

A special problem in interest aggregation in games and online communities is that the current users of the system may not be representative of the users that the developer would like to attract to the system. For example, the early adopters of a new online game might be more dedicated gamers who prefer harder gameplay than those who arrive to the game later. If the developer adopts policies that favor this small segment, those policies might be unattractive to potential followers from other segments. In this case, listening to users will not help the system grow; on the contrary, it will prevent further growth.

There are three approaches to going around this pitfall. The first is to listen to the whole potential user base (the target group) instead of just the existing users. The problem with this is that people who have never tried the system will not be able to express their preferences accurately. The second approach is to listen to existing users, but give extra weight to the interests of the kinds of users that the developer would like to attract more of. The third approach is for designers to just use their intuition, in which case success depends on how well they are in tune with the needs of their target group. All three approaches come with one big risk: if the aggregation is unsuccessful, the system might not only fail to gain new users, but also lose its existing ones, since their preferences are sidelined.

Policy process

Despite all the difficulties in interest aggregation, policymakers usually can gather some credible information about what the public wants them to do. The next question is, How should the new rules and mechanics be designed?

Do you involve the users?

One form of policy process, common in the game industry, is to go into a room, close the doors, and design whatever systems you wish. This policy is then tested and released. Governments, however, have learned to involve the citizens in policymaking. While this muddies the policymaking process considerably, it has some undeniable advantages.

Citizens are involved in offline policymaking in several ways. First, in most countries, the citizens have a voice in determining who the policymakers are (or who their bosses will be). Democratic governance systems ensure that policymakers who design policies in ways that citizens dislike will eventually lose their jobs. A similar process exists for designers of for-profit community economies: if the policies are bad, people vote with their feet and leave. The problem with electing policy designers is that often the people on the design team represent very different groups of people and have very different ideas about what should be done. Policies come out looking like sausage.

Citizens are sometimes more directly involved in drafting new policies. Public meetings are sometimes held at which draft regulations can be commented on and suggestions made. This would be like rolling out a new design specification to the public and soliciting feedback from forums.

Testing

Game companies are famous for testing new policies before implementing them. This is perhaps the best way to make user interest a central part of the policymaking process. When you test a new system, the people who enter it are exhibiting genuine behavior, not answering surveys about hypothetical situations. At the same time, the users are not able to confuse or distort the process of policy design.

The best way to test a policy is to make an exact copy of the environment and subject it to one small change of policy. Let a random sample of the population play that experimental environment for a substantial amount of time. Survey this population about their satisfaction or record data about their expenditures, time use, and so on. If the experimental group exhibits energy, excitement, and enthusiasm, the policy has worked well. This kind of testing where different user groups are exposed to slightly different versions of a feature or a service is called A/B testing or split testing.[1]

1. For advice on how to implement A/B testing, see Kohavi et al. (2009).

Policy implementation

Policy scientists have discovered that the implementation of policy is often overlooked as an element in an overall successful policy plan. To the naive policymaker, implementation is "detail." It turns out that these details often matter significantly.

As an example, Pressman and Wildavsky analyzed the implementation of a plan to "Save the City of Oakland" immediately following riots there in the late 1960s.[2] National politicians were enthusiastic about bringing new jobs and new hope to the blighted, run-down neighborhoods that were the center of the problems. They quickly voted a great deal of money to a program of public works. They then turned the program over to bureaucrats for implementation. These officials had to decide who was going to get the money and for doing what. There was no system in place in Oakland for deciding what kind of public works needed to be done. There was no way to know if the people who got the money would use it to hire people from the bad neighborhoods. These and many other informational and organizational problems prevented the money from being spent in any useful way for a period of several years. During that time, the urban problems that caused the riot remained unsolved. The story of "Save Oakland" is a good cautionary tale about the need to be careful about how a policy will actually be done.

Communication

In virtual environments, a major cause of policy success or failure has nothing to do with policy design and everything to do with expectations. If people expect a rule change to greatly hurt them, they will raise a tremendous cry about it. If the success of a policy requires that people basically go along with it, this kind of public opposition can cause severe problems. For example, perhaps a game world wants to create a new way of grouping for dungeon content. A rumor goes around that the new system does not work. When the new system is launched, no one uses it because they'd "heard" that the system was broken. The few people who do try it out report that they can't find a group. The system is not broken in fact, but because the rumors have driven all the potential group members away, it seems broken. So nobody uses it.

Expectations can be managed only through communication. A policy must be explained well in order to succeed. It must be justified. Concerns of damaged groups must be addressed. Descriptions of likely consequences should be offered. Inaccurate rumors should be squashed. All of this must be done without the policymakers becoming defensive or argumentative. This can be difficult if the policymakers are not elected representatives but rather owners of the world. Owners may resent the fact that users are complaining about "their" world. The users may not technically have the "right" to complain, but complain they will, and it is no fun to be a dictator of an empty world.

---

2. Pressman and Wildavsky (1984).

As a result, most policymaking bodies put great effort into communicating their policies to the public in honestly, simply, and accurately.

Execution

Actually doing the policy is also tricky. Overnight surprises are generally a bad idea. If there is a need to reduce the number of rooms each user is able to build on their house, the way to do this is not to have a tornado suddenly appear and destroy every house with more than five rooms. While such methods might save the policymaker from having to listen to complaints and suggestions in advance and might be fun to watch, it destroys the trust of users who now can have no faith that you won't change everything again tomorrow.

Policies that affect lots of people should be enacted on all of them at the same time to avoid accusations of unfairness. And, needless to say, the execution of the policy should be considered part of the policy itself. If credits or gold are to be given out, or prices changed, or zoning restricted, the specifics of all of these changes need to be determined before any part of the policy is executed.

Policy assessment

Careful assessment of past policies is a crucial element of a successful policymaking process. It may sometimes be the case that a policy "obviously didn't work," but such coarse judgments are often not very helpful. If you're rejecting only policies that apparently didn't work, you're leaving in place all bad policies whose negative consequences were not very obvious. Moreover, by relying only on the obvious, you're not open to the possibility that the "obvious" negatives might have been outweighed by some not-so-obvious positives.

Careful scientific approaches to policy assessment help decision makers see the effects that are not so obvious. They also are an important planning tool. A designer who has a good command of ex post policy assessment is in a better position to use those same tools to predict the likely effects of future policies.

The tool kit for policy assessment can include a wide variety of statistical and analytical methods, but all of these methods should focus on three kinds of indexes: what the effects are, who they hit, and when they happened.

Benefit-cost analysis

Benefit-cost analysis (BCA) is a method for quantifying the good and bad effects of any policy decision. The basic BCA protocol is to:

- Enumerate: List all of the consequences of a policy
- Quantify: Measure the effects of each consequence in terms of dollars
- Combine: Add the benefits and subtract the costs to get an overall impact number.

The overall impact number is called the net benefit (NB) of the policy. If the benefits greatly exceeded the costs, the policy worked. If the costs exceeded the benefits, the policy failed. If the benefits and costs are close, then the policy was neutral. The NB number gives decision makers an unbiased assessment of what really happened; it is a powerful weapon against special interest claims.

The overall impact number is not the main source of value in doing a BCA, however. Designers can obtain a great deal of clarity about their policies simply by the enumeration step, listing all of the things the policy will do. The enumeration part can be much harder than it looks. Suppose I reduce the drop rate on copper ore in my economy. The first effect of this is a reduction of productivity among those who harvest: it takes them more time to get their ore. But this primary effect causes all kinds of second- and third- and fourth-order effects. The price of copper ore will rise. The prices of things that are built with copper ore will rise. People who make items using copper ore will see their profits fall. And so on. Thankfully there is a general rule to follow here: count only the first effect. You should not count secondary effects of a policy. The reason is that these secondary effects all wash one another out: the people who make things with copper ore do pay more for the ore, but they pass that cost on to their customers. All of the secondary effects are, in fact, the passing on of the initial hit to the economy. The initial hit to the economy, and the creation of the cost that is being passed on, occurs at the first effect: the reduction of harvesting productivity of copper ore harvesters. By thinking hard about the mere enumeration of effects, designers can have a better handle on what those effects really are.

Quantification is also an important step. In principle, every effect should be quantified. In practice, many effects of policies are hard to quantify or simply cannot be. At times, special quantification methods may be needed. In the offline world, economists and policy analysts have developed numerous methods for quantifying seemingly unquantifiable things. For example, you can quantify the dollar value of cleaner air by measuring the difference in price between equivalent houses in towns with clean or poor air. You can value the economic cost of an injury by doing a statistical analysis of lost earnings. You can discover something about the value of a public park by having people imagine that the park had an entrance fee and then asking them how much they would be willing to pay to go in. By these and similar methods, scientists have developed methods for quantifying many seemingly intangible effects of policies.

Once again, the mere act of explicitly attempting to quantify something is itself valuable for a decision maker. The special interests will claim that there is some terrible effect of a policy; if so, any reasonable quantifying method should produce a large cost number. Representatives of the special interest have every incentive to cook the process so as to produce a big negative, but even in doing that, the special interests give the decision maker a way to make a reasonable assessment. Methods can be good, or bad, or just plain crazy. Well-trained neutral experts can fairly easily judge whether a measurement method is genuine or hocus-pocus. The decision maker can see which special interests are making serious arguments and which ones are just blowing hot air. By forcing the special interests to make their argument in the form of assessable measurements rather than emotional appeals in words the policymaker has a better chance of coming to the right decision.

Quantification is also an important step for decision makers to decide what it is they really care about. Throughout this discussion, it is assumed that the decision makers care mostly about the dollar value of effects on users. This is indeed the kind of metric you want to use if your goal is to increase the overall well-being of the people in your system. It could be thought of as the best way of measuring whether your environment is going to be long-run successful: an economy that produces positive net benefits for its members will succeed in the long run. However, some economy builders may want to target different goals, such as the net revenue earned by the builder. Or the benefits and costs may be enumerated in terms of some social objective, such as exposure to a certain work of art or commitment of funds to a political candidate. The same BCA protocol can be applied in these cases, but the quantification step is different.

Finally, adding everything up is in itself valuable. Arguments in words tend to make every effect seem equal. So, for example, proponents of a new railway might say that it will:

1. Increase trade

Opponents might counter that the railway will:

1. Increase accidents
2. Increase noise pollution
3. Displace homes
4. Displace wildlife

This simple listing seems to tilt the decision against the railway. Suppose, however, that the BCA analyst comes up with these numbers:

Benefits
1. Increase trade: +$7,200 million

Costs
1. Increase accidents: −$3 million
2. Increase noise pollution: −$5 million
3. Displace homes: −$9 million
4. Displace wildlife: −$20 million

Even if we take account of the displacement of people and animals from their homes, these costs are completely swamped (in this hypothetical example) by the benefits to be had by everyone else in the increase in trade. The difference is so big that it seems very unlikely that even the most generous assessment of the cost calculations, with every assumption tilted in their favor, would produce a cost number that approaches the trade benefit in gross magnitude.

In the three steps of enumerating, quantifying, and combining, BCA gives the policymaking process much more detailed information about what is happening. BCA can also be used in advance to try to estimate the net effects of a future policy. In some cases, the final outcome of the BCA, the net benefit number, may even be the key part of a decision. Some builders may want to enact every policy that passes a BCA and reject all those that fail. Doing this is usually not advisable, however. The bottom line of a BCA is not nearly as informative as the process that created it. Moreover, there are circumstances in which a net-negative policy makes sense. For example, suppose some group in your world has had a very hard time of it, with all kinds of unpleasant things happening to them. You might want to do something to provide some support or a reward. For example, your intervention might involve a price increase in something that this group often sells. A BCA will probably determine that the total cost of the price increase on other people in the society is higher than the benefit the target users receive. You may still want to go through with the policy; the BCA tells you, however, how much it costs *other people* for you to go ahead. In fact, you may want to consider three or four different ways of helping the target population and use BCA to decide which one offers the most benefit for the least cost—the most bang for the buck.

Incidence

One of the most important pieces of information from a BCA is in fact this information about who is being affected. The "who" of a policy effect is called its *incidence*. Incidence usually makes no difference to the bottom line of a BCA, but it can make a huge difference in the politics of the policy and its eventual success. We have already described the way that a policy with concentrated benefits and spread-out costs can result in vocal special interests badgering the decision maker in favor of the policy.

The reverse also holds. A policy whose benefits are spread widely among a group of people but whose costs are targeted to a few is sure to generate loud opposition. This will happen even if the net benefits of the policy are huge. Suppose, for example, that a change to the auction house will make it a little easier for everyone in the world to do their trading but will also destroy profit opportunities for the small number of users who like to do day trading on the auction house as their main form of play. The traders will be up in arms about the change, while supporters will be few and far between. It may still be the right policy, but the political challenge is very much harder than it would be for a policy with broader incidence of costs.

Dealing with incidence is a matter of politics, and BCA has a role to play here as well. Incidence, as determined by a BCA, should be part of the communication strategy. In the example, the world's user community could be informed fully of the measured incidence data. This admits honestly that traders will be harmed. But it allows everyone to compare the costs of the traders to the much larger benefits everyone else receives. The designers thus have a chance to emerge from the policy change with a reputation for taking care of all their users. BCAs and incidence analysis help world owners from seeming to be capricious dictators.

Incidence analysis also allows builders to engage the community in a dialog about compensation for policy changes. Perhaps in the above case, a deal could be struck whereby the traders get some percentage of the auction house proceeds to restore their profit margins. This has the effect of diverting some of the benefit of the change from all players back to the traders, somewhat reducing the nasty politics of targeted cost and diffuse benefit. Society as a whole still shows net benefits, but the traders get to share a bit more in the benefit and a bit less in the cost.

Time effects

Another dimension of policy assessment in general and BCA in particular involves time. There will be policies that have a disjointed time structure in costs and benefits. A city that builds a new stadium will pay a lot of costs at the start and then reap benefits over the course of many years. A foundation that takes a big chunk of its endowment to pay for a huge celebration will enjoy a big benefit now and a cost that runs over many years in the form of reduced endowment income.

BCA analysts borrow from the world of finance to deal with time issues. The core concept is *present value* (PV). PV is the value today of a stream of effects that run into the future. At the simplest level, this is about adding up the effects in future years and comparing them to the effects in the current year. In the stadium example, let's say the stadium costs $50 million to build this year, but produces a benefit of $5 million every year for twenty years. If we add up the benefits, we get $100 million, which is higher than the cost.

However, just adding up future effects is incorrect. The PV has to take into account two extremely important aspects of the future.

1. The future is unknown.
2. The future is not today.

Both of these aspects reduce the value of future effects. The unpredictably of the future means that future consequences may be very different than the estimate suggests. What if the stadium is built on a fault line? If there is a chance that an earthquake will destroy the stadium, then the probable benefit of the stadium is going to get lower and lower as the years pass. If the probability of a disaster is just 5 percent, the likelihood that the stadium will even be there twenty years from now is much less than half. This means you cannot count the twentieth-year benefit as $5 million. It should be less than half that amount.

Even if there are no future risks to a project, the distance of the future *in the future* is still an issue. An apple tomorrow is worth less to me than an apple today. The reason is simple: I can go ahead and eat today's apple, but I can't eat tomorrow's apple. I have to wait until tomorrow. And waiting is costly.

The offline economy puts a price on waiting, called the interest rate. The interest rate is what a bank will pay you to set your money aside and wait to use it until later. The existence of interest rates in the economy shows that time is indeed money. Because of this, however, BCA effects in future years are worth less than BCA effects right now. BCA analysts (and experts in finance) use a concept called *discounting* to adjust downward the value of future effects. If the annual interest rate is 3 percent, it means that a dollar next year is worth 3 percent less than one right now. Therefore, a BCA effect that happens in a year counts for 3 percent less than its face value. BCA effects happening in years further out are further reduced. This is not the place to get into the formulas, but the basic notion of discounting is important for everyone involved in economic policy to understand.

As a general rule, a decision maker would be well served by an assumption that effects more than ten years in the future have to be quite large to have any meaning for decisions made today. If those future effects are quite large, then it would make sense to consult with experts in finance and BCA to come up with more precise numbers.

Policy and game testing

Policymaking is its own science. It combines design knowledge with economics and politics. The design element makes the rules, the economic element quantifies the impacts of the rules, and the political element communicates the effects to the users. The professional field of policy analysis has existed for more than 100 years and its studies have shown again and again that a "fire and forget" approach to making changes is unlikely to lead to long-run success. Experts in the game industry and the software development industry have learned many of the same lessons and therefore insist that users be a critical part of new product development. The future of policy analysis may lie in combining the insights of past policy experts with the user-centered approach of software developers. A repeated BCA of a policy that has been tested in many different formats and populations would be more informative than a BCA alone or a test alone.[3]

3. To learn more about user-centered design in modern online business, see Johnson (2013).

The global economy is in trouble. Besides constant financial crises, stagnation, unemployment, and poverty, the economy is starting to face an even graver set of problems: dwindling natural resources and a looming global environmental disaster. The International Panel on Climate Change estimates that in order to avoid a catastrophic level of global warming, we need to cut global carbon emissions not by a quarter, not even by half, but by up to 85 percent over 1990 levels by 2050.[1] Even before that deadline, we are likely to see more and more wars and struggles over increasingly scarce natural resources, such as oil, rare earth metals, and even clean water. Here's the rub: our methods for solving the first set of problems exacerbate the second set of problems, and vice versa. The harder we drive our economy to grow, the closer to collapse we push our ecology. The more we protect our environment, the harder it is for the economy to grow and create prosperity. The solution to this dilemma seems nowhere in sight. As we write this, Canada has just pulled out of the Kyoto Protocol, and the world's economic leaders are in disarray.

In the history of economic studies and policies, there is a well-known pattern where a crisis in the real economy results in a change in the dominant approach used to comprehend it. The Great Depression of the 1930s resulted in neoclassical dogma being replaced with Keynesian economics. The oil crisis of the 1970s resulted in the Keynesian system being scrapped in favor of monetary economics. The latest and perhaps gravest global economic conundrum yet in terms of potential consequences has ignited a similar shakedown. On the one hand, the current economic mainstream is blamed for causing frequent crises and uneven growth around the world. On the other hand, it is denounced for locking us in on a path of infinite growth on a finite planet.

The outcome of this turmoil remains out of sight, but many leading economists believe that at least one aspect of the solution needs to be a more humane understanding of the economy. Nobel laureate George Akerlof and Yale economist Robert Shiller express this need as follows:

1. IPCC (2007).

To understand how economies work and how we can manage them and prosper, we must pay attention to the thought patterns that animate people's ideas and feelings. . . .We will never really understand important economic events unless we confront the fact that their causes are largely mental in nature.[2]

While poverty and pollution are certainly tangible phenomena, our economy that gives rise to them is ultimately the work of human minds. The hope is that by developing a better understanding of this human aspect of the economy, we could find ways to overcome or circumvent the current paradigm, which places economic prosperity on a collision course with ecological survival.

In the remainder of this chapter, we are going to be so bold as to suggest that insights to the global economy's perils might be drawn from virtual economies—that is, to apply orc economics to the real world. What could virtual economies possibly teach the real economy? After all, in a virtual economy, poverty and pollution are easy to tackle: just create things out of thin air and destroy them without a trace. But there is one thing that both types of economies share: people. The same people who make decisions in virtual economies make decisions in the global economy. If there is anything that we can learn about the mental nature of economic events in virtual economies, then those learnings should be transferable to the real economy.

You could argue that many people act differently in virtual economies, taking more risks, acting more on intuition, and maximizing short-term benefits more than in business or at work, and you would be right. But these are all differences of degree rather than kind. In empirical studies, we have found no discrepancies in the fundamentals of economic behavior in virtual and real settings, and indeed there are no theoretical reasons to expect any.[3] Thus, in the following sections, we make observations about the mental and social underpinnings of virtual economic phenomena and consider their implications for the global economy. To be fair, almost any such underpinnings have already been recognized by at least some social scientist somewhere. What we can do here is to help reaffirm and highlight the important ones and provide readers with a way to use their newly acquired virtual economic knowledge to understand where the real global economy is headed.

Economic institutions as consumable goods

In chapter 2, we told you that in virtual economies, economic activities are not just means to an end; they can also be ends in themselves. People don't produce virtual

2. Akerlof and Shiller (2009, p. 1).
3. Castronova et al. (2009a, 2009b). Note that we are not claiming that computer-mediated social interaction is no different from face-to-face interaction. This is not an issue of digital versus physical interaction. Both virtual and real online shopping and stock trading are computer mediated. The issue is whether the human decision-making apparatus somehow changes when the good is a virtual item instead of a digital stock. It doesn't.

goods just to earn a profit, as mainstream economic theory posits. They do it because they enjoy producing things, or because it is part of their role, or because they feel that it boosts their social status. In other words, the economic process is itself an end, a consumable good. A theory that doesn't account for this fact will fail to explain the participants' behavior.

The real economy is of course no game. When people's real income is at stake, they will certainly focus on the profit and regard economic institutions as mere tools, not as ends in themselves. Or will they? Let's take an example: stock markets. In Finland, almost a third of all households directly own stocks.[4] Thanks to the rise of online trading platforms, it has become very common for investors to actively manage their stock portfolio, that is, to actively buy and sell stocks. The ostensible goal of such investment activities is profit. According to financial theory, investors aim to maximize their value by choosing the best alternatives in light of expected return, risk, and personal risk tolerance.

There's a problem in applying this theory to practice. For most people, active stock trading is a terrible strategy for maximizing value. Studies of active traders show that on average, they perform significantly worse than the market.[5] In other words, their returns can be beaten simply by buying and holding a weighted average of the stock market. In one study, the most active traders underperformed the market by a whopping 5 percentage points, leading the researchers to conclude that "trading is hazardous to your wealth."[6]

Poor performance stems from the way active traders behave. They prefer to invest directly in individual stocks instead of diversifying their investments through mutual funds. They shift positions frequently, racking up transaction fees. They also trade speculatively, which means that they take bigger risks. And in many cases they may well do all this despite knowing that it is likely to result in poor performance. Researchers have sought to explain this behavior with behavioral economics, positing that certain biases and flaws in human decision making could cause perfectly profit-seeking individuals to go systematically down the wrong path.

Our observations from virtual economies suggest a complementary explanation: that the stock market is not merely a means to pursue profits but itself a consumable good that provides value to traders independent of any profits. This explanation is supported by a recent series of studies that for the first time sought to explore individual investors' motivations outside the finance-theoretical frame.[7] The studies showed that contrary to financial theory, financial value is not the only thing that investors seek. They are also motivated by, among other things, the positive emotions that they

4. Finnish Foundation for Share Promotion survey conducted in 2011.

5. See, for example, Barber et al. (2009) and Barber and Odean (2000).

6. Barber and Odean (2000).

7. Puustinen (2012).

experience from trading, such as enjoyment, thrills, and excitement, as well as by how investing activities contribute to their self-esteem and image toward others. In other words, the economic activity of investing is also a consumable good in itself, like a game or a sport.

Through this perspective, the investors' rather odd behavior suddenly becomes understandable. Investing in stocks directly rather than through a mutual fund is a bid to position oneself as an independent-minded person or even an expert. Taking big risks is a way to seek thrills, in the same way gamblers do. And excessive trading naturally follows from the desire to enjoy the game frequently. The damage that these choices do to the investor's financial performance can be seen as the cost of this entertainment in money. Buying and holding an average portfolio might be financially prudent, but it's also inescapably boring.

What are the implications of adopting this kind of a gaming perspective to the real economy? New angles are opened up in financial marketing, forecasting, and, not least, in regulation. Consider the following example. A bank where we have a checking account advertises an investment product structured as follows: if at the end of the investment term, the stock prices of three unrelated companies—China Construction Bank, McDonalds, and a small insurance company—are higher than at the beginning of the term, the investor gains a bonus interest. But if even one stock closes below its initial price, the bonus interest is forfeit and the investor loses money in real terms. From a financial perspective, this product makes no sense. It's like betting on dice— roll a six and you win. In the end, the only winner is likely to be the house. But from the perspective of the psychology and sociology of gaming, the product makes a lot of sense: it allows buyers to feel some of the prestige associated with having an interest in how stock market prices develop, it provides them with the thrill of risk taking, and so on.

Indeed, products designed similar to our bank's product are also offered by gaming companies, only under different names. At least one online casino allows betting on stock market indexes, which is pretty much the same thing our bank offers. And like gaming companies, banks are now starting to offer their products as mobile apps, because that's where the users are. Yet despite these similarities, banks and gaming companies are regulated very differently. Financial regulation, drawing on financial theory, simply seeks to ensure that products are accurately described and leaves the choice up to consumers, who are assumed to be rational decision makers. Gambling regulation, drawing on studies of addiction, tends to prohibit the same kinds of games outright, no matter how accurately they are described. This is not the place to argue which approach is better. There are no simple answers. The point here is that by looking at our economy as we do a virtual economy, it becomes possible to see through established categories and labels and recognize institutions for what they are, whether you are a regulator or an individual player.

Know what you measure

Now let's move upward from individual institutions to say something about the mental and social underpinnings of the entire macroeconomy. In chapter 12, we talked about economic indicators in a virtual economy. Among other indicators, we introduced the gross virtual product (GVP), which measures the total value of virtual goods produced in a virtual economy as measured in virtual currency. Gross virtual product is the virtual counterpart of the gross domestic product (GDP), which measures the total value of production in a national economy. Despite measuring similar things, these two indicators are used in very different ways in economic management. In a game economy, managers try to keep the GVP per capita relatively stable. In a national economy, policymakers do everything they can to keep the GDP per capita in constant growth. It turns out that by analyzing this difference, we can tease out some interesting facts about today's macroeconomic fundamentals.

GDP is probably the most closely followed economic indicator among economists and policymakers. It is an important measure, because it reflects a nation's ability to provision for the material needs of its population. Nations that produce a lot relative to their population are able to provision for their inhabitants better than nations that produce little. Policymakers mindful of their nation's prosperity consequently try to maximize GDP, sometimes even when doing so is at odds with ecological sustainability. Another reason that GDP matters is that nations with a high productive capacity have an edge in wars, as they can churn out more bombs than their rivals can. This type of production obviously does not contribute to addressing human needs; in the worst case, it adds to them.

GVP doesn't measure material provision. It measures the provision of virtual goods, the uses of which are mental and social in nature. We discussed these uses in chapter 3. Virtual goods are used to fulfill personal whims, establish identity positions, and communicate values. They are used to constitute and take part in perpetual fashion cycles and races for social status and decency—keeping up with the J'Kars (akin to keeping up with the Joneses in the world of the fantastical). They are used to overcome virtual dangers and challenges, for which evolution rewards us with feelings of relief and satisfaction.

The important thing about all these benefits is that they are not necessarily increased by increasing provisioning. More powerful items can make virtual challenges too easy. Greater quantities can make status goods worthless. Every novel frivolity is a potential chink in our virtual self-image that needs to be mended. For these reasons, the relationship between virtual production and user satisfaction can be modeled as a parabolic curve: up to a certain point, production and satisfaction increase together, but after that, additional increases in production will begin to detract from satisfaction instead of adding to it. Virtual economy managers know this, and that is why they try to keep their GVP relatively stable per capita instead of maximizing it (in the long run match-ing it with depreciation). Maximizing virtual goods production would be easy: just reprogram the system to produce ten or a million times as many goods as before. But the resulting economy wouldn't satisfy anyone.

So real-world policymakers seek to maximize GDP because it measures material production that can alleviate poverty, while virtual economists seek to stabilize GVP because it measures virtual production that caters to social and mental uses. But here's the next question: To what extent is GDP really a measure of material production? To what extent has it actually become a measure of virtual production, especially in postindustrial societies? Here are a few examples of activities that help make up the global GDP today: production and sales of artificially scarce brand items, development of ever new varieties of ice cream and soda, production and sales of Twitter followers and Facebook likes, and sales of treadmills with graphics that simulate real walks.

It is clear that many people in the world's richest countries today live in a more or less virtual economy, where our well-being is no longer constrained by any material lack or need but is rather tied to the mental pleasures, anxieties, and status games of consumerism. In such a situation, increases in GDP represent not so much relief from need and suffering, but increases in the availability of signs and symbols, just as with GVP. And just as with GVP, increases past a certain point will do little to increase our well-being. This idea is supported by empirical studies in the budding field of happiness economics.[8] Cross-country comparisons, longitudinal studies of individual countries, and surveys of individual people all suggest that increases in production and income increase happiness only up to a certain point.[9] By looking at what happens inside vir-tual economies, we can get a good sense of the social and psychological mechanisms that explain why this should be so.

In virtual economies, GVP is not a very prominent measure, certainly nothing like GDP. Most virtual economy managers don't even calculate GVP, as balancing can be achieved via simpler means. Instead, they consider it much more important to keep a close eye on indicators that reflect user interestedness and satisfaction. In the same way, social scientists are developing new measures to track the health and progress of real societies. The GDP was developed in the United States to help policymakers steer the country through two major crises, the Great Depression and World War II. It replaced earlier measures like tons of steel produced and number of railroad boxcars rolled out, which reflected the needs of the industrial revolution. Now the economy has moved on, and an update to the measures is due again.

8. See Layard (2006) for an introduction to this field. Given how fundamental a concept happi-ness is, it is striking that social scientists have only quite recently started serious attempts to measure it.

9. Inglehart et al. (2008), Easterlin et al. (2010), Kahneman and Deaton (2010).

The end of materialism?

Even if our national economies are already highly virtual in the sense that our uses for goods and our reasons for participating in economic institutions are largely mental and social in nature, their environmental impact is still very real. We use the planet's expendable resources to create a mind-boggling variety of symbolic goods. We turn those goods into waste as soon as they have lost their symbolic value, even if they remain functionally intact. We aspire to expand our economic institutions even when they are already beyond what can be sustained. And so the cycle continues. Ecological economists implicate consumerism as a major driver of unsustainable economic practices.[10]

There are some signs that the warning has been heard and things are changing. During the past decade, carbon emissions in developed countries stopped growing and even turned into a small decline. But this decline is still too small and in large part illusory, as many polluting activities have simply been outsourced to developing countries. Global carbon emissions continue to increase in pace with the GDP. Perhaps a more fundamental sign of hope is that social scientists are reporting a decline of materialistic values in Western countries, especially in the rich Northern Europe.[11] People in Finland are no longer compelled to assert themselves through luxury handbags in quite the same way as people do now in emerging China. Focus has shifted more toward free time, family, and health. Could the solution to the economic-environmental dilemma be that we simply give up the use of goods for frivolous symbolic purposes, reducing the economy to a simple life support system?

There are two major problems with this notion. One is that our capitalist economic system is predicated on growth. Stagnation, let alone significant reductions in the size of the economy for whatever reasons, would result in massive unemployment. Others have argued convincingly that services and cultural activities alone cannot sustain growth and employment.[12] The growing goods economy is what keeps money flowing in today's world. It is one thing to say that in many places, this economy no longer contributes to increased human welfare and an entirely different matter to come up with a way of changing it without forfeiting everything that is good about it. Still, through either policy or crisis, economic systems do change. Perhaps virtual economies and alternative digital currencies turn out to be catalysts of such change.

10. Jackson (2009). Tim Jackson is an influential British environmental economist. A key thesis in his book, *Prosperity without Growth: Economics for a Finite Planet*, is that "prosperity—in any meaningful sense of the word—transcends material concerns."
11. Inglehart (1997).
12. Jackson (2009).

The second and more fundamental problem with the notion of a postmaterialistic life support economy is that using goods as a system of signification may be an essential feature of human society. Although our full-blown consumer society is a relatively recent invention, archeological and anthropological studies show that to a greater or lesser extent, goods have always been a part of human culture. Right across history and culture, goods have been imbued with symbolic meanings and fetishized beyond their utilitarian purposes. Goods have been a language through which people not only communicate with each other but also articulate their concept of self to themselves. Perhaps this should not be surprising, given that humans developed into conscious beings in a world full of material objects. But it means that asking someone to give up consumption for symbolic purposes may be like asking them to give up an innate psychological process. The relative emphasis on goods and consumption may fluctuate with socioeconomic conditions and currently seems in decline in some parts of the world even as it grows in others. But the notion of an entirely postmaterialistic culture may be impossible.

Human attachment to material culture is vividly illustrated by the brief history of cyberspace. Author William Gibson famously coined the term in 1982 to describe the graphical representation of data as a space where users roam. Digital theorists like John Perry Barlow adopted the term to real digital environments and predicted that since cyberspace was not restricted by material scarcity, a postmaterialistic society would arise. In his *A Declaration of the Independence of Cyberspace*, Barlow wrote:

Your legal concepts of property . . . do not apply to us. They are all based on matter, and there is no matter here. . . . In our world, whatever the human mind may create can be reproduced and distributed infinitely at no cost. The global conveyance of thought no longer requires your factories to accomplish.[13]

Today, decades later, virtual spaces somewhat similar to Gibson's cyberspace have indeed emerged, and some come close in scale and population to what he envisioned. But contrary to Barlow's declaration, all of these spaces, barring some marginal ones, retain the concept of property by introducing artificial scarcity. In fact, it seems almost as if scarcity and the ability to own something is a prerequisite for a virtual environment to become popular. Completely open-ended 3D environments have been developed, but they have failed to attract users. Outside the literal space metaphor, in text and 2D visual communication, Barlow's declaration has been much more successful. But even in discussion forums, social networking sites and two-dimensional online communities, different kinds of virtual property, from points to badges, are on the increase rather than declining. It is as if scarcity was a missing feature that is only now

13. Barlow (1996).

being reinvented. Perhaps some aspects of our sociability and personality, developed in the physical world, do after all require the trappings of materiality for their full conveyance.

However, the material culture of virtual spaces does differ from conventional material culture in one crucial aspect: ecological impact. Digital networks and hardware obviously do have an ecological footprint, by some estimates as large as air travel. The constant cycle of new hardware replacing functional but obsolete devices is no more sustainable than throwaway consumerism in general. But the cycle of virtual consumerism that takes place inside virtual environments is different. New virtual goods can be created, used, and, when their symbolic value runs out, dumped—all with practically no marginal impact on the environment at all. If we so desire, we can speed up the cycle of consumerism almost indefinitely, and yet its ecological impact will stay the same. In other words, in virtual economies, we have for the first time managed to decouple economic growth from ecological impact.

Here may lie our biggest hope for solving the economy-ecology dilemma. If we fail to transform the global economic system or simply find ourselves too addicted to consumerism, then at least we might be able to virtualize it. As we noted above, huge portions of the economy are already virtual in the sense that they serve uses that are purely mental in nature. All that is needed is to take this virtualization to its conclusion of replacing the material markers used in today's consumption games with digital ones. In fact, this process may already be underway. As people spend more and more of their time on digital networks, the personal and social significance of virtual possessions and achievements increases, while at least the relative significance of physical possessions decreases. When one of us was young, the boys in the neighborhood used to brag to each other about their action figures. Today they brag about their *World of Warcraft* avatars. Some judgments that were previously made based on a person's attire or automobile are now based on their choice of operating system. Consumption and leisure time activities that are considered worthwhile are becoming increasingly virtualized.

This prediction does not mean that in the future we will all sit behind our desks and interact only through virtual environments. Mobile and augmented reality technologies are already bringing virtual economies in the form of games and social media applications into everyday social situations. Even if we would prefer it didn't, the hardware upgrade cycle will no doubt still continue long enough to ensure that tabletops, other surfaces, and perhaps even clothing materials will soon be connected to the Net. The digital world is intertwined with everyday life, and virtual economies are just as present in everyday experience as the material economy. In this situation, perhaps our consumerist status games and markers can finally become just that: compelling games that need not have any material impact on the world.

How the virtual informs the real

We sense that the possibilities we have just raised are merely a preamble to much bigger changes that information technology will bring. When a hurricane is coming, the wind rises, hour by hour. Tracking the effects of these changes on the larger society is one last area in which virtual economies may have a role to play. This can happen in several ways.

Basic research in the economic and social sciences is beginning to use data from virtual worlds. Dmitri Williams of the University of Southern California acquired data from the game *EverQuest II* and made it available to scholarly researchers from many disciplines. To date, more than thirty academic papers have been produced from this data set, including an article in the world's leading sociological journal.[14] One of us (Lehdonvirta) similarly negotiated access to *EVE Online*'s data, which has so far been used in at least five academic papers. For instance, Juha Tolvanen at the Helsinki Institute for Information Technology is using the *EVE* data to study a difficult problem in insurance markets: distinguishing between moral hazard and adverse selection. Outside virtual economies, data sufficiently comprehensive for addressing this problem are simply not available. Virtual economies are allowing scholars to do research that previously was not possible. They may yet be used to discover important foundational truths about human behavior and society.[15]

Moreover, game and social media developers are themselves busy conducting research. The people who run virtual economies are developing their own methods of analyzing them, and those methods often are indistinguishable from basic research. As a result, we would not be surprised if virtual economists came to important discoveries about economics and society in general in the course of their private analysis of their own economies. At this moment, thousands and thousands of companies and private individuals own pocket communities, and they have every incentive to improve them. The power of this incentive shows in the breathtaking advances in game metrics and social media data analysis that we have seen in just the past few years. All of this experimentation and innovation is bound to produce discoveries about human behavior and society. It is only a matter of time.

Fundamentals don't change

In writing this book, we have been ever-mindful of how rapidly many elements of the virtual world are changing and have attempted to focus on things we believe will not change. There is no likelihood, in our view, that the invisible hand will suddenly

14. Burt (2012).
15. See also Schroeder (2011, chapter 7).

cease to move prices. We do not expect people to stop caring about their goods and their wealth—virtual or tangible. We doubt very much that humanity will tire of its affection for trading and accumulating and comparing. We do not expect the world's economy to collapse into the trade of a few goods; rather, we expect the diversity of offerings to only grow. For the foreseeable future, there will be vast macroeconomies composed of hundreds of thousands of markets, driven by incentives and the evolution of human desire. These are the topics we sought to keep at the core of the book, because we are confident that knowing about them will always be a good thing, no matter how the winds blow.

References

Aarseth, Espen. 1997. *Cybertext: Perspectives on Ergodic Literature*. Baltimore, MD: Johns Hopkins University Press.

Akerlof, George A., and Robert J. Shiller. 2009. *Animal Spirits: How Human Psychology Drives the Economy, and Why It Matters for Global Capitalism*. Princeton, NJ: Princeton University Press.

Allais, Maurice. 1953. Le comportement de l'homme rationnel devant le risque: critique des postulats et axiomes de l'école Américaine. *Econometrica* 21 (4): 503–546.

Anderson, Chris. 2010. *Free: How Today's Smartest Businesses Profit by Giving Something for Nothing*. New York: Hyperion.

Ariely, Dan. 2009. *Predictably Irrational: The Hidden Forces That Shape Our Decisions*. London: HarperCollins.

Atkins, Barry. 2003. *More Than a Game: The Computer Game as Fictional Form*. Manchester, UK: Manchester University Press.

Au, W. James. 2010. *Snoop Dogg Sells $200K+ in Virtual Items, Demonstrating Value of Branded Goods*. http://socialtimes.com/snoop-dogg-sells-200k-in-virtual-items-demonstrating-value-of-branded-goods_b19293.

Balkin, Jack. 2004. Virtual Liberty: Freedom to Design and Freedom to Play in Virtual Worlds. *Virginia Law Review* 90 (8): 2043–2098.

Barber, Brad M., Yi-Tsung Lee, Yu-Jane Liu, and Terrance Odean. 2009. Just How Much Do Individual Investors Lose by Trading? *Review of Financial Studies* 22 (2): 609–632.

Barber, Brad M., and Terrance Odean. 2000. Trading Is Hazardous to Your Wealth: The Common Stock Investment Performance of Individual Investors. *Journal of Finance* 55 (2): 773–806.

Barlow, John Perry. 1996. A Declaration of the Independence of Cyberspace. http://homes.eff.org/~barlow/Declaration-Final.html.

Barnard, Malcolm. 2002. *Fashion as Communication*, 2nd ed. London: Routledge.

Bartle, Richard. 2003. *Designing Virtual Worlds*. San Francisco: New Riders Games.

Bauman, Richard. 1975. Verbal Art as Performance. *American Anthropologist,* 77 (2): 290–311.

Bauman, Zygmunt, and Tim May. 2001. *Thinking Sociologically,* 2nd ed. Oxford: Blackwell.

Belk, Russell W. 1995. *Collecting in a Consumer Society.* London: Routledge.

Belk, Russell W. 2004. The Human Consequences of Consumer Culture. In *Elusive Consumption,* edited by K. M. Ekström and H. Brembeck, 67–86. Oxford: Berg.

Bloomfield, Robert, and Young Jun Cho. 2011. Unregulated Stock Markets in Second Life. *Southern Economic Journal* 78 (1): 6–29.

Bogost, Ian. 2006. *Unit Operations: An Approach to Videogame Criticism.* Cambridge, MA: MIT Press.

Bollen, Johan, Huina Mao, and Xiao-Jun Zeng. 2011. Twitter Mood Predicts the Stock Market. *Journal of Computational Science* 2 (1): 1–8.

Bourdieu, Pierre. 1984. *Distinction: A Social Critique of the Judgment of Taste.* New York: Routledge.

Bourdieu, Pierre. 1998. *Practical Reason: On the Theory of Action.* Stanford: Stanford University Press.

Braithwaite, Brenda, and Ian Schreiber. 2008. *Challenges for Game Designers.* Newton Center, MA: Charles River Media.

Burt, Ronald. 2012. Network-Related Personality and the Agency Question: Multi-Role Evidence from a Virtual World. *American Journal of Sociology* 118 (3): 543–591.

Castronova, Edward. 2002. On Virtual Economies. *CESifo* working paper series no. 752. http://ssrn.com/abstract=338500.

Castronova Edward, Mark W. Bell, Marc Carlton, Robert Cornell, James J. Cummings, Will Emigh, Matthew Falk, Michael Fatten, Paul LaFourest, Nathan Mishler, Justin Reynard, Sarah Robbins, et al. 2009a. A Test of the Law of Demand in a Virtual World: Exploring the Petri Dish Approach to Social Science. *International Journal of Gaming and Computer-Mediated Simulations* 1(2): 1–16.

Castronova, Edward, and Joshua Fairfield. 2007. Dragon Kill Points: A Summary Whitepaper. http://dx.doi.org/10.2139/ssrn.958945

Castronova, Edward, Dmitri Williams, Yun Huang, Cuihua Shen, Brian Keegan, Rabindra Ratan, Li Xiong, and Noshir Contractor. 2009b. As Real as Real? Macroeconomic Behavior in a Large-Scale Virtual World. *New Media and Society* 11:685–707.

China Internet Network Information Center. 2009. 中国网络游戏市场研究报告 2009年度 [Chinese Online Game Market Research Report 2009]. Beijing: China Internet Network Information Center.

Crawford, Chris. 1984. *The Art of Computer Game Design.* New York: McGraw-Hill.

Davenport, Thomas H., and John C. Beck. 2001. *The Attention Economy: Understanding the New Currency of Business.* Boston: Harvard Business School Press.

Dibbell, Julian. 2006. *Play Money. Or, How I Quit My Day Job and Made Millions Trading Virtual Loot.* New York: Basic Books.

Dijkman, Jessica. 2011. *Shaping Medieval Markets: The Organization of Commodity Markets in Holland, c. 1200–c. 1450.* Leiden: Brill.

Douglas, M., and B. Isherwood. 1978. *The World of Goods.* New York: Basic Books.

Dovidio, John F., Jane A. Piliavin, David A. Schroeder, and Louis A. Penner. 2006. *The Social Psychology of Prosocial Behavior.* Hillsdale, NJ: Erlbaum.

Duranske, Benjamin. 2008. *Virtual Law: Navigating the Legal Landscape of Virtual Worlds.* Chicago: American Bar Association.

Easterlin, R., L. Angelescu McVey, M. Switek, O. Sawangfa, and J. Smith Zweig. 2010. The Happiness-Income Paradox Revisited. *Proceedings of the National Academy of Sciences of the United States of America* 107 (52): 22463–22468.

Eskelinen, Markku. 2004. Towards Computer Game Studies. In *First Person: New Media as Story, Performance, and Game,* edited by Noah Wardrip-Fruin and Pat Harrigan. Cambridge, MA: MIT Press.

Espey, Molly. 1996. Explaining the Variation in Elasticity Estimates of Gasoline Demand in the United States: A Meta-Analysis. *Energy Journal* 17 (3): 49–60.

Fairfield, Joshua. 2005. Virtual Property. *Boston University Law Review,* 85:1047–1102.

Farrell, Graham, and John Roman. 2006. Crime as Pollution: Proposal for Market-Based Incentives to Reduce Crime Externalities. In *Crime Reduction and the Law,* edited by Kate Moss and Mike Stephens, 135–155. New York: Routledge.

Featherstone, Mike. 1991. *Consumer Culture and Postmodernism.* London: Sage.

Flegal, K. M., M. D. Carroll, C. L. Ogden, and L. R. Curtin. 2010. Prevalence and Trends in Obesity among US Adults, 1999–2008. *Journal of the American Medical Association* 303 (3): 235–241.

Frederick, Shane, George Loewenstein, and Ted O'Donnel. 2002. Time Discounting and Time Preference: A Critical Review. *Journal of Economic Literature* 40 (2): 351–401.

Fullerton, Tracy. 2008. *Game Design Workshop,* 2nd ed. San Francisco: Morgan Kaufmann.

Gabriel, Y., and T. Lang. 1995. *The Unmanageable Consumer. Contemporary Consumption and Its Fragmentations.* London: Sage.

Galbraith, John Kenneth. 1975. *Money: Whence It Came, Where It Went.* Boston: Houghton Mifflin.

Granovetter, Mark. 1985. Economic Action and Social Structure: The Problem of Embeddedness. *American Journal of Sociology* 91 (3): 481–510.

Greene, William H. 2011. *Econometric Analysis,* 7th ed. Upper Saddle River, NJ: Prentice Hall.

Hamari, Juho. 2011. Perspectives from Behavioral Economics to Analyzing Game Design Patterns: Loss Aversion in Social Games. Paper presented at the CHI'2011 Social Games Workshop, Vancouver, Canada. http://www.hiit.fi/u/hamari/2011-perspectives_from_behavioral_economics.pdf.

Hamari, Juho, and Vili Lehdonvirta. 2010. Game design as marketing: How game mechanics create demand for virtual goods. *International Journal of Business Science and Applied Management* 5 (1):14–29.

Harris, Larry. 2003. *Trading and Exchanges: Market Microstructure for Practitioners*. New York: Oxford University Press.

Hawdon, James, Pekka Räsänen, and Atte Oksanen. 2013. Social Responses to Collective Crime: Assessing the Relationship between Crime-Related Fears and Collective Sentiments. *European Journal of Criminology* 10. doi: 10.1177/1477370813485516.

Hotelling, H. 1929. Stability in Competition. *Economic Journal* 39 (153): 41–57.

Huhh, Jun-Sok. 2005. Empirical Study on the Decline of Lineage 2 in Korea. http://ssrn.com/abstract=833847.

Ingham, G. 2004. *The Nature of Money*. Cambridge: Polity Press.

Inglehart, R. 1997. *Modernization and Postmodernization: Cultural, Economic, and Political Change in Forty-Three Societies*. Princeton, NJ: Princeton University Press.

Inglehart, R., R. Foa, C. Peterson, and C. Welzel. 2008. Development, Freedom, and Rising Happiness: A Global Perspective (1981–2007). *Perspectives on Psychological Science* 3 (4): 264–285.

Intergovernmental Panel on Climate Change (IPCC). 2007. *Climate Change 2007: Synthesis Report*. Geneva, Switzerland: Intergovernmental Panel on Climate Change.

Jackson, Tim. 2009. *Prosperity without Growth: Economics for a Finite Planet*. London: Earthscan.

Johnson, Mikael. 2013. How Social Media Changes User-Centred Design: Cumulative and Strategic User Involvement with Respect to Developer–User Social Distance. Helsinki: Aalto University. https://aaltodoc.aalto.fi/handle/123456789/8842.

Juul, Jesper. 2005. *Half-Real: Video Games between Real Rules and Fictional Worlds*. Cambridge, MA: MIT Press.

Kahneman, Daniel. 2011. *Thinking, Fast and Slow*. New York: Farrar, Straus and Giroux.

Kahneman, D., and A. Deaton. 2010. High Income Improves Evaluation of Life But Not Emotional Well-Being. *Proceedings of the National Academy of Sciences of the United States of America* 107 (38): 16489–16493.

Kahneman, Daniel, and Amos Tversky. 1984. Choices, Values, and Frames. *American Psychologist* 39 (4): 341–350.

Kaplan, Robert S., and David P. Norton. 1996. *The Balanced Scorecard: Translating Strategy into Action*. Boston: Harvard Business School Press.

Klemperer, Paul. 2004. *Auctions: Theory and Practice*. Princeton, NJ: Princeton University Press.

KOCCA. 2010. 2010대한민국 게임백서. [White Paper on Korean Games]. Korea Creative Content Agency: Seoul.

Kohavi, Ron, Roger Longbotham, Dan Sommerfield, and Randal M. Henne. 2009. Controlled Experiments on the Web: Survey and Practical Guide. *Data Mining and Knowledge Discovery* 18 (1): 140–181. http://link.springer.com/content/pdf/10.1007%2Fs10618-008-0114-1.pdf.

Koster, Raph. 2004. *A Theory of Fun for Game Design*. Scottsdale, AZ: Paraglyph.

Krebs, B. 2009. The Scrap Value of a Hacked PC. *Washington Post Security Fix*. http://voices.washingtonpost.com/securityfix/2009/05/the_scrap_value_of_a_hacked_pc.html.

Lanham, Richard A. 2007. *The Economics of Attention: Style and Substance in the Age of Information*. Chicago: University of Chicago Press.

Lastowka, Greg. 2010. *Virtual Justice: The New Laws of Online Worlds*. New Haven, CT: Yale University Press.

Lastowka, Greg, and Dan Hunter. 2004. The Laws of the Virtual Worlds. *California Law Review* 92 (1): 1–73.

Layard, R. 2006. *Happiness: Lessons from a New Science*. London: Penguin.

Lehdonvirta, Vili. 2009a. Virtual Item Sales as a Revenue Model: Identifying Attributes That Drive Purchase Decisions. *Electronic Commerce Research* 9 (1): 97–113.

Lehdonvirta, Vili. 2009b. *Virtual Consumption*. Turku: Turku School of Economics. http://info.tse.fi/julkaisut/vk/Ae11_2009.pdf.

Lehdonvirta, V., and M. Ernkvist. 2011. *Knowledge Map of the Virtual Economy*. Washington DC: World Bank. http://www.infodev.org/en/Document.1056.pdf.

Lehdonvirta, V., and E. Joas. 2012a. *Social Games Virtual Goods and Currencies Pricing Report 2012*. Helsinki: Virtual Economists Ltd. http://virtualeconomists.com.

Lehdonvirta, V., and E. Joas. 2012b. *Mobile Games Virtual Goods and Currencies Pricing Report 2012*. Helsinki: Virtual Economists Ltd. http://virtualeconomists.com.

Lehdonvirta, V., and E. Joas. 2013. *PC F2P Games Virtual Goods and Currencies Pricing Report 2013*. Helsinki: Virtual Economists Ltd. http://virtualeconomists.com.

Lehdonvirta, Mika, Yosuke Nagashima, Vili Lehdonvirta, and Akira Baba. 2012. The Stoic Male: How Avatar Gender Affects Help-Seeking Behaviour in an Online Game. *Games and Culture* 7 (1): 29–47.

Lehdonvirta, Vili, and Perttu Virtanen. 2010. A New Frontier in Digital Content Policy: Case Studies in the Regulation of Virtual Goods and Artificial Scarcity. *Policy and Internet* 2 (3): 7–29.

Lehdonvirta, Vili, Terhi-Anna Wilska, and Mikael Johnson. 2009. Virtual Consumerism: Case Habbo Hotel. *Information, Communication and Society* 12 (7): 1059–1079.

Lury, Celia. 2011. *Consumer Culture*, 2nd ed. Cambridge: Polity.

Malaby, T. M. 2006. Parlaying Value: Capital in and beyond Virtual Worlds. *Games and Culture* 1 (2): 141–162.

Mankiw, N. Gregory. 2009. *Macroeconomics*, 7th ed. New York: Worth.

Mankiw, N. Gregory. 2011. *Principles of Microeconomics*, 6th ed. Boston: South-Western.

Mauss, Marcel. 1990. *The Gift: The Form and Reason for Exchange in Archaic Societies*. New York: Norton.

Mayer-Schönberger, Victor, and Kenneth Cukier. 2013. *Big Data: A Revolution That Will Transform How We Live, Work, and Think*. Boston: Houghton Mifflin Harcourt.

McConnell, Campbell, Stanley Brue, and Sean Flynn. 2011. *Microeconomics*, 19th ed. New York: McGraw-Hill.

Mercuro, Nicholas, and Steven G. Medema. 2006. *Economics and the Law: From Posner to Postmodernism and Beyond*. 2nd ed. Princeton, NJ: Princeton University Press.

Mnookin, Jennifer L. 1996. Virtual(ly) Law: The Emergence of Law in LambdaMOO. *Journal of Computer-Mediated Communication* 2 (1). http://jcmc.indiana.edu/vol2/issue1/lambda.html.

Murray, Janet. 1997. *Hamlet on the Holodeck: The Future of Narrative in Cyberspace*. Cambridge, MA: MIT Press.

Nash, J., and E. Schneyer. 2004. *Virtual Economies: An In-Depth Look at the Virtual World of Final Fantasy XI: Online*. http://lgst.wharton.upenn.edu/hunterd/VirtualEconomies.pdf.

Nicolas, Gaelle, Benoit Durand, Rene Rakotondravao, and Veronique Chevalier. 2013. Description and Analysis of Cattle Trade Network in the Madagascar Highlands: Potential Role in the Diffusion of Rift Valley Fever Virus. *Acta Tropica* 126 (1): 19–27.

North, Peter. 2007. *Money and Liberation: The Micropolitics of the Alternative Currency Movement*. Minneapolis: University of Minnesota Press.

Polanyi, Karl. 2001. *The Great Transformation: The Political and Economic Origins of Our Time*. Boston: Beacon Press.

Pressman, Jeffrey L., and Aaron Wildavsky. 1984. *Implementation: How Great Expectations in Washington Are Dashed in Oakland; Or, Why It's Amazing that Federal Programs Work at All*. Berkeley: University of California Press.

Puustinen, Pekka. 2012. Towards a Consumer-Centric Definition of Value in the Non-Institutional Investment Context—Conceptualization and Measurement of Perceived Investment Value. Academic Diss. *Acta Electronica Universitatis Tamperensis 1195*. Tampere, Finland: Tampere University Press.

Robischon, Noah. 2006. *Station Exchange: Year One*. http://vili.lehdonvirta.com/files/oosa8403/SOEStationExchangeWhitePaper1.19.pdf

Rollings, Andrew, and David Morris. 2003. *Game Architecture and Design*. San Francisco: New Riders.

Rubin, Paul H., and C. Monica Capra. (2011) The Evolutionary Psychology of Economics. In *Applied Evolutionary Psychology*, edited by S. C. Roberts. New York: Oxford University Press.

Rubinstein, Ariel, and Yuval Salant. 2008. (A, f): Choice with Frames. *Review of Economic Studies* 75 (4): 1287–1296.

Salen, Katie, and Eric Zimmerman. 2003. *Rules of Play: Game Design Fundamentals*. Cambridge, MA: MIT Press.

Scheck, Justin. 2008. Mackerel Economics in Prison Leads to Appreciation for Oily Fillets. *Wall Street Journal*, October 2. http://online.wsj.com/article/SB122290720439096481.html.

Schell, Jesse. 2008. *The Art of Game Design: A Book of Lenses*. San Francisco: Morgan Kaufmann.

Schroeder, Ralph. 2011. *Being There Together: Social Interaction in Shared Virtual Environments*. Oxford: Oxford University Press.

Shapiro, Carl, and Hal Varian. 1999. *Information Rules: A Strategic Guide to the Network Economy*. Boston: Harvard Business School Press.

Simmel, Georg. 1957. Fashion. *American Journal of Sociology* 62 (6): 541–548.

Taylor, Greg. 2013. Scarcity of Attention for a Medium of Abundance: An Economic Perspective. In *Society and the Internet: How Information and Social Networks are Changing Our Lives*, edited by W. H. Dutton and M. Graham. Oxford,: Oxford University Press.

Tversky, Amos, and Daniel Kahneman. 1981. The Framing of Decisions and the Psychology of Choice. *Science* 211 (4481): 453–458.

Varian, Hal. 2009. *Intermediate Microeconomics: A Modern Approach*, 8th ed. New York: Norton.

Veblen, Thorstein. 1899. *The Theory of the Leisure Class: An Economic Study of Institutions*. New York: Macmillan. http://www.gutenberg.org/etext/833.

Wilkinson, Richard G., and Kate Pickett. 2009. *The Spirit Level: Why More Equal Societies Almost Always Do Better*. London: Penguin.

Yee, Nick. 2005. *The Daedalus Project*, vols. 3–5 (10/19/2005). http://www.nickyee.com/daedalus/archives/pdf/3-5.pdf.

Yomiuri Shimbun. 2012. "Kompu gacha" [Online Games May Be Illegal]. May 6. http://www.yomiuri.co.jp/dy/national/T120505002978.htm.

Zorpette, G., ed. 2012. The Beginning of the End of Cash. *IEEE Spectrum* 49 (6): 27–72.

Index